Solving the Mystery of Reading

Carolyn L. Davidson

Butte Community College

PEARSON
Longman

New York   San Francisco   Boston
London   Toronto   Sydney   Tokyo   Singapore   Madrid
Mexico City   Munich   Paris   Cape Town   Hong Kong   Montreal

Senior Acquisitions Editor: Susan Kunchandy
Development Editor: Janice Wiggins-Clarke
Senior Marketing Manager: Melanie Craig
Senior Supplements Editor: Donna Campion
Production Manager: Donna DeBenedictis
Project Coordination, Text Design, and Electronic Page Makeup: Nesbitt Graphics, Inc.
Cover Design Manager: John Callahan
Cover Designer: Maria Ilardi
Cover Photo: Getty Images, Inc.
Graphic Artist: Joshua Siegel
Photo Researcher: Photosearch, Inc.
Manufacturing Manager: Mary Fischer
Printer and Binder: Quebecor World/Dubuque
Cover Printer: Phoenix Color Corporation

For permission to use copyrighted material, grateful acknowledgment is made to the copyright holders on p. 387, which is hereby made part of this copyright page.

Library of Congress Cataloging-in-Publication Data

Davidson, Carolyn L.
    Solving the mystery of reading / Carolyn L. Davidson.
        p. cm.
    Includes index.
    ISBN 0-321-27339-7
    1.   Developmental reading I. Title
LB1050.53.D37 2005
372≥41--dc22

                                            2005019315

Please visit us at http://www.ablongman.com

ISBN 0-321-27339-7

1 2 3 4 5 6 7 8 9 10—QWD—08 07 06 05

This book is dedicated to my son, Joshua A. Siegel,
in thanks for all his love, support, and assistance.

Contents

Preface

For the developmental college student, reading even simple text may seem as difficult as deciphering Egyptian hieroglyphs. It does not need to be. The purpose of this text, *Solving the Mystery of Reading*, is to demystify the process of reading while providing the developmental student with the strategies, practice, and critical thinking skills necessary to become a successful reader. Here are the chapter topics:

- An Introduction to the Reading Process
- Decoding Symbols
- Decoding the Sounds/Pronunciation
- Finding Facts
- Using Context Clues to Improve Vocabulary and Comprehension
- Mastering Dictionary Skills
- Using Roots and Affixes to Improve Vocabulary and Comprehension
- Understanding Organization
- Finding the Main Idea of a Paragraph
- Using Graphics and Other Aids
- Five-Step Strategies for Comprehending Long/Complex Readings
- Noting the Central Idea of a Reading

Each chapter has a reading pertaining to a "mystery" of sorts and covering topics from history to science to sociology. Following each reading are exercises to practice strategies and skills that were introduced in this chapter or in previous chapters. There are also optional activities at the end of each chapter such as "Just for Fun" and "Enhancing Your Thinking Skills." At the end of the text are eight additional readings with exercises that allow the student to practice all the strategies and skills they have learned to that point. Additional types of activities are added once the strategy has been covered.

Solving the Mystery of Reading is different from other developmental reading texts. Some reading texts are what instructors call skill-and-drill. These are often repetitive and can become boring for adult students. Other texts emphasize instruction with readings. Unfortunately, these readings are often personal narrative essays. These may be interesting but are often filled with idioms that are difficult for developmental students. Even in some of the texts using a thematic approach, the exercises provide little opportunity for the repetition of new vocabulary and concepts that are critical for language development. They frequently also assess skills that have not yet been covered.

So how is *Solving the Mystery of Reading* different? This text:

- is based on language acquisition research.
- has been carefully organized and written to provide both a step-by-step development of vocabulary and comprehension strategies and the frequent repetition and use of these strategies.
- demystifies the process of reading, which empowers the students to take charge of their own learning.
- uses a supportive, encouraging tone.
- provides 20 "mystery" readings intended to be of interest to and at a suitable readability for a developmental adult reader; these readings will hopefully not only build the reader's background knowledge but also allow students to develop a more global worldview.
- has three different assessment levels for some activities; this allows students of different abilities to work to their greatest potential and gives the instructor more options for both instruction and assessment. For example, teams or partners might be working on a Challenge or Mastery exercise while the instructor works with students who need more assistance at the basic level.
- offers a wide variety of activities for students with different abilities and learning styles.
- provides critical thinking and problem-solving activities.
- can be used independently or in the classroom, with individuals, partners, or teams.
- encourages the use of a variety of resources such as the dictionary, the Internet, the library, maps and other graphics, and so on.
- offers quick, easy-to-read boxed material: Secrets to Success, Caution, and FYI.
- has an appendix that provides a collection of maps.
- empowers the student whether his or her goal is personal, vocational, or academic.
- is demanding yet allows students the opportunity to see that reading/learning can be both valuable and fun.

Supplements

Longman is pleased to offer a variety of support materials to help make teaching reading easier on teachers and to help students excel in their coursework. Many of our student supplements are available free or at a greatly reduced price when packaged with a Longman reading or study skills textbook. Contact your local Longman sales representative for more information on pricing and how to create a package.

For Instructors

The Instructor's Manual and Answer Key (Instructor/0-321-27340-0)

This supplement accompanies *Solving the Mystery of Reading* and is available to adopters.

Printed Test Bank for Developmental Reading (Instructor/0-321-08596-5)

Offering more than 3,000 questions in all areas of reading, this test bank includes vocabulary, main idea, supporting details, patterns of organization, critical thinking, analytical reasoning, inference, point of view, visual aids, and textbook reading. (An electronic version is also available; see below.)

Electronic Test Bank for Developmental Reading (Instructor/CD 0-321-08179-X)

Offering more than 3,000 questions in all areas of reading, this test bank includes vocabulary, main idea, supporting details, patterns of organization, critical thinking, analytical reasoning, inference, point of view, visual aids, and textbook reading. Instructors simply choose questions, then print out the completed test for distribution *or* offer the test online.

The Longman Instructor's Planner (Instructor/0-321-09247-3)

This planner includes weekly and monthly calendars, student attendance and grading rosters, space for contact information, Web references, an almanac, and blank pages for notes.

For Students

Vocabulary Skills Study Card (Student/0-321-31802-1)

Colorful, affordable, and packed with useful information, Longman's Vocabulary Skills Study Card is a concise, eight-page reference guide to developing key vocabulary skills, such as learning to recognize context clues, reading a dictionary entry, and recognizing key root words, suffixes, and prefixes. The study card is laminated for durability, so students can keep it for years to come and pull it out whenever they need a quick review.

Reading Skills Study Card (Student/0-321-33833-2)

Colorful, affordable, and packed with useful information, Longman's Reading Skills Study Card is a concise, eight-page reference guide to help students develop basic reading skills, such as concept skills, structural skills, language skills, and reasoning skills. The study card is laminated for durability, so students can keep it for years to come and pull it out whenever they need a quick review.

The Longman Textbook Reader, Revised Edition (with answers, Student/0-321-11895-2; without answers, Student/0-321-12223-2)
Offering five complete chapters from our textbooks in the disciplines of computer science, biology, psychology, communications, and business, this reader's chapters include additional comprehension quizzes, critical thinking questions, and group activities.

The Longman Reader's Portfolio and Student Planner (Student/ 0-321-29610-9)
This unique supplement provides students with a space to plan, think about, and present their work. The portfolio includes a diagnostic area (including a learning-style questionnaire), a working area (including calendars, vocabulary logs, reading response sheets, book club tips, and other valuable materials), and a display area (including a progress chart, a final table of contents, and a final assessment), as well as a daily planner for students including daily, weekly, and monthly calendars.

The Longman Reader's Journal, by Kathleen McWhorter (Student/ 0-321-08843-3)
The first journal for readers, *The Longman Reader's Journal* offers a place for students to record their reactions to and questions about any reading.

The Longman Planner (Student/0-321-04573-4)
Ideal for organizing a busy college life, this planner includes hour-by-hour schedules, monthly and weekly calendars, an address book, and an almanac of tips and useful information.

10 Practices of Highly Effective College Students (Student/ 0-205-30769-8)
This study skills supplement includes topics such as time management, test taking, reading critically, stress, and motivation.

***Newsweek* Discount Subscription Coupon (12 weeks) (Student/ 0-321-08895-6)**
Newsweek gets students reading, writing, and thinking about what's going on in the world around them. The price of the subscription is added to the cost of the book. Instructors receive weekly lesson plans, quizzes, and curriculum guides as well as a complimentary *Newsweek* subscription. The price of the subscription is 59 cents per issue (a total of $7.08 for the subscription). *Package item only.*

Interactive Guide to *Newsweek* (Student/0-321-05528-4)
Available with the 12-week subscription to *Newsweek*, this guide serves as a workbook for students who are using the magazine.

Research Navigator Guide for English, by H. Eric Branscomb and Doug Gotthoffer (Student/0-321-20277-5)
Designed to teach students how to conduct high-quality online research and to document it properly, Research Navigator guides provide discipline-specific academic resources in addition to helpful tips on the writing process, online research, and finding and citing valid sources. Research Navigator guides include an access code to Research Navigator™—providing access to thousands of academic journals and periodicals, the *New York Times* Search by Subject Archive, Link Library, Library Guides, and more.

Penguin Discount Novel Program
In cooperation with Penguin Putnam, Inc., Longman is proud to offer a variety of Penguin paperbacks at a significant discount when packaged with any Longman title. Excellent additions to any developmental reading course, Penguin titles give students the opportunity to explore contemporary and classical fiction and drama. The available titles include works by authors as diverse as Toni Morrison, Julia Alvarez, Mary Shelley, and Shakespeare. To review the complete list of titles available, visit the Longman–Penguin Putnam website: http://www.ablongman.com/penguin.

The New American Webster Handy College Dictionary (Student/ 0-451-18166-2)
This paperback reference text contains more than 100,000 entries.

The Oxford American College Dictionary (Student/0-399-14415-3)
Based on the *New Oxford American Dictionary* and drawing on Oxford's unparalleled language resources (including a 200-million-word database), this college dictionary contains more than 75,000 entries and more than 1,000 illustrations, including line drawings, photographs, and maps.

Multimedia Offerings

Interested in incorporating online materials into your course? Longman is happy to help. Our regional technology specialists provide training on all of our multimedia offerings.

MySkillsLab 2.0 (www.myskillslab.com)
This exciting new website houses all the media tools any developmental English student will need to improve their reading, writing, and study skills, and all in one easy-to-use place. Resources for reading and study skills include:

- **Reading Roadtrip 4.0 Website.** The best-selling reading software available, Reading Roadtrip takes students on a tour of 16 cities and landmarks throughout the United States, with each of the 16 modules corresponding to a reading or study skill. The topics include main idea, vocabulary, understanding patterns of organization, thinking critically, reading rate, notetaking and highlighting, graphics and visual aids, and more. Students can begin their trip by taking a diagnostics test that provides immediate feedback, guiding them to specific modules for additional help with reading skills.

- **Longman Vocabulary Website.** The Longman Vocabulary Website component of MySkillsLab features hundreds of exercises in ten topic areas to strengthen vocabulary skills. Students will also benefit from "100 Words That All High School Graduates Should Know," a useful resource that provides definitions for each of the words on this list, vocabulary flash cards, and audio clips to help facilitate pronunciation skills.

- **Longman Study Skills Website.** This site offers hundreds of review strategies for college success, time and stress management skills, study strategies, and more. Students can take a variety of assessment tests to learn about their organizational skills and learning styles, with follow-up quizzes to reinforce the strategies they have learned.

- **Research Navigator.** In addition to providing valuable help to any college student on how to conduct high-quality online research and to document it properly, Research Navigator provides access to thousands of academic journals and periodicals (including the *New York Times* Archive), allowing reading students to practice with authentic readings from college-level primary sources.

MySkillsLab 2.0 is available in the following versions: Website, CourseCompass, WebCT, and Blackboard.

Reading Road Trip 4.0 Plus Website (www.ablongman.com/ readingroadtrip) is also available as a stand-alone site.

State-Specific Supplements
For Florida Adopters

Thinking Through the Test: A Study Guide for the Florida College Basic Skills Exit Test, by D. J. Henry
This workbook helps students strengthen their reading skills in preparation for the Florida College Basic Skills Exit Test. It features both diagnostic tests to help assess areas that may need improvement and exit tests to help test skill mastery. Detailed explanatory answers have been provided for almost all of the questions. *Package item only—not available for sale.*

Available Versions:

Thinking Through the Test (A Study Guide for the Florida College Basic Skills Exit Tests: Reading and Writing), Second Edition (0-321-27660-4)

Thinking Through the Test (A Study Guide for the Florida College Basic Skills Exit Tests: Reading and Writing), with Answers, Second Edition (0-321-27756-2)

Thinking Through the Test (A Study Guide for the Florida College Basic Skills Exit Tests: Reading) (0-321-27746-5)

Thinking Through the Test (A Study Guide for the Florida College Basic Skills Exit Tests: Reading), with Answers (0-321-27751-1)

Reading Skills Summary for the Florida State Exit Exam, by D. J. Henry (Student/0-321-08478-0)
An excellent study tool for students preparing to take Florida College Basic Skills Exit Test for Reading, this laminated reading grid summarizes all the skills tested on the Exit Exam. *Package item only—not available for sale.*

CLAST Test Package, Fourth Edition (Instructor/Print ISBN 0-321-01950-4)
These two 40-item objective tests evaluate students' readiness for the Florida CLAST exams. Strategies for teaching CLAST preparedness are included.

For Texas Adopters

The Longman THEA Study Guide, by Jeannette Harris (Student/ 0-321-27240-0)
Created specifically for students in Texas, this study guide includes straightforward explanations and numerous practice exercises to help students prepare for the reading and writing sections of THEA Test. *Package item only—not available for sale.*

TASP Test Package, Third Edition (Instructor/Print ISBN 0-321-01959-8)
These 12 practice pre-tests and post-tests assess the same reading and writing skills covered in the Texas TASP examination.

For New York/CUNY Adopters

Preparing for the CUNY-ACT Reading and Writing Test, edited by Patricia Licklider (Student/0-321-19608-2)
This booklet, prepared by reading and writing faculty from across the CUNY system, is designed to help students prepare for the CUNY-ACT exit test. It includes test-taking tips, reading passages, typical

exam questions, and sample writing prompts to help students become familiar with each portion of the test.

Acknowledgments

As with most things in life, this textbook was a collaboration. From its conception at a textbook adoption meeting through the years of content development to the final days of editing and text preparation, *Solving the Mystery of Reading* has been a team effort. I would like to take this opportunity to thank my colleagues at Butte Community College for their understanding, patience, and suggestions during this process, particularly Nicole LaGrave, Julie Nuzum, and Jerry Chandler.

Special thanks to my friend and mentor Stan Kane and to my son, Joshua Siegel, for their hard work and confidence in me.

And, of course, none of this would have been possible without my incredible editors Janice Wiggins, Susan Kunchandy, and Kathy Dvorsky. Most of all, though, I would like to thank the students at Butte College; you were my inspiration and my best critics.

Last, but certainly not least, I want to acknowledge my reviewers: Frances Boffo, St. Philip's College; Bernice Brown, Sinclair Community College; Karen H. Davis, Austin Community College; Raymond DeLeon, California State University–Long Beach; JoAnn M. Foriest, Prairie State College; Betty Fortune, Houston Community College; Marty Frailey, Pima Community College; Laura B. Girtman, Tallahassee Community College; Gail Hannan, Butte College; Derrick W. Harding, Ivy Tech State College; Marie Heath, Collin County Community College; Sue Hightower, Tallahassee Community College; Kimberly James, Rowan-Cabarrus Community College; Diane Lerma, Palo Alto College; Kathleen Riehle, Sinclair Community College; Charis Sawyer, Johnson County Community College; Cynthia Shermeyer, University of Delaware; Frederick Shorter, Albany Technical College; and Sandra Thomson, Northwest Vista College. Though I admit there were times their comments made me cry or scream in frustration, it was their honest and insightful criticisms and suggestions that forced the evolution of *Solving the Mystery of Reading* from nothing more than a "good idea" into this fully developed text. Thanks from me and all the students who will use your input to better their lives.

CAROLYN L. DAVIDSON

Solving the Mystery of Reading

Life is full of mysteries. Reading should not be one of them. The purpose of this book is to give you, the reader, **strategies** (plans for success) to help you find the truth hidden in the words you read.

As you begin, remember that reading is a complex and often difficult **process** (series of actions). Reading requires you to think actively. How much knowledge you already have about a subject also affects how well you understand what you read. That is why it is important to read—because reading helps your knowledge grow. The more you read, the easier it becomes to read.

Symbols

Fortunately, humans are born with a talent for understanding language. Even people who cannot read a written language can interpret **symbols**. For example, most people knew that a red eight-sided sign means *stop*, even if they cannot read the letters. Symbols are a common part of your everyday life. See how many of these common symbols you can "read."

Exercise 1-1 Recognizing Symbols

Place the letter next to each symbol on the line next to its meaning.

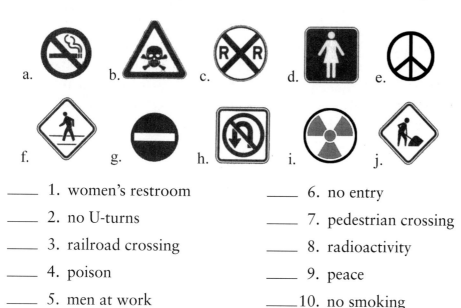

a.   b.   c.   d.   e.

f.   g.   h.   i.   j.

_____ 1. women's restroom

_____ 2. no U-turns

_____ 3. railroad crossing

_____ 4. poison

_____ 5. men at work

_____ 6. no entry

_____ 7. pedestrian crossing

_____ 8. radioactivity

_____ 9. peace

_____ 10. no smoking

Copyright © 2006 Pearson Education, Inc.

In English, letters are nothing more than symbols that represent sounds. We combine these sound symbols into words to make meaning. The first step in reading is learning to **decode** (figure out) these symbols. Decoding, however, may be difficult if you do not know the English language well or if you have a learning disability. Chapters 2 and 3 will help you learn to decode the symbols and sounds of English.

Becoming a Reading Detective

Decoding words is only the first step in reading. **Comprehension** (understanding what you read) is the next and most important step. As you read, you are constantly looking for clues to the meaning of what you are reading. To find meaning, you should think like a reading detective.

Below is a story about a police detective who has a crime to solve. As you read, or listen to your instructor read, the following story, notice any strategy you see Detective Lee using to solve the mystery.

The Case of the Missing Necklace

Late one afternoon, Detective Lee received a phone call at the police station. A woman was calling to report that her diamond necklace had been stolen. Detective Lee asked the woman for her name and address, and for other important information. The detective wrote down the facts in her notebook.

A short time later, Detective Lee arrived at Mrs. Jones' home. Before going to the front door, she glanced around at the neighborhood and then at the house and yard and wrote down a few more notes. It was important to have an overview of the crime scene.

Next, Detective Lee questioned Mrs. Jones. What did the necklace look like? How much was it worth? When was the last time she had seen the jewelry? Where was the safe, and who knew that she kept the necklace there? Again, the detective wrote the answers in her notebook. The names and addresses of all the people who worked in the house or who had visited recently were also added to the growing list of facts.

Detective Lee spent the next hour looking for clues and gathering information. No detail was too small not to notice. She dusted the entire house for fingerprints. She checked for strands of hair. She even looked outside for footprints, tire tracks, or other **evidence**. From the fire escape, she scraped a flake of dried mud into a tiny plastic bag.

Later, back at the police station, Detective Lee used many different **resources** to help her study the evidence: the crime lab, the computer, people with special knowledge, books, and much more. She needed the information they provided to help her understand the clues she had found.

From these clues, Detective Lee made **deductions** (educated guesses) about what she thought happened. Over and over, the detective checked her ideas about what might have happened to the necklace against what she already knew.

Her only real clues were a fingerprint from the bedroom window and the bit of mud from the fire escape that was just outside the bedroom window. Tests proved that the mud had come from the vegetable garden and that the fingerprint matched the gardener's. When a background check on all of Mrs. Jones' employees found that the gardener had a $200,000 gambling debt, Detective Lee searched the man's apartment and found the necklace. The gardener was arrested.

Detective Lee's work was not done yet. She still had to write up a report. She wrote her report carefully because she knew that she might be called to court later to present her evidence. The detective also filed away in her mind all that she has learned from this case to help her with the next mystery.

Exercise 1-2 Self-Check

Read the list of detective skills below and put a check next to the ones you think might help you understand what you are reading.

_____ previewing

_____ collecting and
       organizing facts

_____ taking notes

_____ finding clues

_____ interpreting clues

_____ using available resources

_____ organizing information

_____ making deductions

_____ thinking about what
       you've learned

_____ using what you've learned

If you checked them all, you are right. A good reader uses many of the same strategies that a detective uses. If you want to become a better reader, think of yourself as a reading detective. Learn and practice the exercises in this textbook, and hopefully you will find you can solve the mystery of reading.

The Many Kinds of Reading

Just as Detective Lee used different strategies on different kinds of crimes, so too will you as a reader have to use different techniques depending on what you are reading. There are many different kinds of reading—job applications, classified ads, newspapers and magazines, letters, the Internet, both **fiction** (short stories and novels) and **nonfiction** (biographies, histories, how-to manuals, and others) books, and **textbooks** like this one. This textbook, for example, emphasizes the strategies you can use for reading the type of nonfiction writing that you will find in a college or university textbook.

The Purpose of Reading

Keeping in mind your **purpose** (reason) for reading is important in deciding on which strategies you will need to use. If you are reading a novel for pleasure, you only need to work as hard as you like. However, if your instructor has assigned Chapter 10 of your biology textbook, and if you will be tested on that material, comprehension is very important. You will have to work hard and use many of your strategies in order to understand and remember what you have read.

Choosing a Dictionary

Detective Lee depended on her tools and equipment to gather information. A reading detective's most important tool is a quality dictionary. Any of the following **collegiate** (college level) dictionaries would be a good choice:

> *The American Heritage College Dictionary*
>
> *Random House Webster's College Dictionary*
>
> *Webster's New World College Dictionary*

If you are not a native English speaker or have reading problems or a learning disability, you might consider using *The American Heritage English as a Second Language Dictionary*. This intermediate-level dictionary has clear, easy-to-understand definitions. Unfortunately, it does not have all the information available in a college-level dictionary. If you have the money, owning both versions of a dictionary—intermediate and college—is the most helpful.

Caution

ELECTRONIC DICTIONARIES

To date, electronic dictionaries, translators, and spellcheckers do *not* have the amount or quality of information provided by a good dictionary. These electronic resources can, however, be used for extra help.

Solving the Mystery of Using Your Textbook

VOCABULARY

bold-faced—darkened

emphasize—to show importance

resource—something you use for help

assess—to test or judge value

challenge—something difficult

mastery—in full command (of a subject)

recommended—suggested

THE PURPOSE OF THIS TEXTBOOK

1   The purpose of this textbook is to help you learn and practice the strategies and skills needed to be a successful reader. It can also help you improve your vocabulary and provide you with valuable practice in critical thinking. Once you have learned the strategies and put them to use, both your comprehension and memory of what you have read should improve.

Vocabulary

2   Did you notice that some of the words in the story are in **boldface** (darkened)? The bold-facing is to **emphasize** (show importance) new words that are necessary for comprehension. In the first few chapters, definitions will be given to you for most of the bold-faced words. Once you have completed the chapters on vocabulary in context and on how to use your dictionary, you will be expected to find the correct definitions yourself. Vocabulary words are repeated from paragraph to paragraph and chapter to chapter to give you extra practice using them. You will also be learning word parts and word families to help you more quickly understand vocabulary.

Chapter Organization

3   After the title page of this book, you will find the **Table of Contents**. The Table of Contents lists the titles of each chapter. It gives you the strategies taught in each chapter, the titles of the readings, and an extra **resource** (help) provided for you at the end of the chapter. The titles of the additional readings at the back of the book are also listed.

4   Within each chapter you will find new reading strategies and practice exercises. Each reading selection is accompanied by exercises. The strategies you have learned in previous chapters will continue to be **assessed** (tested) as you move from one chapter to the next.

5   Some of the exercises are offered at three levels. Exercises are at a basic level for everyone. The **Challenge** Exercises are just that— challenging. Your instructor may want you to work with a partner or team when doing these. **Mastery** Exercises are the most difficult. These will take effort, problem-solving strategies, and often the use of a college-level dictionary. Your instructor will decide which level (or levels) you should do.

6   Each chapter includes at least one reading with exercises that check your vocabulary, comprehension, and more. There is also an additional section near the end of each chapter titled **Going Beyond**. Here you can find research topics if you are interested in finding out more about the information discussed in the reading. There are often also **recommended** websites, books, or movies listed. After Going Beyond, there are one or more optional sections such as **Writing About What You've Read, Study Strategies, Just for Fun, Enhancing Your Thinking,** and **Organizing In-formation**. Again, your instructor will decide whether or not these will be assigned. If they are not required, you can still do them for fun or to improve your skills. There will also be opportunities to write and use your problem-solving skills throughout the book. Each chapter ends with a **Chapter Review**, which includes a summary of the important in-formation.

Symbols in the Text

7   This book will use several symbols to help you quickly find, use, or review important information. Study the meanings of the symbols below so that you will recognize them when you see them in this chapter and following chapters.

8   **Caution** (be careful): English has many "exceptions to the rules." This symbol will call attention to any possible prob-lems or points for confusion.

9   **Secrets to Success:** This is critical information that will help you become a better student.

10   **For Your Information:** These are hints or suggestions that are not **essential** (necessary) for the reader but are ideas that may help you understand or remember something more easily.

Additional Readings

11   Once you have learned the strategies of being a successful reader, you will have the opportunity to use all your strategies on the additional read-ings. With these eight extra readings will be exercises to assess all the skills and strategies you have learned in the text.

Appendix

12   An **appendix** is a section that has been attached to the end of the main text. Near the end of this book, you will find an Appendix that includes maps of the world and each of the continents, a view of the world from the North Pole and the South Pole, plus a map of the United States. This Appendix is an excellent resource; use it for necessary background information to support the Readings.

Doing Your Part

13   While this textbook offers strategies and practice to help you become a more successful reader, reaching that goal takes hard work, patience, and determination. Like every skill, reading takes time and practice to develop. Do the best you can each day and never give up. You, your instructor, and the text are a team. But, in the end, you are the one who must do the work.

Exercise 1-3 Checking New Vocabulary

Choose a word from the Answer Box to correctly complete each sentence below. Use the information in Reading 1 to find your answers.

ANSWER BOX

appendix	Mastery	strategies	symbols
Challenge	additional	bold-faced	purpose

1. The purpose of this book is to help you learn and practice the

    _____ and skills needed to be a successful

    reader.

2. Certain words in the textbook have been _____

    to emphasize that they are new and important for comprehension.

3. At the end of the book is an _____ that includes maps and other useful information you may need.

4. Some strategies are assessed at three levels:

    Exercises, _____ Exercises, and

    _____ Exercises.

5. A stop sign, a label with a skull and crossbones to warn us of poison,

    and the letters of the alphabet are all _____.

Exercise 1-4 Checking Comprehension

Write the letter of the correct answer on the line provided. Use Reading 1 to find your answers.

_____ 1. Which of these would you find in the Table of Contents of your textbook?
a. a chapter review
b. a reading
c. titles of chapters
d. maps

_____ 2. Which of the following is *not* one of the levels of assessment?
a. exercises
b. beginner's exercises
c. Challenge exercises
d. Mastery exercises

_____ 3. Where would you find the chapter review?
a. at the beginning of the chapter
b. at the beginning of the reading
c. at the end of the reading
d. at the end of the chapter

_____ 4. What kind of information would you find in a box marked **FYI**?
a. interesting but not essential information
b. very important information that you should learn
c. a new study strategy
d. a warning to be careful about something

_____ 5. Who or what plays the most important part in your reading improvement?
a. the teacher
b. the class
c. the textbook
d. you

Exercise 1-5 Getting to Know Your Textbook

Use this textbook to complete the following. You may find many of the answers by using the Table of Contents.

1. On which page does the Table of Contents begin?

_____

2. In which chapter will you learn how to use context clues to improve your vocabulary and comprehension? _____

3. In which chapter will you read a story about the brain?

   _____

4. What is the title of the third Additional Reading?

   _____

5. List three different maps found in the Appendix of this textbook.

   _____

   _____

   _____

Writing About What You've Read

Writing about what you have read or learned is an excellent way to help test your comprehension, because in order to write about something effectively, you must know the subject's vocabulary and general concepts. Writing about a subject also helps you organize your thoughts.

Exercise 1-6 Writing About Yourself

As practice, write about the one thing you know best—yourself. Take a few moments to think about your history as a reader. Did your parents read to you as a child? Do you read now? What is your favorite kind of reading? Is English your native language? If not, what kinds of problems are you having learning to read English? Do you think you have any special problems that make reading difficult? Is there some kind of reading you have to do, for example, on your job or in school? Why do you want to improve your reading? Are there any problems that might make it difficult for you to improve your reading? What are your strengths as a reader? What do you hope to accomplish by using this book? How can you help your classmates, family, or friends improve their reading skills?

On your own paper, use the answers to the questions above or other related questions to write a brief description of your history as a reader—past, present, and future. Share specific examples or ideas if you can.

Study Strategy

Getting to Know Your Textbook

If you are taking another course that uses a textbook, flip through that book and see if you can find any of the following parts. Check off any you find. Getting to know a textbook can help you be a better student.

_____ introduction

_____ table of contents

_____ chapter preview

_____ bold-faced vocabulary

_____ chapter review

_____ chapter review questions

_____ appendix

_____ **index** (list near back of book of internal subjects with page numbers)

_____ **bibliography** (list of resources used to write book)

_____ additional resources

_____ answer key

_____ other parts: _____

CHAPTER 1 REVIEW

- **Introduction to the Mystery of Reading**
  Reading is a complex process. You need strategies to help you understand what you are reading.

- **Symbols**
  The first step in reading is to recognize symbols. The next is to decode them.

- **Becoming a Reading Detective**
  The reading strategies you need to improve comprehension are much like those used by detectives to solve crimes. The goal of this text is to teach you to use those strategies.

- **The Many Kinds of Reading**
  There are many different kinds of reading. The strategies you use will depend on what you are reading. This textbook will focus on **academic** (school) reading.

- **The Purpose of Reading**
  Your purpose for reading is important in deciding which strategies you need to use and how hard you will have to work.

- **Choosing a Dictionary**
  Having the right tools makes any job easier. An up-to-date, quality dictionary is **essential** (absolutely necessary) for all readers.

The Secrets of Decoding English Symbols

Written Language

Written language is nothing new. Early humans drew pictures and other symbols on cave walls. These pictures were called **petroglyphs** (stone writing). No one is sure of the meaning of these ancient drawings, but they probably showed important events in the lives of the people who drew them.

Later, people began to draw symbols that had meaning. For example, if you wanted to communicate the word ox you just drew a picture of an ox. A picture that has meaning is called a **pictograph**. The earliest known pictographic writing system came from the country **Mesopotamia** (which is now called **Iraq**). Pictographs were etched into tiny pillow-shaped clay tablets.

Pictographs

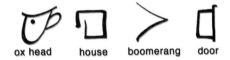

ox head   house   boomerang   door

The Phoenicians, neighbors of the Egyptians, used these pictographs to create the first true **alphabet** 4,000 years ago. A true alphabet is a group of symbols that represent sounds. The Phoenicians, who were sea traders, needed a faster way than using pictographs to keep records of their buying and selling. That is why they invented letters to represent the sounds of words. It was faster and easier than picture writing.

Phoenician Letters

Greece was also a trading nation along the Mediterranean Sea. This ancient people often traded with the Phoenicians and soon learned the Phoenician alphabet. The Greeks, however, used this new writing form for more than just business. The Greeks were great storytellers and used this new alphabet to write plays, songs, and great epic adventures. Over many centuries, the Greeks changed the old Phoenician alphabet. The word **alphabet** comes from a combination of the Greek letters: alpha + beta.

Greek Letters

Α Β Γ Δ

In Italy, another great civilization was developing that would eventually become the Roman Empire. These early Romans borrowed the Greek letters, made some changes to them, and added letters of their own. Today, this Roman alphabet is still used not only in the Italian language but also in English, Spanish, French, and several other languages.

Roman Letters

A B C D

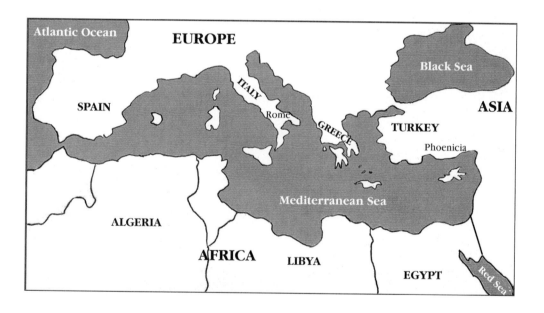

Around the world, other families of languages developed using symbols very different from the Roman alphabet, which uses letters to represent sounds. Chinese is an example of a very different language that uses **ideographs** (symbols that represent ideas rather than sounds).

Chinese Ideographs

Some languages were used for many years, then lost. For centuries, people tried to translate ancient Egyptian hieroglyphs. It took **linguists** (people who study languages) hundreds of years and the discovery of a "code book" to decipher the hieroglyphs. Even today, the hieroglyphic writing of the Mayan people of South America is still a mystery.

Reading

Reading in any language is a process of being able to decode symbols and to know how those symbols go together. In English, we read from left to right. In Hebrew, and several other languages, they read right to left. Some languages read from top to bottom or bottom to top in long columns. Besides knowing the direction in which the text is read, it is also helpful to know the language's special punctuation symbols, such as the English period and question mark.

Sometimes learning to read English, even if it is your native language, can seem as difficult as reading Egyptian hieroglyphs. However, it doesn't have to be so hard, not if you understand how the language works and learn the strategies you need to discover the meaning in the words. The first step is to learn to decode.

Decoding

Here is a sentence written in a code that looks a little like Egyptian hieroglyphs. Can you read the sentence?

Probably not. Don't give up. Study the symbols carefully. Do you see any **patterns** (repeated letters or words) or other clues that might help you decode this mysterious language?

In most languages, certain letters and even words are used much more often than others. What six letters do you think are used most often in English? _____ In English, the letters a, e, o, n, s, and t are the most common.

Common words in a language are sometimes called **sight words** because we recognize them when we see them. Words like a, I, the, you, is, no, not, and, he, and she are some of the English sight words. Can you think of any others?

_____

Now look at the coded sentence again.

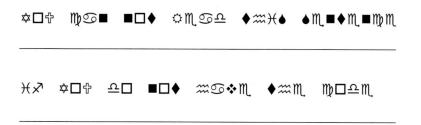

Do you think you see any of these common words used? _____

If you do, try to use the letters that make up that word to decode the rest of the sentence. Still having a hard time? Don't give up! Here's a clue that might help: □ represents the letter o and ♦ represents the letter t.

Try again. Write the letters you know on the line directly below each symbol then see if you can figure out any of the missing letters from the clues you have.

For some people, decoding may seem easy; for others, very hard. As with any skill, whether it is playing the piano, riding a horse, or fixing a car, different people have different abilities. Some people are natural **decoders**. Others aren't.

Don't worry! Decoding is much easier for everyone if you have the code book with the **key** to the symbols.

THE KEY (◆≈♏ ♍□⌐♏)

♋ A	♑ G	M	■ N (S ◆ T)	✡ Y					

♋ A	♑ G	● M	● S	✡ Y
♌ B	≈ H	■ N	◆ T	⌘ Z
♍ C	♓ I	□ O	☩ U	
♎ D	℔ J	⚑ P	❖ V	🖃 .
♏ E	& K	➳ Q	⚷ W	✪ ?
♐ F	● L	☼ R	⊠ X	

Exercise 2-1 Decoding Letters

Use the key above to decode the sentence below.

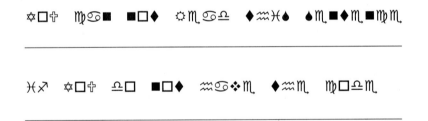

_____

_____

Did Exercise 2-1 take some effort and concentration to complete? Reading is not easy, and decoding is only the first step. Before a child can learn to read, he or she must first recognize not only the symbols but also the fact that the symbols in combination make words. A reader also needs to recognize punctuation marks like the 🖃 for a period and the ✪ for a question in this code.

Learning to read well is a complex and often difficult process. A non-native student learning a new language or a student who has dyslexia or a learning disability often feels the same difficulty and frustration that you might have felt trying to decode this new language. Even good readers who are trying to read about a new or difficult subject go through much the same process. Learning new words takes time and repetition. Just remember, the more you read in any language the easier it becomes.

If you like challenges and would like to read and write more of this language, go to the **Just for Fun** section at the end of this chapter.

Decoding English

Every language has special rules of its own. If you understand the rules, decoding new or difficult words will be easier. Here are a few simple facts about the English language that may be helpful. You probably already know some of the rules.

Letters

The English language has 26 letters:

A B C D E F G H I J K L M
N O P Q R S T U V W X Y Z

These letters can be represented in a variety of ways. Here is a small sample of the many different ways the letter A can be written.

A a A a a *a*

These 26 letters can be used alone or together to make almost 50 distinct sounds.

Words

A **word** is made up of a letter or a group of letters. These letters correspond to sounds, and combinations of letters have meaning. Look at the word dog, for example.

- It is made up of three letters: d + o + g.
- Each of those letters has a sound; these sounds are blended together to say the word dog.
- Most important of all, the letters d-o-g carry a meaning, a meaning that is different from other combination of letters like c-a-t or h-o-r-s-e.

Sentences

A sentence is a group of words that starts with a capital letter and ends with a period, question mark, or exclamation point. A sentence must have a **subject** and a **predicate** (for example, a noun + a verb).

Caution
THE COMMAND!
Sometimes you don't see the subject as in a command sentence like: Jump! In your mind, you know the subject. <u>You</u> jump!

Most important, each sentence represents a complete thought.

Paragraphs

A paragraph is a series of related sentences. Each paragraph should have a main idea or organizing thought. The beginning of a new paragraph is usually **indented,** set in to the right several spaces.

Longer Readings

Use what you know about the English language to solve this riddle.

When we put letters together, we get words.

When we put words together, we get sentences.

When we put sentences together, we get paragraphs.

What do we get when we put paragraphs together?

In your life, you will need to read a wide variety of things. Some may be easy. Some may be very hard. With an understanding of the English language, with the strategies of a reading detective, and with effort, you should be able to understand even the most difficult writing.

Decoding the Meaning of Words

Do you remember the definition of a word? It is a group of letters that has meaning. Your job as a reading detective is not only to decode the letters but also to find the meaning of that combination of letters. That may be easy or very difficult.

In English, words can be short and simple like hot or dog. Others can be long and difficult like hieroglyph. Some words have a single definition like the word hat, while others like the word run have more than 50 definitions. And sometimes two or more words are put together to make a new word called a **compound word** (a word made up of two words), like hotdog or firehouse.

Recognizing Compound Words

Whether you are trying to say a new word correctly or trying to guess its meaning, you must first notice whether the word is a compound word or just a collection of syllables. Check to see if you already have this skill by completing Exercise 2-2.

Exercise 2-2 Compound Words

Put a check next to any word in the list below that is a compound word.

1. ____ woodpile	7. ____ shoestring	13. ____ fingerprint
2. ____ syllable	8. ____ headache	14. ____ horsetail
3. ____ thunderstorm	9. ____ checkbook	15. ____ schoolhouse
4. ____ adventure	10. ____ aviation	16. ____ freshman
5. ____ computer	11. ____ important	17. ____ wallet
6. ____ desktop	12. ____ raindrop	18. ____ bulletproof

Secrets to Success

WATCH THOSE COMPOUND WORDS

For some compound words, the meaning is obvious as in such words as headache (a pain in your head) or raindrop (a small drop of rain). Others, however, like cowboy only hint at the meaning. A cowboy certainly does not mean a boy who is a cow or a cow who is a boy. A cowboy is a person, often a male in earlier times, who works with cows. Still other words like hotdog have very different meanings from their parts. A hotdog may be hot, but it certainly is not a dog.

If the compound word does *not* make sense when you put the parts together, you will have to use context clues or your dictionary to find the meaning.

Types of Compound Words

Compound words can be even more difficult because there are several types.

Simple Compound Words. These are the most common kind of compound words. Here are a few examples: **rainbow, dishwater, airplane.** In your dictionary, simple compound words are often written with a dot between the syllables, for example: **rain•bow, dish•water, air•plane.**

Hyphenated Compound Words. Some compound words must have a **hyphen** (-) placed between the words. For example: **e-mail, re-elect, father-in-law, self-service, one-sided, well-being.** In your dictionary, hyphenated words should show the hyphen plus syllable breaks, for example: **e-mail, re-e•lect, fa•ther-in-law, self-ser•vice, well-be•ing.**

Spaced Compound Words. Other compound words are actually **spaced words.** A spaced word actually looks like two or more separate words but is, in fact, only one. Here are some examples: **health care, vice president, word processing, ground water, time saver.** In your dictionary, spaced compounds should look like this: **health care, vice pres•i•dent, word proc•es•sing, ground wa•ter, time sav•er.**

Exercise 2-3   Checking Compound Words

Use your dictionary to check the following compound words. If the word is already correct, just copy it on the line that follows. If it is wrong, rewrite it correctly. Here's an example:

quarter back (which is listed as **quar•ter•back**) ___quarterback___

1. face value _____

2. man kind _____

3. broken down _____

4. mother in law _____

5. practical joke _____

6. soda pop _____

7. skate board _____

8. fire engine _____

9. foot step _____

10. wall to wall _____

Caution

HYPHENATED AND SPACED COMPOUND WORDS
You must be very careful with hyphenated or spaced compound words. The same combination of letters with or without a hyphen may mean something very different. For example:
   It is warm up in the attic.
   Always warm-up your body before you exercise.

In this chapter, you have learned to decode a new language. Now read about how the mysterious code of the Egyptian hieroglyphs was finally translated.

The Rosetta Stone: The Key to Egyptian Hieroglyphs

PART I

VOCABULARY

pyramid—a large, often stone structure used as a royal tomb or burial place

pharaoh—an Egyptian king

hieroglyph—a sacred/holy writing symbol

official—someone in power, or something authorized by the people in power

papyrus—early form of paper made from reeds

Middle Ages—time period from 500 to 1450 CE (Common Era)

scholar—a person who studies a particular subject

bitumen—a medicine made of ground up mummies

mummy—a body preserved after death

sarcophagus—a stone coffin

THE MYSTERIOUS HIEROGLYPHS

1   Egypt is an ancient land of many mysteries. How were the great **pyramids** built? Who killed the boy **pharaoh** King Tut? Did the famous queen Cleopatra kill herself rather than be taken prisoner by the Romans? For nearly 1,400 years, the greatest mystery of all was the meaning behind the Egyptian hieroglyphs.

2   **Hieroglyph** means "sacred or holy carving." These pictures of animals, objects, and other unusual symbols were used by the Egyptian pharaohs and queens, priests, and government **officials** to record history, laws, business, and religious ceremonies. Hieroglyphs were written on rolls of **papyrus**, one of the earliest forms of paper. They were also carved into the stone walls of temples, pyramids, and other ancient Egyptian holy sites.

3   For more than a thousand years, hieroglyphs were the only form of written language in Egypt. Then, in the year 334 **BCE** (**Before the Common Era**—the time before the birth of Jesus), the Greek general Alexander the Great and his army defeated the Egyptians. Afterward, Greek became the language of the Egyptian rulers, priests, and businesspeople of Egypt. Several hundred years later, the Roman general Octavian defeated Egypt's Queen Cleopatra. After that, Latin was the **official** language of Egypt. Fewer and fewer people used or remembered the ancient hieroglyphs. As the centuries passed, the meaning of the ancient hieroglyphs was completely forgotten.

4   Nearly a thousand years later during the **Middle Ages,** European **scholars** became interested in hieroglyphs. At that time, doctors often gave their patients a medicine called **bitumen.** Bitumen was a powder made from ground-up Egyptian **mummies.** The mummies often arrived in Europe still in their **sarcophaguses.** Carved on the sides of these stone coffins were hieroglyphs. Curious people wanted to know what these strange symbols meant.

5   As early as 1633, a German priest named Anthanasius Kircher tried to translate this mysterious writing. He was unable to find a way to decipher the hieroglyphs, so he finally gave up. For the next 200 years, European scholars studied the Egyptian symbols. Without a "code book" to help them translate the symbols, however, all they could do was guess at the meaning of the strange symbols.

Exercise 2-4   Checking New Vocabulary

Choose a word from the Answer Box to correctly complete each sentence below. Use an answer only once.

ANSWER BOX

scholars	pharaoh	hieroglyphs
papyrus	officials	sarcophagus

1. King Tut was the famous Egyptian boy _____.

2. Egyptian _____ would write important information on rolls of _____ just as we write on paper.

3. The symbols used in ancient Egyptian writing are called

_____.

4. For many years, _____ studied the ancient

   Egyptian language trying to decode the strange symbols.

5. A mummy was put in a _____ because this

   stone covering protected the body.

Exercise 2-5 Finding Facts

Use the information in Reading 2, Part I, or the maps in the Appendix to answer the following questions.

1. On what continent is Egypt? _____

2. What famous Egyptian was queen when the Romans invaded Egypt?

   _____

3. Did Alexander the Great live before or after Jesus?

   _____

4. What was the name of the medicine made from ground-up mummies?

   _____

5. From what country was Anthanasius Kircher?

   _____

PART II

> ### VOCABULARY
>
> **linguist**—a person who studies languages
> **royalty**—pharaohs, queens, and their families
> **demotic**—hieroglyphs used by the common people
> **democracy**—rule by the people

THE AMAZING DISCOVERY

6   In 1798, the French Army of General Napoleon Bonaparte invaded Egypt. A year later, Napoleon's soldiers made an amazing discovery near the mouth of the **Nile River**. Just outside the small Egyptian town of Rosetta, they found a block of black stone.

7   The stone, which was about the size of a tabletop, had strange writing on it. The soldiers took the stone to the scholars that Napoleon had brought with him to study Egypt's ancient culture. The linguists were very excited about the discovery. There was something very remarkable about the Rosetta Stone. On the black slab of rock was the same story written in three different languages.

8   On the top third of the stone were lines of Egyptian hieroglyphs. The middle section was written in a language unknown to **linguists**. Most important, the bottom third was written in ancient Greek, a language that the linguists could still read. At last a code book had been found to decipher the mysterious hieroglyphs.

9   By studying the Greek writing on the stone, these language scholars were able to learn that the Rosetta Stone was written in 196 CE by Egyptian priests. The stone was carved to honor their ruler Pharaoh Ptolemy V (the fifth). Ptolemy was one of the Greek pharaohs. At that time, both hieroglyphs and Greek were being used in Egypt. That explained why his story was written in both languages. Scholars still could not understand the meaning of the middle language.

10   For many years, this strange language was a mystery. After much study, linguists finally decided these symbols were nothing more than a simpler form of hieroglyphs. True hieroglyphs were symbols of a sacred language that could only be used by priests, **royalty** (pharaohs, queens, and their families), and a few selected others. This simpler form of Egyptian writing could be used by the common people. For that reason, the second form of hieroglyphs was called **demotic**. The Greek root **demo-** means "of the people," like the word **democracy**, which means "rule by the people."

11   Even with the Rosetta Stone, solving the mystery of the ancient Egyptian hieroglyphs was very difficult because not all the symbols needed to decode this ancient language were on the stone. Many scholars tried but gave up. The problem was that most people believed that hieroglyphs were a kind of picture writing, similar to the Chinese language. In 1814, Dr. Thomas Young suggested a new idea. He thought that there might be a relationship between the symbols and the sounds, like in the English language. But he too gave up his studies.

12   Finally, in 1822, a young Frenchman named Jean-Françoise Champollion succeeded in breaking the code. He had seen a copy of the Rosetta Stone when he was a boy and was determined to solve its mystery. Champollion spent most his life studying ancient languages and cultures. With that knowledge and another newly discovered piece of writing similar to the Rosetta Stone, the young linguist proved that hieroglyphs are based both on phonics and picture meaning.

13   The key to understanding Egyptian hieroglyphs was finally found. At last, linguists could read this forgotten language. In those strange symbols, scholars discovered something even more remarkable—the lost history of an ancient civilization.

Exercise 2-6 Noticing Compound Words

Six of the words in the Answer Box are compound words—either regular, hyphenated, or spaced. The others are not. Write the compound words on the lines provided.

ANSWER BOX

Egyptian	tabletop	bitumen	ground-up
outside	Frenchman	scholar	linguists
demotic	underline	code book	conquer

1. _____   4. _____

2. _____   5. _____

3. _____   6. _____

Exercise 2-7 Vocabulary Check

Most of the new vocabulary words in this chapter were defined for you. Go back to the text or use your dictionary to define any word you can't remember or are unsure of. Then match the correct definition to each word by putting the letter of that definition on the line by the word.

_____ 1. symbol

_____ 2. linguist

_____ 3. officials

_____ 4. pharaoh

_____ 5. hieroglyph

_____ 6. papyrus

_____ 7. decipher

_____ 8. demotic

_____ 9. democracy

a. an early form of paper

b. male ruler of Egypt; Egyptian king

c. a person who studies languages

d. rule by the people

e. a written figure or sign that represents something else

f. an early form of Egyptian writing used by royalty

g. form of Egyptian writing used by common people

h. to decode or translate

i. people in power

Exercise 2-8 Checking Comprehension

Use words from Exercise 2-7 to complete the following sentences. You can use the Reading or Chapter 2 if you need information.

1. The ruler Ptolemy V was a Greek _____. The Rosetta Stone was carved to honor him.

2. A _____ is someone who studies languages.

3. Common people were never allowed to use hieroglyphs. Instead they had to use _____ writing.

4. After the Roman general Octavian defeated Queen Cleopatra, Latin became the language used by the government _____ of Egypt.

5. The form of government in the United States is called a _____ because people elect most of their officials.

6. Hieroglyphs were often written on _____, an early form of paper.

7. An ankh is an Egyptian _____ that represents life or fertility.

8. It is possible that linguists would never have been able to _____ ancient Egyptian hieroglyphs if the Rosetta Stone had not been found.

Exercise 2-9 Finding Places

Use the map of Egypt in Reading 2, Part II, the map of the Mediterranean area in the earlier part of the chapter, or the maps in the Appendix to answer the following questions.

1. What great river flows through Egypt? _____

2. Is the town of Rosetta in the northern (upper) or the southern (lower) part of Egypt? _____

3. What large body of water lies to the north of (above) Egypt?

   _____

4. What large body of water lies to the east (right) of Egypt?

   _____

5. Which is closer to Egypt, Greece or Italy?

   _____

Exercise 2-10 Writing About What You've Read

Writing about what you read is a good way to check your comprehension. On your own paper, write a short paragraph or two explaining how Egyptian hieroglyphs were finally decoded. Go back to Reading 2 if you have trouble remembering the details.

Going Beyond

Research

Check out the following key names and words on the Internet or at your local library.

mummies	hieroglyphs	the Rosetta Stone
King Ptolemy V	Cleopatra	King Tut (Tutankhamen)

Recommended

If you are fascinated by Egyptian history and artifacts go to the ancient Egypt website of the British Museum (www.ancientegypt.co.uk/menu.html) or visit the Egyptian Museum in Cairo's collection at www.egyptianmuseum.gov.eg.

Just for Fun

Decoding

For those of you who like to decode, here is the key again, plus some of the more common words you might use.

THE KEY

♋ A	♑ G	M	S	✡ Y
♌ B	♒ H	■ N	♦ T	⌘ Z
♍ C	♓ I	□ O	☦ U	
♎ D	♊ J	⚑ P	❖ V	
♏ E	& K	⇁ Q	⚢ W	
♐ F	● L	☼ R	⊠ X	

Common Words

a ♋   at ♋♦   as ♋♠   it ♓♦   in ♓■   on □■   is ♓♠

no ■□   not ■□♦   I ♓   you ✡□☦   your ✡□☦☼   he ♒♏   she ♠♒♏

Exercise 2-11

Try to read this paragraph without looking up at the key.

_____

_____

_____

_____

_____

_____

Challenge 2-11

In the passage below, some of the symbols have been changed. Can you decode this new writing? Hint: Why are some letters written differently in English?

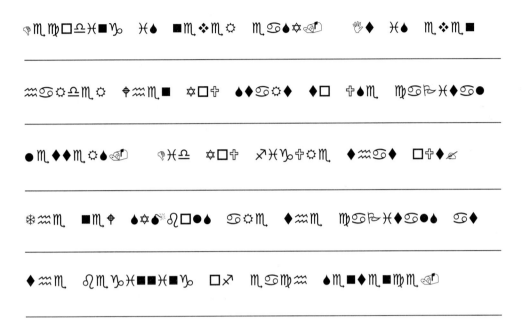

Mastery 2-11

Try using the key on page 28 to write a message of your own, then share it with a friend or fellow student.

CHAPTER 2 REVIEW

- Written Language

  Petroglyphs were the first known form of writing.

  In Mesopotamia, petroglyphs evolved into **pictographs**.

  The Phoenicians changed pictographic writing into the first true **alphabet**.

  The Greeks improved the Phoenician alphabet for storytelling.

  The Romans borrowed the Greek alphabet, changed and added letters.

  Today's English letters are very similar to the Roman alphabets.

  Other cultures such as the Chinese culture created different forms of language, like **ideographs**.

- Reading

  The process of reading in any language includes decoding and knowing how the symbols of that language are used together plus knowing other language rules, like in which direction to read and what punctuation marks to use. Decoding includes recognizing the symbols (letters) and combinations of letters (words). You should learn to recognize short, easy, common words by sight without having to decode each letter.

- Decoding

  Letters combine to make words, words combine to make sentences, sentences combine to make paragraphs, paragraphs combine to make different kinds of longer pieces of writing.

- Decoding the Meaning of Words

  The first step is to recognize a collection of letters as a unit of thought. Compound words are two words that have been created to make one. Compound words may be simple, hyphenated, or spaced.

The Secrets of Decoding the Sounds of English

The Sounds of English

In many languages like Spanish or Italian, a letter or symbol represents only one sound. That makes the language easier to write, speak, hear, and read. Unfortunately, that is not true of English. Because the English language has a very complicated history and because even modern English borrows words from other languages, you cannot depend on spelling to help you pronounce a new word.

Here are three words that look like they should sound the same except for the first letter: tough, bough, dough. But do they sound the same? No! Tough sounds like cuff. Bough sounds like cow. Dough sounds like no.

When English is so unpredictable, how can you ever expect to sound out new words? Here are a few suggestions.

Start with What You Know!

As with all the reading strategies you will learn in this book, start with what you already know. With one-syllable words, it is usually possible to sound out a new word by **rhyming** it with a similar word you know. One word **rhymes** with another when they have similar sounds. For example,

in	bin	din	fin	gin	kin	pin	sin	tin	win	grin	spin
bar	car	far	gar	mar	par	tar	char	spar	star		
at	bat	fat	hat	mat	pat	rat	sat	vat	spat	that	

Exercise 3-1 Noting Patterns—One Syllable

Add as many more words as you can to each of these patterns.

1. an, can, _____

2. cap, scrap, _____

3. end, bend, _____

4. bet, get, _____

5. but, cut, _____

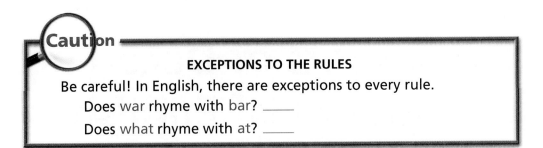

EXCEPTIONS TO THE RULES

Be careful! In English, there are exceptions to every rule.

Does war rhyme with bar? _____

Does what rhyme with at? _____

Use Your Dictionary to Find Pronunciation of New Words

Obviously, if you must know the correct **pronunciation** of a new word, there is only one thing to do. Use your dictionary. How do you do that? Here are a few simple steps.

Step 1

Look up an unknown word in your dictionary. Let's use the word quiche. The dictionary entry for quiche would look something like this:

> **quiche** (kēsh) *n.* A rich, unsweetened custard baked in a pastry shell.

In the dictionary, the pronunciation is immediately after the **entry word** (the word you looked up) and is usually in **parentheses**, such as quiche (kēsh). You may not know all the sounds that the symbols stand for, but you will once you learn to use the pronunciation key in your dictionary.

Step 2

Use your dictionary's pronunciation key to decode the sounds of the new word. Here is a sample pronunciation key. With each sound's symbol there is a common word that has that sound. Your dictionary may use slightly different symbols and words than this sample or other dictionaries.

SAMPLE PRONUNCIATION KEY

ă	cat	j	job	sh	shut
ā	may	k	kite	t	tall
âr	air	l	line	th	thick
ä	father	m	man	*th*	then
b	boy	n	no	ŭ	nut
ch	chat	ng	sing	ûr	sir
d	dog	ŏ	hot	v	vine
ĕ	get	ō	toe	w	wet
ē	we	ô	paw	y	yell
f	fun	oi	oil	z	zoo
g	go	o͝o	good	zh	treasure
h	hot	o͞o	food	ə	carton
hw	which	ou	out	ər	butter
ĭ	hit	p	pan		
ī	my	r	run		
îr	here	s	sit		

In the word quiche (kēsh), the q sounds like a k as in the word kite. The ui sounds like an ē as in the word we, and the ch sounds like the sh in shut. The e is silent.

Caution

PHONETIC SYMBOLS

Remember these symbols are *not* letters of the alphabet. They are **phonetic** (sound) symbols. Do not depend on the spelling of a word to give you its pronunciation. Letters such as the s in the word sugar has a different sound than you would expect. Also, certain letters are often silent in modern English such as the w in the word write and the b in the word comb. That is why it is always important to check your dictionary for the correct pronunciation.

Step 3

Once you check all the pronunciation symbols, blend the sounds together. For example, quiche (kēsh) sounds like: k + ē + sh = kēsh.

Exercise 3-2   **Pronouncing the Sounds of English**

After listening to your instructor say the sound for each symbol in the sample pronunciation key above, find a partner or team and take turns reading aloud the words that represent each sound. If you are not a native

English speaker, some of these sounds may be difficult for you to say. Do your best. If you have difficulty, keep practicing.

Exercise 3-3 Using your Dictionary to Pronounce New Words

Look up the following words and write their pronunciation on the line. Use the pronunciation key to try to sound out these new words. This may be difficult, so you may want to work with one or more partners.

1. mystery _____   6. official _____

2. pyramid _____   7. scholar _____

3. pharaoh _____   8. sarcophagus _____

4. hieroglyph _____   9. current _____

5. papyrus _____   10. era _____

Exercise 3-4 Using the Pronunciation Key to Decode

Use your knowledge of the pronunciation key to decode the phonetically written words. Write the letter of the correct pronunciation on the line beside each word.

_____ 1. code   a. (kē)

_____ 2. decode   b. (ĕn kōd´)

_____ 3. encode   c. (rīm)

_____ 4. key   d. (dē kōd´)

_____ 5. read   e. (sĭm´ bəl)

_____ 6. decipher   f. (rēd)

_____ 7. linguist   g. (wûrd)

_____ 8. word   h. (kōd)

_____ 9. rhyme   i. (dĭ sī´ fər)

_____10. symbol   j. (lĭn´gwĭst)

Get to Know the Sounds of the English Language

As you learned earlier, there are only 26 letters in the English alphabet, but, as you can see in the pronunciation key, there are nearly 50 different sounds.

You do not need to memorize all the sound symbols. If you can't remember a symbol, just look it up in the key.

For Your Information
YOUR DICTIONARY'S PRONUNCIATION KEY

Every dictionary uses slightly different symbols for those sounds. For that reason, it is very important that you get to know the symbols used in your dictionary's pronunciation key.

Exercise 3-5

Find the pronunciation key in your dictionary. It is usually near the front. Sometimes it is on the inside of the front cover. Some dictionaries even put the key at the bottom of each page. Where is yours located?

Consonant and Vowel Sounds

Linguists have divided the 26 English letters into two groups: consonants and vowels. **Consonants** are letters whose sounds are made by using your tongue, lips, or teeth.

CONSONANT SOUNDS									
b	ch	d	f	g	h	hw	j	k	l
m	n	ng	p	r	s	sh	t	th	*th*
v	w	y	z	zh					

For Your Information
THE DIFFERENCE BETWEEN th AND *th*

If you are wondering what the difference is between th and *th,* put your hand in front of your mouth and say the word thick. Do you feel breath on your hand? Now say the word then. Do you feel air now?

When you say thick, the tip of your tongue is outside your teeth. Air can blow between your tongue and teeth. When you say then, the tip of your tongue is up behind your teeth. No air can escape.

- The sound in thick (with air) is written th.

- The sound in then is written *th* (no air).

Vowel Sounds

A sound made without using your tongue, lips, or teeth is a **vowel**. Here are the vowel sounds of English.

VOWEL SOUNDS									
ă	ā	âr	ä	ĕ	ē	ĭ	ī	îr	ŏ
ō	ô	oi	oŏ	ōō	ou	ŭ	ûr	ə	ər

Special Sounds

Notice that several consonant sounds—ch, hw, ng, sh, th, *th*, zh—and several vowel sounds—âr, îr, oi, oŏ, ōō, ou, ûr, ər—are made up of more than one letter. Each of these symbols represents one distinct sound. For example, the phonetic symbol sh is *not* a blending of an s + an h sound. The phonetic symbol sh stands for the sound sh as in ship.

Say these words and listen to the sounds of the bold-faced letters.

ch—**ch**at	hw—**wh**ich	ng—si**ng**	sh—**sh**ut
th—**th**ick	*th*—***th***en	zh—televi**s**ion	
âr—**air**	oi—**oi**l	oŏ—g**oo**d	ōō—f**oo**d
ou—**ou**t	îr—**ear**	ûr—s**ir**	ər—butt**er**

Exercise 3-6 Finding the Pronunciation

Look up the words below and write their pronunciations on the line beside each word.

1. write _____
2. sleigh _____
3. pier _____
4. nose _____
5. exam _____

6. quit _____
7. roam _____
8. chute _____
9. magic _____
10. bowl _____

Did you notice again that spelling is not a good clue for pronunciation, particularly for vowel sounds? Even consonants can have several different sounds; the letter c can sound like an s as in the word cell (sĕl) or k as in the word cat (kăt) or even ch as in the word cello (chĕl′ ō). That is why it is so important for you to learn to use your dictionary's pronunciation key.

Rhyming Words

As you learned earlier, words often rhyme. There are many one-syllable words that rhyme like fat (făt), cat (kăt), sat (săt), mat (măt). Did you notice that the rhyming words all had the same vowel sound and a similar consonant pattern? Words with more than one syllable can rhyme too if they also have the same vowel or vowel sounds and similar consonant patterns. Here's an example: rabbit (răb´ ĭt) and habit (hăb´ ĭt).

Here are four words that look very different, yet they all rhyme.

moo (mo͞o)   you (yo͞o)   stew (sto͞o)   blue (blo͞o)

Exercise 3-7 Using Your Dictionary to Find Rhyming Words

Look up the words below and write their pronunciation on the line provided. If the word rhymes with the bold-faced word, circle it. Remember that words that rhyme should have the same vowel sound and a similar consonant pattern. Number 1 has been done for you.

1. **ham** (hăm)   lamb __lăm__   lame __lām__   ram __răm__
2. **play** (plā)   whey _____   sleigh _____   may _____
3. **mend** (mĕnd)   friend _____   waned _____   send _____
4. **meek** (mēk)   chic _____   teak _____   pique _____
5. **dim** (dĭm)   time _____   hymn _____   slim _____
6. **write** (rīt)   byte _____   height _____   fright _____
7. **pox** (pŏks)   rocks _____   knocks _____   hoax _____
8. **home** (hōm)   hum _____   comb _____   roam _____
9. **rum** (rŭm)   come _____   dumb _____   from _____

Challenge 3-7

10. **balm** (bäm)   psalm _____   calm _____   qualm _____
11. **air** (âr)   bear _____   square _____   heir _____
12. **hear** (hîr)   beer _____   sir _____   weir _____
13. **cross** (krôs)   rose _____   sauce _____   floss _____
14. **pour** (pôr)   tore _____   soar _____   floor _____

Mastery 3-7

15. **boil** (boil)   royal _____   toll _____   soil _____
16. **out** (out)   route _____   mount _____   doubt _____
17. **good** (go͝od)   should _____   rude _____   would _____
18. **you** (yo͞o)   hue _____   slew _____   flu _____

Syllables

A **syllable** is a part of a word. Each syllable has only one vowel sound. Every time there is a new vowel sound in a word, there is another syllable. For example:

cap   (kăp´) 1   slippery   (slĭp´ ə rē) 3

party   (pär´ tē) 2   photographer   (fə tŏg´ rə fər) 4

Secrets to Success

CHECK YOUR DICTIONARY FOR SYLLABICATION

When listing a word, a dictionary often puts dots between the syllables, for example: po·ta·to. Other dictionaries might use dashes: po-ta-to. Some just leave a space between letters: po ta to. Be sure to check your dictionary to see how words are divided into syllables.

Exercise 3-8   Noting Syllables

Sound out the word or check your dictionary to find the number of syllables in each of the following. Write the number of syllables on the line beside the word. Example: __3__ potato

1. _____ pharaoh   6. _____ papyrus

2. _____ queen   7. _____ mystery

3. _____ decode   8. _____ mummy

4. _____ pyramid   9. _____ linguist

5. _____ Tut   10. _____ Roman

Challenge 3-8

11. _____ hieroglyph   13. _____ Alexander

12. _____ Egypt   14. _____ sarcophagus

Mastery 3-8

15. _____ Ptolemy   17. _____ Cleopatra

16. _____ Rosetta   18. _____ Renaissance

Accents

The accent mark in the pronunciation of a word tells you where to put the **punch** on that word. The accent mark is usually placed at the end of the syllable that gets this emphasis, for example, carrot (kâr´ ət).

Where a word is accented can change the pronunciation of a word. For instance, in the sentence "I have an old 45 record of Frank Sinatra," the word record, which is used as a noun, is pronounced rek´ ərd. In the sentence "I think I'll record that movie to watch later," the word record, which is used as a verb, is pronounced rĭ kôrd´.

Sometimes there are two accent marks. The darker one is called the **primary**. It is the stronger of the two. The lighter one is called **secondary**. You often find primary and secondary accent marks on compound words like dogfight (dôg´ fĭt´).

Secrets to Success

HEARING THE ACCENTED SYLLABLE

Here's a trick to help you with accents. When you pronounce a word, tap your finger or fist on something when you say the accented syllable. Say the accented syllable louder and with more punch than the unaccented syllable.

Exercise 3-9 Accented Syllables

Try sounding out the following words. Put the emphasis on the accented syllable. On the line beside each word, write the number of the syllable or syllables accented. Example: __1__ sequel (sē´ kwəl)

____ 1. balloon (bə loon´)

____ 2. butterfly (bŭt´ ər flī´)

____ 3. equal (ē´ kwəl)z

____ 4. cassette (kə sĕt´)

____ 5. rhyming (rī´ mĭng)

____ 6. mission (mĭsh´ ən)

____ 7. ticket (tĭk´ ət)

____ 8. American (ə mĕr´ ĭ kən)

____ 9. motor (mō´ tər)

____ 10. injunction (ĭn jŭngk´ shən)

Caution

CHECK YOUR DICTIONARY FOR USE OF ACCENT MARKS

Again, it is important to check how your dictionary shows accented syllables. Some can be very different, particularly if you are using an international dictionary.

Schwa

Did you notice in the words above that there was often a symbol that looks like an upside down and backward e (ə)? That symbol is called **schwa** (shwä). The schwa actually represents the most common sound in the American English language. Its pronunciation is exactly like ŭ. The symbol ər, which is the schwa combined with an r, is pronounced exactly like ûr. Can you figure out why the same sounds have different symbols? Here's a clue: You will never find an ə or an ər in a one-syllable word.

Exercise 3-10

Look up the pronunciation of each of the following words in your dictionary and write it on the line beside the word:

1. about _____

2. pilot _____

3. vacant _____

4. master _____

5. corner _____

6. flutter _____

Have you figured out the mystery of schwa yet? Schwa and ər are only found in **unaccented** syllables. That means you will never find a schwa in a one-syllable word.

For Your Information

NOTE TO NONNATIVE ENGLISH SPEAKERS

One reason spoken English is so difficult for nonnative speakers to understand is because, unlike other languages that have a single vowel sound for each vowel letter, American English uses the schwa sound for most vowels in unaccented syllables. Other English speakers, like the British, Canadians, Australians, and others, tend to pronounce more of the vowel sounds than Americans do.

Decoding the pronunciation of new words sometimes seems as difficult as trying to decipher the Egyptian hieroglyphs. Remember it takes time, practice, and patience to master a new skill. In Reading 3, you will discover another language that is far more difficult to decode than English. Take a moment to look over the title, bold-faced headings, and illustrations before you begin to read.

Mayan Hieroglyphs: The Unsolved Mystery

VOCABULARY

astronomy—the study of the stars and outer space

flourish—to do well

city-state—a city that is an independent political unit

archeologist—a person who studies ancient human cultures

altar—a structure of wood or stone used for religious practices

excavation—professional diggings by archeologists

logograph—a symbol that represents an idea rather than a sound

glyph—a symbol that represents a sound

codex—a Mayan book

bishop—a high-ranking leader of the Catholic Church

comet—a ball of ice with a long tail of gas that travels through space

solar—related to the sun

lunar—related to the moon

eclipse—when sun or moon is covered by shadow

technology—the use of science in business or industry

unravel—come apart

WHO WERE THE MAYANS?

1   Hidden under the thick jungles of **Mexico** and **Central America** are the ruins of a once-great civilization: the **Maya** (mä´ yə). The first Mayan people lived in this area known as **Meso-America** as early as 2000 BCE. Over the centuries, the Maya had slowly developed into a highly evolved culture. These amazing people were experts at **astronomy** and mathematics and had developed a unique and complex form of hieroglyphic writing. From around 250 to 900 CE, the Mayan civilization **flourished**. Then, for reasons scientists are still studying, their crowded **city-states** were suddenly abandoned. The jungle quickly buried the once-magnificent temples, pyramids, and ball courts.

2   Today, **archeologists** working in Guatemala, Honduras, El Salvador, Belize, and the Yucatán Peninsula of Mexico are slowly uncovering some of the Mayan ruins. In these ruins, they have discovered the secret to Mayan

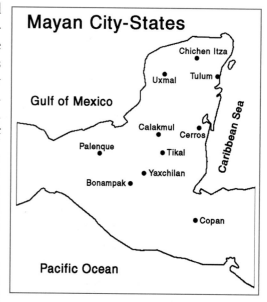

Mayan City-States

Chichen Itza

Uxmal   Tulum

Gulf of Mexico

Calakmul
Cerros

Palenque   ● Tikal

● Yaxchilan

Bonampak ●

Caribbean Sea

● Copan

Pacific Ocean

history. Written on stairways, **altars**, pyramids, walls, and doorways; painted on pottery; and carved into bones and shells are hieroglyphs, Mayan writing. **Excavations** have also uncovered many stelae. **Stelae** are large, freestanding stone **columns** that are covered with hieroglyphic writing. Now, archeologists are working to discover the secrets of the Mayan people's culture, their traditions, their rulers, their science, and their history, but first they must completely decipher the Mayan hieroglyphs.

MAYAN HIEROGLYPHS

3   Modern research on Mayan hieroglyphs did not begin until 1962. Since that time scholars have interpreted about 60 to 70% of the Mayan hieroglyphs. This has not been easy. Today, researchers are using computers to help decipher this complex language.

4   Why is the Mayan writing so difficult to translate? There are several reasons. First, the Mayans had no alphabet. Like the Egyptians, the Maya used a combination of **logographs** that represent ideas and **glyphs**

or symbols that stand for sounds. A logograph is like our $ symbol. Even someone who cannot speak English can understand the meaning of this symbol. The Mayan writing system has more than 3,000 logographs. So far, over 800 glyphs have also been discovered. The incredible number of Mayan symbols is not the only problem. Mayan logographs and glyphs can be combined in many different ways to form words or sentences.

5   Some of the symbols could also have more than one meaning. For example, in English, a tie might be something you wear with a suit or something that happens when two teams have scored the same number of points.

6   There is another reason the Mayan hieroglyphs have been so difficult to decode. Unlike English, which is only read from left to right, Mayan hieroglyphs were read left to right, right to left, top to bottom, or bottom to top.

DECIPHERING THE MAYAN HIEROGLYPHS

7   Mayans did write books. Their **scribes** wrote on pages of bark. A Mayan book was called a **codex**. Historians believe there may have been hundreds or thousands of these codices—bark books—at one time. The hot, humid climate of the jungle caused many of them to rot. The invading Spaniards destroyed most of the rest. In 1562, a Spanish **bishop** ordered all the Maya's books gathered up and burned. He believed that the strange symbols in these books were the work of the devil. Today, only four major Mayan books have been found. They have helped somewhat in decoding the hieroglyphs.

8   Researchers actually began their translation of the hieroglyphs using the Mayan calendar. Because the calendar is based on astronomical events such as **comets** and **solar** and **lunar eclipses**, scientists were able to decipher many of the glyphs written there. They could then use these to begin trying to comprehend the complex Mayan writing system.

9   Though more and more is being understood every day about Mayan hieroglyphs, the language is still only partially understood. Perhaps, one day, someone will discover a "Rosetta Stone" for this forgotten language. Until then, researchers around the world, aided by computer **technology**, will continue trying to **unravel** the mystery of Mayan hieroglyphs.

Exercise 3-11 Pronouncing New Words

Look up the following words in your dictionary and write down the word's correct pronunciation. Then practice saying the word correctly.

1. flourish _____

2. solar _____

   3. lunar _____

   4. scribe _____

   5. archeology _____

   6. astronomy _____

   7. altar _____

   8. excavation _____

   9. eclipse _____

10. technology _____

Exercise 3-12 Decoding Pronunciation Symbols

Use the pronunciation of words in Exercise 3-11 to answer the following questions:

1. List all the two-syllable words. _____

2. Does the u sound in lunar sound the same as the vowel sound in bun or the vowel sound in moon? _____

3. Does the i sound in scribe sound like the i in write or the i in bit?

_____

4. How many syllables does the word archeologist have?

_____

5. Does the last syllable of the word technology rhyme with by or with me? _____

6. Which words have the schwa sound (ə) found in unaccented syllables?

_____

7. On which syllable is the noun eclipse accented?

_____

8. Does the g in archeologist sound like a g or like a j?

_____

9. Does the vowel sound in the first syllable of flourish sound like the vowel sound in flour or the vowel sound in girl?

_____

10. Does the a in altar sound like the a in all or the a in art?

_____

Exercise 3-13 **Noting Compound Words**

Six of the words in the Answer Box are compound words; the others are not. Write the compound words on the lines provided.

ANSWER BOX

freestanding	astronomer	writing system	comprehension
archeologist	once-great	technology	doorway
city-state	hieroglyph	ballcourt	inscription

1. _____   4. _____

2. _____   5. _____

3. _____   6. _____

Exercise 3-14 **Vocabulary Check**

Use a word from the Answer Box to complete each sentence.

ANSWER BOX

archeologists	astronomical	eclipses
stelae	technology	bishop
flourished	scribes	excavation

1. The Mayan civilization _____ for hundreds of years then suddenly disappeared.

2. Before the _____ of a Mayan ruin can begin, all the jungle plants must be cut away so that the workers can start to dig.

3. A _____ is a stone column covered with Mayan hieroglyphs.

4. The Mayan priests knew so much about astronomical events that they could predict both solar and lunar _____ and the arrival of comets.

5. A Spanish _____ ordered all of the Maya's books burned because he thought they were the work of the devil.

6. Mayan _____ had to write each codex by hand.

7. _____ study both the ancient Mayan and Egyptian cultures.

8. Today, computer _____ is used to study Mayan hieroglyphs.

Exercise 3-15 Comprehension Check

Write the letter of the correct answer on the line provided.

_____ 1. Why have so few Mayan books been found?
   a. They were destroyed by angry Mayan priests.
   b. Because each codex took so long to write, only a few were written.
   c. They were destroyed by a flood.
   d. They were destroyed by the Spaniards.

_____ 2. During what time period did the Mayan civilization flourish?
   a. from 2000 BCE to the present
   b. from 2000 BCE to 250 CE
   c. from 250 to 900 CE
   d. from 900 to 1962

_____ 3. What percent of the hieroglyphs have now been deciphered?
   a. 0%   b. 50–60%   c. 60–70%   d. 70–80%   e. 100%

_____ 4. About how many Mayan logographs are there?
   a. 26   b. 300   c. 800   d. 1,000   e. 3,000

_____ 5. When did modern research on Mayan hieroglyphs first begin?
   a. 2000 BCE   b. 1962 BCE   c. 250 CE   d. 900 CE
   e. 1962 CE

Challenge 3-15

_____ 6. Where would you *not* find Mayan hieroglyphs written?

a. doorways   b. stelae   c. codex   d. papyrus
e. pottery

_____ 7. A Mayan logograph represented:

a. a vowel   b. a consonant   c. a number
d. a picture   e. an idea

_____ 8. Why have the Mayan hieroglyphs been so hard to decode?

a. There are over a thousand symbols to decipher.
b. Mayan writing uses both logographs and glyphs.
c. Mayan writing can be read in several different directions.
d. Few Mayan "books" survived to help decode the language.
e. All of the above.

Mastery 3-15

_____ 9. In which area would you not have found the Maya?

a. Yucatán Peninsula   b. Peru   c. Honduras   d. Belize
e. Guatemala

_____ 10. Which of these areas is known as Meso-America?

a. Part of Central America and the Yucatán Peninsula of Mexico
b. Mexico   c. South America   d. Yucatán Peninsula

Exercise 3-16   Map Check

Use the map of North America in the Appendix to answer the following questions:

1. What country is just north of (above) Mexico?

   _____

2. Of these countries where Mayan ruins are found—Belize, Guatemala, Honduras, El Salvador, and Mexico—which is the farthest north (toward top of the map)? _____

3. What is the small country that lies east of Guatemala?

   _____

4. What ocean is west (to the left) of Meso-America?

_____

5. What sea is east (to the right) of Meso-America?

_____

Exercise 3-17 **Writing About What You've Read**

On your own paper, explain why translating the Mayan hieroglyphs has been so hard to do.

Going Beyond

Resources

If you are interested in learning more about the Maya, look up any of the following key words on the Internet or at your local library.

Chichen Itza	Spanish conquistadors
Tulum	Mayan ballgames
stelae	Bishop Diego de Landa

Recommended

Though it may be difficult to find, there is an excellent book titled _Incidents of Travel in the Yucatán_ (1842), written by John Lloyd Stephens. In this travel book, the author shares his adventures as he searches for and discovers "the lost civilizations" of the Yucatán.

Just for Fun

Roman Numerals

Letters are not the only thing the English borrowed from the Romans. Roman numerals or numbers are also a part of your world. You often see them as dates, on clock faces, or in the preface, introductions, or chapter headings of books. Roman numbers are also used when making outlines or preparing study guides.

Just as hieroglyphs slowly disappeared, Roman numerals are becoming rarer and rarer in the modern world. This is probably because Roman numerals take longer to write and are more difficult to use. Whatever the reason, most schools do not even teach students how to read them anymore. If you don't know how and want to learn, you can—just for fun!

The Roman counting system is different from the Arabic numerals we use today. The Roman counting system used the following symbols, which are combined to make numbers.

I = 1   V = 5   X = 10   L = 50   C = 100   D = 500   M = 1,000

Here's how you would count to twenty in Roman numerals:

I = 1	VI = 6	XI = 11	XVI = 16
II = 2	VII = 7	XII = 12	XVII = 17
III = 3	VIII = 8	XIII = 13	XVIII = 18
IV = 4	IX = 9	XIV = 14	XIX = 19
V = 5	X = 10	XV = 15	XX = 20

Do you see a pattern that helps you understand how this number system works? Here are a few more examples that might help.

XL = 40	LIX = 59	CXXXVIII = 138	CMIII = 903
XLIV = 44	XC = 90	CCCXXXIV = 339	MXXXIV = 1,034
XLIX = 49	LXXXIX = 89	DXLIII = 543	MCMXCIX = 1,999
LIV = 54	XCIX = 99	DCCLXXXIX = 789	MMI = 2,001

Do you see the pattern now? It is based on addition and subtraction. Here's how it's done. Remember to work from left to right just like when you are reading English, using only these symbols.

I = 1   V = 5   X = 10   L = 50   C = 100   D = 500   M = 1,000

If a smaller number follows a larger number, the numbers are added.

VII = 7

If a smaller number comes before a larger number, the numbers are subtracted.

IX = 9

The parts are then totaled.

XLIII = (XL = 40) + (III = 3) = 43

MCMLXXXIV = (M = 1,000) + (CM = 900) + (L = 50)
         + (XXX = 30) + (IV = 4) = 1984

Exercise 3-18

Try matching the Roman numbers with the equivalent Arabic symbols.

_____ 1. 23   a. XCIV

_____ 2. 45   b. MMDCLVIII

_____ 3. 94   c. DLI

_____ 4. 132   d. XXIII

_____ 5. 465   e. MMMV

_____ 6. 551   f. XLV

_____ 7. 692   g. MD

_____ 8. 1,500   h. CXXXII

_____ 9. 2,658   i. CDLXV

_____ 10. 3,005   j. DCXCII

CHAPTER 3 REVIEW

- **The Sounds of English**
  Because of English's complex history, spelling is not usually helpful when trying find the correct pronunciation of a word. Compare new words or parts of new words to words you already know. See if you can make the new sound by rhyming. Learn the pronunciation symbols in your dictionary and use them to sound out new words.

- **Consonant and Vowel Sounds**
  Practice the sounds of English.

  Consonant sounds: b, ch, d, f, g, h, hw, j, k, l, m, n, ng, p, r, s, sh, t, th, *th*, v, w, y, z, zh

  Vowel sounds: ă, ā, ä, ĕ, ē, ĭ, ī, îr, ŏ, ō, ô, ŭ, ə

  Special sounds: ch, hw, ng, sh, th, *th*, zh, âr, oi, o͝o, o͞o, ou, ər, îr, ûr

- **Syllables**
  A syllable is a part of a word; it has only one vowel sound.

- **Accents**
  An accent mark tells you where to put the "punch" on a word when you say it.

- **Schwa**
  The symbol schwa (ə) sounds like the short u sound (ŭ) in unaccented syllables.

Finding the Basic Facts

Asking the Right Questions

Remember the first thing Detective Lee did in the story "The Case of the Missing Necklace"? (See Chapter 1.) She asked Mrs. Jones questions: Who? What? When? Where? Why? How? and more. Even as the detective hunted for clues and tried to interpret them, she asked herself more questions. Some of the answers to those questions were easy to find. Some were impossible. However, finding the facts to answer her questions is what helped Detective Lee solve the mystery.

If you are an **active** reader, you must do more than just decode the words. You must also constantly ask yourself questions based on what you are reading. To solve the mystery of reading, you must first learn to ask the right questions about the reading to find the facts that you need for comprehension.

The Simple Questions

The types of questions you ask yourself as you read depend on what you are reading and why you are reading. Here are examples of the kinds of questions that usually have simple answers:

Who or what is this about?

Where does this take place?

When does this take place?

The answers to simple questions are usually names of people, places, things, or times. Here are examples of simple questions with their answers:

- Who had the first true alphabet?
  The Phoenicians had the first true alphabet.
- In what country is Rome?
  Rome is in Italy.
- Where was Phoenicia?
  Phoenicia was east of Egypt.
- When was the first alphabet invented?
  The first alphabet was invented 4,000 years ago.

The Complex Questions

Other questions have longer or more complicated answers. Some questions lead you to other questions.

How?

When you ask a how question, your answer will be a **process**, a series of actions that bring about some result.

> How were the Egyptian hieroglyphs finally deciphered?
>
> Champollion used the Rosetta Stone, which had writing in both ancient Greek and Egyptian hieroglyphs, to decipher the symbols.

Why?

When you ask a why question, your answer will be what is called a **cause-and-effect** relationship—one action causes another. Your answer will often have the word because in it.

> Why were the common people of Egypt not allowed to use hieroglyphs?
>
> The common people of Egypt were not allowed to use hieroglyphs because hieroglyphs were holy symbols to be used only by royalty, priests, or government officials.

What?

When you ask a what question, your answer may be:

- a simple fact,

> What alphabet does English use?
>
> English uses the Roman alphabet.

or

- a process,

> What did the Romans do to change the Greek alphabet?
>
> The Romans first changed some of the letters and added others.

Answering Questions

Did you notice that the answers, even the simple ones, were presented in complete sentences? You too should develop the habit of answering questions in complete sentences. If you repeat the question in your answer, the answer is easier to understand and you will remember the answer better. For example, if the question is "When did Christopher Columbus discover America?" don't write "1492." If you answer, "Christopher Columbus discovered America in 1492," you are more likely to remember both the date and why that date is important.

Secrets to Success

ANSWERING QUESTIONS

There are times when it is perfectly okay to answer a question with a word or phrase. For example, spoken questions are often informal, so you may answer them with a short answer. When answering written questions, always follow the directions. If no specific directions are given and if room allows, write your answer in a complete sentence.

Exercise 4-1 Asking the Right Questions

*Using the information in Reading 2, "The Rosetta Stone: The Key to Egyptian Hieroglyphs," or Reading 3, "Mayan Hieroglyphs: The Unsolved Mystery," or both, write a question that begins with each of the types of questions discussed. Here's a helpful hint! Think like a teacher who is writing questions for a test. You **don't** have to answer the questions. Number 1 has been done as an example.*

1. Who? <u>Who was Alexander the Great?</u>

2. Where? _____

3. When? _____

4. How? _____

5. Why? _____

6. What? (fact) _____

7. What? (process) _____

Finding the Facts You Need for Comprehension

Accessing Your Own Background Knowledge

Whenever you read, your first and best resource is yourself. Always start with what you know. For example, if you are going to read a story titled "The Mummies of Ancient Egypt," take a moment before you start reading to **access** (get to) your background knowledge about this topic. Do you know what a mummy is? Perhaps you even know how people were mummified. Do you know where Egypt is on a map? Do you remember anything about the history of Egypt?

Take a moment to preview the reading, then think of what you know or don't know about the subject. Self-questioning before you read should tell you how easy or difficult the reading will be. It will also give you a foundation on which to build comprehension.

One of your first jobs as an active reader is to note whether or not you are familiar with the subject you are about to read. If you are *not*, be aware of the following:

1. You will have to do more work to find the necessary facts, so give yourself extra time to do the reading.

2. You will have to use outside resources to find the necessary facts.

3. Your comprehension may not be as complete as you want. That's okay! The next time you read about that subject, you will have a deeper understanding.

For Your Information

INCREASING YOUR BACKGROUND INFORMATION

Remember that the more you read, the more you know. Learning is like a snowball rolling down a hill. The more you read and experience, the bigger and bigger your background knowledge becomes. Try to think of every day as an opportunity to grow—as a person and a reader.

Finding Facts in the Text

Unless you have a photographic memory, you will never remember every detail of what you have read. However, if it is important to you to know specific facts, you can always go back to the text and find the facts you need. The secret is to find them quickly and easily.

Scanning for Key Words

Let's say you want to look up the phone number for a Janet Jones. Would you start at the beginning of the phone book? Of course not. You would flip to the Js in the phone book and find the page or pages that list the Jones. You would then **scan** (run your eyes quickly) over the list of Jones looking for the name Janet.

When you are looking for a particular fact, such as an answer to a question, you do the same thing. First you start with a **key word** or words. Like the key to a code, a key word helps you find what you are looking for.

Look at the following question: Where do manatee live? What word in the question do you think is the key word? Did you guess manatee? Then you're right.

You may also need to examine other words in the question to help find the answer. For example, you know you are looking for a place where the manatee lives. However, you would not find the answer to the question by looking up the word live.

Exercise 4-2   Noting Key Words

In the questions below, <u>underline</u> the key word(s) that you would use to find the answer to each question. You do not *need to look up the answer.*

1. What is the atomic number of iodine?
2. When did President Rutherford B. Hayes die?
3. Is a camellia a plant or an animal?
4. What is another name for Independence Day?
5. Can you eat a shallot?
6. Where did the Tlingit people live?
7. Is DDT a medicine used to treat a cold?
8. Do you need a deck of cards to play gin rummy?
9. To what religion does a caliph belong?
10. Does an ornithologist study fish?
11. Does Passover occur in the spring or fall?
12. What part of the body does a dermatologist work with?
13. Who uses a cleaver?
14. In what sport would you use a springboard?
15. From what is lanolin made?
16. When do you use an asterisk?
17. Where is Barbados?
18. How many players are on a baseball team?
19. What does the field of orthography study?
20. Of what is bronze made?

Using the Key Word(s)

Once you have found a key word or words in the question, it is time to use that key word to find your answer in the text. Remember, do not read word for word. Let your eyes run down the page until you see the key word you are looking for.

Exercise 4-3   Scanning Text for Information

Read each of the short paragraphs (A to E) below. Next, read the questions that follow each set. Underline the key word(s) in each question, then use that key word(s) to scan for the correct answer. Write the answer on the line beside the question.

A.   Across the whole of North Africa, from the Atlantic Ocean in the west to Egypt in the east, stretches the world's largest desert—the

Sahara. This hot, arid landscape covers more than 3 million square miles. When most people think of the Sahara, they picture huge, white sand dunes. Surprisingly, only 15 percent of the Sahara is sand. Almost 70 percent is stone deserts, plateaus of naked rocks. Mountains, oases, and the semi-arid regions on the borders of the great desert make up the remaining 15 percent.

1. What ocean is west of the Sahara Desert? _____

   _____

2. How many square miles is the Sahara Desert? _____

   _____

3. What percent (%) of the Sahara are stone deserts? _____

   _____

4. Mountains, oases, and the semi-arid regions make up what percent of the Sahara?_____

   _____

B.   Before the invention of the telegraph, people had to communicate over distances by using either sight or sound. Bonfires and smoke signals were used on land. Ships at sea often used flags of different colors and shapes. Pounding on drums or hollowed trees was a good way to send messages in jungles or forests where it was more difficult to see long distances. Church bells and whistles were also used to communicate over a distance.

1. What two objects were used for communication in jungles or forests? _____

   _____

2. Where were flags of different colors and shapes used to communicate? _____

   _____

3. For what purpose were church bells and whistles used?

   _____

   _____

4. How did people communicate before the invention of the telegraph? _____

   _____

C.   During a top-secret **photomapping** (mapping a place from the air by photographing it) of China during World War II, an American pilot made an amazing discovery—a gigantic pyramid. Today, researchers know that there are hundreds of pyramids in China. Unlike the pyramids of Egypt and the Americas, the Chinese pyramids are made of hardened clay instead of stone. Some are nearly as big as the Egyptian pyramids. One Chinese pyramid that has been studied is as tall as a 15-story building. As in Egypt, these pyramids were built as royal tombs or burial chambers.

1. When did Americans first discover the Chinese pyramids?

   _____

   _____

2. The Chinese pyramids are made of what material?

   _____

   _____

3. How tall are the Chinese pyramids?   _____

   _____

4. Why were the Chinese pyramids built?   _____

   _____

D.   The Earth is not a ball of solid rock. There are actually three distinct regions to our planet. The center, called the core, is very hot because it is under extreme pressure. The rock here is a semiliquid. The outer layer of the planet is called the crust. The crust is mostly solid rock. In places, this crust is covered by water, soil, sand, or cities. Between the hot core and crust is the thickest layer, called the mantle. Most of the mantle is solid rock, but at the very top is a thin semiliquid layer. This molten hot rock, floating between the mantle and crust, is called magma. If there is a crack in the crust, the magma can squeeze upward. When magma reaches the Earth's surface, it is called lava. At the surface, the magma cools back into rock. This magma erupting from the Earth creates volcanoes.

1. What is the center of the Earth called?   _____

   _____

2. What is the outer layer of the Earth called?   _____

   _____

3. Where would you find magma?   _____

   _____

4. How does magma reach the Earth's surface?   _____

   _____

E.   Do you think the people of the United States are the richest in the world? If you do, then you are wrong. The United States is not even in the top five countries if you compare the average incomes of the world's people. Europe has four of the five countries with the highest incomes. The tiny country of Luxembourg has the highest level of income in the world. In U.S. dollars, the average person in Luxembourg earns over $45,000 a year. Switzerland, Japan, Liechtenstein, and Norway—in that order—finish out the top five. The five poorest countries are all in Africa—Mozambique, Somalia, Eritrea, Ethiopia, and Congo DNC. In these countries, the average person makes $100 a year or less.

1. The citizens of what country have the highest income in the world?

   _____

   _____

2. On what continent are the five poorest countries in the world?

   _____

   _____

3. How much money does the average person in Ethiopia make a

   year? _____

   _____

4. Is Luxembourg a large or small country? _____

   _____

Using Resources to Find Facts

What if the information you need is not in your background knowledge or in the text of what you've read? Here's an example:

> Baby boomer is the name given to a person born between the end of World War II and the election of John F. Kennedy.

You have decoded the words and have a general understanding of the meaning. Is your comprehension complete enough to answer the following question?

> Is a person born in 1969 considered a baby boomer?

You cannot answer the question unless you know when World War II ended and the date of John F. Kennedy's election. What would you do to answer this question if you don't know these facts?

1. You could do nothing! That's your choice. However, a successful reader knows that it takes time and effort to find meaning.

2. You could ask a friend or family member for the information you need. Sometimes that is the easiest thing to do. But, if you do, can you be sure they really know the answer? What if they are wrong?

3. If you must be correct, here's what to do:
   - Identify the key words or key information you need to know.
   - Choose a **reliable** (trustworthy) resource like a college-level dictionary or encyclopedia. You can also use the Internet if you know you have a trustworthy **website** (electronic address). Your library's reference librarian is also a great resource for finding information.
   - Scan for your key word in that resource.
   - Finally, once you think you have found the information you need, check it against what you already know. Does it make sense?

   Now, follow the steps above to answer this question (explain why your answer is correct): Is someone born in 1969 a baby boomer?

   _____

Using Your Dictionary as a Mini-Encyclopedia

Did you know that you can use your dictionary as a mini-encyclopedia? A quality collegiate dictionary is filled with facts about people, places, dates, and much more. Buy the best-quality dictionary you can afford. Your dictionary is your best resource for finding a wide range of information.

Exercise 4-4   **Using Your Dictionary as a Mini-Encyclopedia**

Underline the key word(s), then use your dictionary to find the answers.

1. How many sides does the Pentagon have? _____
2. Name something that would be sold at a kiosk. _____
3. Is a saguaro a cactus or a succulent? _____
4. Is the Tropic of Cancer in the northern or southern hemisphere?

   _____

5. The czar was the ruler of what country? _____
6. Is a gander a male or female? _____
7. What is the atomic number of helium? _____
8. What material is used to make linen? _____
9. Where do you find a hypotenuse? _____
10. How long is a kilometer in miles? _____

Challenge 4-4

Underline the key word(s), then use your dictionary to find the answers. You will need a college-level dictionary to do these exercises.

1. What sea does Pakistan border? _____

2. Name a musical instrument that is related to a cello.

   _____

3. In what year did President Calvin Coolidge die? _____

4. Is a crocodile a reptile or an amphibian? _____

5. If you made an airplane out of balsa, would it fly?

   _____

Mastery 4-4

<u>Underline</u> *the key word(s), then use your dictionary to find the answers. Again, use a college-level dictionary.*

1. Name a country in the Fertile Crescent. _____

2. Lewis Carroll was a **pseudonym** (false name). What was the real name of the author who wrote *Alice in Wonderland*?

   _____

3. Who lived longer, President Lincoln or President Kennedy?

   _____

4. Between what two rivers was the ancient civilization called Mesopotamia found?

   _____

5. Which measurement is longer—a cubit or a yard?

   _____

Noting the Sequence of Events

In some readings, it will be important to notice the order in which the events happened and the time during which each took place. This is called the **sequence** of events. Knowing the sequence will make it easier for you to remember the information you have read.

A story or reading does not have to be told in **chronological** order. The author may wish to start in the present then review the past or any other combination of time sequence. These types of reading can be very difficult. You as a reader must **mentally** (in your mind) put the events in chronological sequence.

Putting events in chronological sequence can be difficult if the reading itself does not follow chronologically. Here is an example of sequencing, again using the events of "The Case of the Missing Necklace" (Chapter 1).

1. A robbery occurs (actually before the story begins).

2. Mrs. Jones reports the robbery of the necklace.

3. Detective Lee investigates the robbery.

4. Detective Lee finds evidence that the gardener is the thief.

5. The necklace is found in the gardener's home.

6. The gardener is arrested.

Exercise 4-5   Sequencing with Words or Numbers

Put these sets of words or dates in chronological order.

A. teenager, baby, adult, senior, child

1. _____
2. _____
3. _____
4. _____
5. _____

B. college, preschool, elementary school, high school, junior high school

1. _____
2. _____
3. _____
4. _____
5. _____

C. today, last week, tomorrow, next year, a month ago

1. _____
2. _____
3. _____
4. _____
5. _____

D. Halloween, New Year's Day, Christmas, Easter, Thanksgiving

1. _____
2. _____
3. _____
4. _____
5. _____

E. 1973, 1924, 1948, 1929, 1951

   1. _____   2. _____   3. _____   4. _____   5. _____

   Did you notice that time sequences can be written top to bottom or left to right? These are the **conventional** (by common agreement) ways to present time sequence in English. Events in chronological order may also be called **time lines**.

Challenge 4-5   Sequencing with Sentences

Place each set of sentences in the Answer Box in correct chronological order on the lines below. One answer has been given to help you.

ANSWER BOX

- After sealing the letter in the envelope, Dan put a stamp on his letter.
- Dan walked to the post office to mail his letter.
- Dan got out some paper and a pen from his desk to write his letter.
- Dan decided to write his mother a letter.
- Dan put the completed letter in the envelope.

A. 1. *Dan decided to write his mother a letter.* _____

   2. _____

   3. _____

   4. _____

   5. _____

ANSWER BOX

- Tonya ate pancakes and fruit for breakfast.
- After school, Tonya went to her part-time job at the mall.
- Tonya woke up at 8:00 a.m.
- After work, Tonya met her friends and went out for a milk shake.
- Tonya went to school.

B. 1. _____

   2. _____

3. _____

4. _____

5. _____

ANSWER BOX

- Though she was still full, Patricia had cookies and milk before bed.
- By 3:00 in the afternoon, Patricia's stomach was already growling.
- The salad Patricia had for lunch left her hungry for more.
- The large dinner she had waited for all day was on the table waiting when she came home.
- Knowing she was going to have a big dinner, Patricia only had a piece of toast for breakfast.

C. 1. _____

2. _____

3. _____

4. _____

5. _____

Mastery 4-5   Sequencing with Paragraphs

Read the short paragraphs, then write the events in the correct chronological order using the summary sentences from the Answer Box. A few of the lines have been done to help you.

A.   The big test is on Friday. Today, I will study the chapter outlines that I made last weekend. Tomorrow I will review my notes. The day before the test, I will reread the chapters.

ANSWER BOX

I will take the test on Friday.
Today, I will study my chapter outlines.
Last weekend, I made chapter outlines.
Tomorrow, I will review for the test.
The day before the test, I will reread the chapters.

1. Last weekend, I made chapter outlines.

2. _____

3. Tomorrow, I will review for the test.

4. _____

5. I will take the test on Friday.

B.   In the forest stands a mighty oak tree. A century ago, a tiny acorn
fell from another oak, now long dead. A squirrel found the acorn and
buried it in the ground, along with many others, but then forgot
about it. In the spring, tiny leaves pushed up through the ground. The
acorn had sprouted. It grew slowly under the shadow of its parent.
Then one day, the older tree fell in a huge wind storm. The young tree
now had lots of sun. It grew quickly and has continued to grow now
for a hundred years.

ANSWER BOX

Today, there is a mighty oak tree in the forest.
It grew quickly once its parent tree fell.
Long ago, the acorn sprouted, and the tree began to grow.
A squirrel found the acorn below the tree and buried it.
A century ago, an acorn fell from a tree.

1. _____

2. A squirrel found the acorn below the tree and buried it.

3. _____

4. _____

5. Today, there is a mighty oak tree in the forest.

C.   Finding a job is never easy. First, you must decide what kind of
job you want and are qualified for. Then you must actively search for
that kind of job. Many people use the newspaper or Internet when
job hunting. Once you find a job you are interested in, you should
neatly fill out the application. If you are lucky enough to be called in
for an interview, you should arrive on time and present yourself well.
After the interview, you might send the employer a note of appreciation. The employer will contact you. Unless the employer has told
you to do so, you should never call the company or institution. Be patient but never give up. Eventually, you will find a job you want.

ANSWER BOX

You should arrive at an interview on time and present yourself well.

Before you start your job search, decide what job you want and are qualified for.

Eventually, you will find a job!

Start your job search.

After the interview, send the possible employer a note of appreciation.

When you find a possible job, fill out an application.

1. _____

2. _____

3. When you find a possible job, fill out an application.

4. _____

5. _____

6. Eventually, you will find a job!

Exercise 4-6 Sequencing Readings

Events from readings in the first three chapters have been listed in the answer boxes below. You need to put them in chronological order. You may go back to the readings if necessary. This exercise may be difficult, so you might want to work with a partner or team.

ANSWER BOX

The Greeks adopted the Phoenicians' alphabet.

Today's English alphabet is still much like the one used by the Romans.

The earliest humans used petroglyphs carved on stone to communicate.

The Romans borrowed then improved the Greek alphabet.

The Phoenicians invented the first alphabet 4,000 years ago.

A. 1._____

2. The Phoenicians invented the first alphabet 4,000 years ago.

3. _____

4. The Romans borrowed then improved the Greek alphabet.

5. _____

ANSWER BOX

The Rosetta Stone was carved to honor Pharaoh Ptolemy V.

Napoleon's soldiers discovered the Rosetta Stone in 1799.

Finally, Jean-Francoise Champollion used the Rosetta Stone to translate hieroglyphs.

Thousands of years ago, hieroglyphs were used by Egyptian priests and royalty.

In the Middle Ages, European scholars first became interested in Egyptian hieroglyphs.

B. 1. Thousands of years ago, hieroglyphs were used by Egyptian priests and royalty.

2. _____

3. In the Middle Ages, European scholars first became interested in Egyptian hieroglyphs.

4. _____

5. _____

ANSWER BOX

Researchers began studies on the newly discovered Mayan hieroglyphs.

The Mayan civilization flourished from around 250 to 900 CE.

Mayan ruins were discovered in the jungle of Meso-America.

Early Mayan villages evolved into city-states.

The attempt to translate Mayan hieroglyphs continues, using computer technology.

The Mayan civilization suddenly vanished.

C. 1. Early Mayan villages evolved into city-states.

2. _____

3. The Mayan civilization suddenly vanished.

4. _____

5. Researchers began studies on the newly discovered Mayan hieroglyphs.

6. _____

READING 4 # Where in the World Did English Come From?

PART I

> VOCABULARY
>
> **adapt**—to change to meet a need or situation
> **ancestor**—a family member who has come before, like father or grandmother
> **sibling**—brother or sister
> **common**—shared, related to all in a group
> **nomad**—a person who moves from place to place looking for food, etc.
> **isolated**—alone, separate
> **Indo-European**—ancient common language of many modern languages
> **Romance languages**—all languages descended from the Roman language (Latin)
> **etymology**—history of a word

1   A language is a living thing. Like people, language grows; it **adapts** to new needs and situations; sometimes a language even dies if there is no one left to speak the language. Languages are like people in another way. Languages have **ancestors** just as people have parents and grandparents. Languages can also be like **siblings**. For example, the English spoken in the United States is the same yet different from the English spoken in England. In Washington, people might say, "I'm taking the elevator to the ninth floor," but in London, "I'm taking the lift to the ninth floor." In the United States, you stand in line, while in England, you queue up.

2   Just like people, each language also has a family tree. Linguists believe that many of the languages used in the world today came from a **common** language that was spoken thousands of years ago. In those ancient times, the few people living on this planet were **nomads**. They moved from place to place looking for food. Over thousands of years, people spread out across the continents of Europe, Asia, and Africa. As farming developed, villages then towns then cities grew. Since travel was difficult and dangerous, distance and natural obstacles like mountains and rivers often kept people **isolated** from each other.

3   As time passed, new words and pronunciations developed differently in each different region. Just as American English has changed from British English, many new languages grew out of the one common language as people separated into different communities. Linguists call this older common language **Indo-European**. Indo-European is the distant **ancestor** of the English that is spoken today. The following family tree shows how some linguists believe many of the languages spoken today are related to each other.

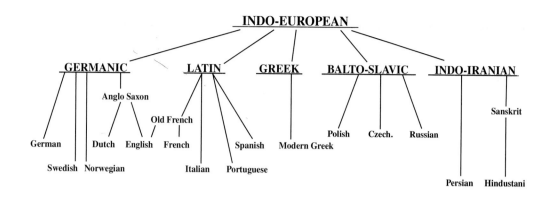

4   As you can see, English and Dutch are close cousins because they are descended from Anglo-Saxon. French, Spanish, Italian, Portuguese, and several other languages that are not listed are also close cousins to each other. They are all descended from Latin. These Latin-based languages are called the **Romance languages** since Latin was the language of Rome.

5   Every language has its own history or **etymology**. Linguists have separated the history of the English language into three stages: Old English, Middle English, and Modern English.

Exercise 4-7 Finding the Correct Pronunciation

Look up the following words in your dictionary and write the pronunciation of each.

1. adapt _____

2. ancestor _____

3. sibling _____

4. common _____

5. nomad _____

Exercise 4-8 Checking Pronunciation—Short Answer

Use the pronunciation of the five words in Exercise 4-7 to answer the following questions.

1. Which words have the schwa sound ə found in words with

   unaccented syllables? _____

2. Which word has the same vowel sound as the vowel sound in the

   word toe? _____

3. Which words have two syllables? _____

4. Is the accent on the word common on the first or on the second

   syllable? _____

5. How many syllables are there in the word ancestor? _____

   _____

Exercise 4-9 Finding Facts

Use Part I of this reading to answer the following questions. Write your answers in complete sentences.

1. From what common language did all the Romance languages

   develop? _____

   _____

   _____

2. Why did the ancient people spread so widely throughout the world?

   _____

   _____

   _____

3. What often isolated the ancient people from each other?

   _____

   _____

   _____

4. How are people and language alike?

   _____

   _____

   _____

5. What language do linguists believe is the common ancestor of many
   languages today?

   _____

   _____

> ### VOCABULARY
>
> **remote**—far from others
>
> **Celts**—early people of the British Isles
>
> **Celtic**—related to the Celts
>
> **Germanic**—related to early tribes from what is now Germany: Angles, Saxons, and Jutes
>
> **Anglo-Saxon**—language of early Germanic tribes
>
> **Old English**—a language that was a combination of Anglo-Saxon and Celtic
>
> **survived**—were not killed
>
> **Normans**—people from the area of Normandy in France
>
> **serf**—servant, worker
>
> **overlord**—rulers, masters
>
> **dialect**—a regional variety of a language
>
> **Old French**—a language from Latin that was once spoken in France
>
> **Latin**—the language of the Roman empire
>
> **Middle English**—a language that was a combination of Old English and Norman

OLD ENGLISH (500–1100 CE)

6   Across the **English Channel** from **France** is a large island known to most people as **England**. The smaller countries of **Scotland** and **Wales** also share this island with England. Together, these three countries make up **Great Britain**. This island nation was the birthplace of the English language. Today, Great Britain, **Ireland**, Australia, and the United States are the main English-speaking countries.

7   Long before there was a Great Britain or even an England, this **remote** island was inhabited by a group of people known as the **Celts**. The Celts spoke the **Celtic** language.

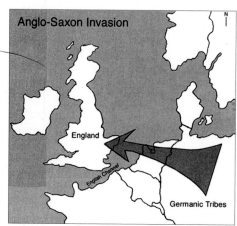

Anglo-Saxon Invasion

8   During the fifth century CE, invaders from the country now called Germany attacked the island. These invaders were from three **Germanic** tribes: the **Angles**, the **Saxons**, and the **Jutes**. All three tribes spoke a very similar language known as **Anglo-Saxon**.

9   The Anglo-Saxon invaders killed many of the Celtic people. The other Celts fled into the wild mountainous lands of Wales or Scotland. Because of this, only a few Celtic words, mostly place names like Thames, Kent, and York, are still part of today's English. As time passed, the Anglo-Saxon language evolved into what linguists call **Old English**.

10   Surprisingly, very few Anglo-Saxon words **survived** either. Only about one-sixth of the words we use today come from Old English. Words like eye, nose, mouth, many of our colors, and all of our numbers from 1 to 100 have come from Old English.

11 Even those words that were the ancestors of modern English were written and pronounced very differently than they are today. You can see the differences in this sample of Old English text.

Old English

Fæder ure Þu Þe art on heofonum si Þin nama

gehalgod tobecume Þin rice

gewurÞe Þin willa on corðan swa swa on heofonum

urne gedæghwamlican half syle us to dæg

and forgyf us ure gyltas swa swa we

forgyfað urum gyltendum

and ne gelæd Þu us on costnunge ac alys us of

yfele soÞlice.

MIDDLE ENGLISH (1100–1500 CE)

12 In 1066, William the Conqueror, the Duke of Normandy, attacked England from across the English Channel. His soldiers defeated the Anglo-Saxons. Unlike the Anglo-Saxons, the **Normans** did not drive the local people away. Instead, the new Norman rulers took possession of the land and forced the Anglo-Saxon people living there to work as their **serfs**. These new Norman **overlords** spoke a **dialect** of **Old French**. Old French had evolved from **Latin**, so many of the new words coming into Old English during these years were from Latin roots.

13 Over the years, the Old English of the Anglo-Saxons began to mix with the Old French of the Normans to create what is called **Middle English**. Linguists say that more than 10,000 Old French words were borrowed during the period of Middle English. With these new words came their Latin roots. It is believed that about 75 percent of those words, or the descendants of those words, are still used in English today.

14 In Middle English, Old English endings were added to French words. For example, the French word gentle plus the Old English word man became gentleman. Frequently, during the era of Middle English, there would be two words for the same things. When you compare similar words from Old English with those from Old French, it is easy to see who was the servant and who was the lord. Look at these pairs and see if you can figure out who was the master and who was the servant: sheep—mutton, swine—pork, ox—beef, calf—veal, house—mansion.

15 Though still very different from today's English, Middle English was evolving into a form that you might be able to recognize as an ancestor of Modern English. Here is the same quote that you read earlier, now written in Middle English.

Middle English

Oure fadir Þat art in heuenes hafwid be Þi name;
Þi reume or kingdom come to be Be Þi will don
in herÞe as it is doun in heuene.
yeue to us today oure eche dayes bred.
And foryeue to us oure dettis Þat is oure
dettouris Þat is to men Þat han synned in us.
And lede us not into temptacioun but delyuere us
from euyl.

Exercise 4-10 **Finding the Correct Pronunciation**

Look up each of these words in your dictionary, write the pronunciation on the line beside the word, then practice sounding out the new word.

1. channel _____
2. serf _____
3. survive _____
4. Celtic _____
5. Saxon _____

Exercise 4-11 **Finding the Facts**

Use Part II of this reading to find the following facts. Again write your answers in complete sentences.

1. Name four English-speaking countries. _____

2. List the three Germanic tribes that invaded England.

3. What language did the Germanic people speak?

4. When did William the Conqueror attack the Anglo-Saxons?

5. Were the Normans serfs or overlords? _____

_____

Challenge 4-11

6. Where did the Celtic people try to hide from the Anglo-Saxon invaders? _____

_____

7. How many Old French words came into English during the Middle English time period? _____

Mastery 4-11

8. Why are there Latin-based words in English today?

_____

9. When the Anglo-Saxons attacked the Celts, from what direction did they come—the north, south, east, or west?

_____

10. Is the word *ear* an Anglo-Saxon or a Norman word? _____

_____

PART III

> ### VOCABULARY
>
> **era**—a specific period of time
> **Dark Ages**—an era of violence and disease from 476 to 1000 CE
> **plague**—a widespread, often fatal disease
> **Black Death**—Fourteenth-century bubonic plagues
> **Renaissance**—an era of the rebirth of culture and civilization
> **ideal**—an honorable or worthy principle
> **equality**—fair and equal treatment of all
> **justice**—the principle of moral fairness
> **literacy**—being able to read and write
> **standard**—the basis on which others are judged
> **standardized**—to change differences to meet the standard
> **New World**—the Americas
> **revolution**—a large and often rapid change

MODERN ENGLISH (1500–PRESENT)

16   After the fall of the Roman Empire, there was an **era** known as the **Dark Ages**. This was a time of violence and disease. In 1349–50, one-third of the English people died during a **plague** known as the **Black Death**.

17   By 1500, life was finally beginning to improve. A new era was beginning. Historians call this time the **Renaissance**. Renaissance means rebirth. The **ideals** of the Greek and Roman civilizations such as **equality** and **justice** were being reborn. The world was beginning to change, and so was language.

18   In 1476, William Caxton brought the first printing press to England. Books written before that time had to be copied by hand. Now they could be printed by a machine. Books became cheaper. **Literacy** increased. More and more people learned to read and write. In the beginning, there were many different spellings and pronunciations for words. To solve that problem, the dialect used in London where most of the books were printed became the **standard** for the English language. Spelling and grammar began to become **standardized** too. Modern English was being born.

Early Modern English

Our father which art in heauen hallowed by thy name.
Thy kingdom come Thy will be done
in earth as it is in heaven.
Giue us this day our daily bread.
And forgiue us oure debts as we forgiue our debters.
And lead us not into temptation, but deliuer us
from euill.

AMERICAN ENGLISH

19   Around 1600, England began to colonize the **New World**. As these American settlements grew, a new form of the English language began to evolve. Many new words, particularly place names, were borrowed from the Native Americans: Mississippi, Iowa, Illinois. Words for plants and animals like raccoon, hickory, and tomato were also borrowed.

20   Over the next 200 years, the new country of the United States began to rapidly expand. Along the way, the settlers borrowed words from their new neighbors. Many Spanish words have come into American English over the years, words like salsa, canyon, ranch, stampede. A few words came from the French in Louisiana

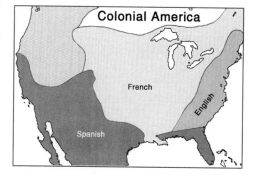

and Quebec, words like armoire, bayou, and fur. Even a few West African words came from the slaves, words like goober, gumbo, and tote.

21   In the 1800s, the industrial and scientific **revolutions** began, both in the United States and England. As new machines were developed and new scientific discoveries made, there was suddenly a need for hundreds of new words. Many of these words, like thermodynamic and hydrocarbon, were created from Greek and Latin roots. Others were simply the combination of existing words like typewriter and horsepower.

22   The medical and technological revolutions of the last 50 years have also caused the creation of many new words. A dictionary that is more than ten years old may not have words like CD-ROM or byte in them. The dictionary of the future will have countless words that are not yet in today's vocabulary. Our language is a living thing. It will continue to grow and change as long as there are people who speak it.

Time Line of the English Language

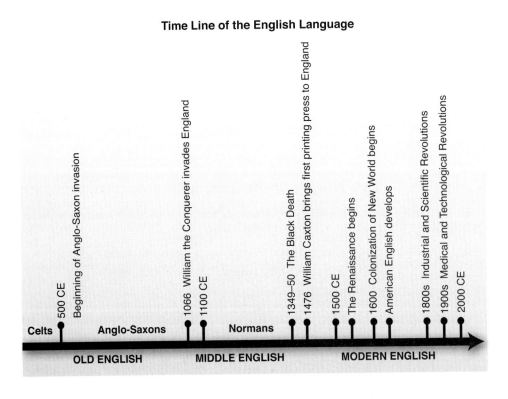

Exercise 4-12 Finding the Correct Pronunciation

Look up each word in your dictionary, and write the correct pronunciation on the line beside it.

1. plague _____

2. era _____

3. equality _____

4. mangle _____

5. Renaissance _____

Exercise 4-13 Vocabulary and Comprehension Check

Choose a word from the Answer Box to correctly complete each sentence below.

ANSWER BOX

standard equality dialect literacy Technological Revolution
plague era Dark Ages Renaissance New World justice

1. The printing press was responsible for a sudden rise in
   _____ because cheaper books meant more
   people had the chance to read.

2. Part of your education is learning the spelling and grammar of
   _____ English, the acceptable academic form
   of the language.

3. The bubonic _____, also called the Black
   Death, killed one-third of all the people living in England.

4. The period after the fall of the Roman Empire was called the
   _____ because life in Europe then was filled
   with violence and disease.

5. People in Australia speak a different _____ of
   English than the people living in the United States.

6. Many new English words were borrowed from the
   _____—French words from Louisiana and
   Canada, Native American words, Spanish words from the old
   Spanish colonies, and even some slave words.

7. Words like computer and microprocessor were invented during the
   _____.

8. _____ and _____ were
   two of the ideals Europeans borrowed from the Greeks and Romans
   during an era known as the _____.

Exercise 4-14 Sequencing

Use the time line at the end of Reading 4 to help you put the events listed in the Answer Box into chronological order. Several have been done to give you a few clues.

ANSWER BOX

- After the Germanic tribes invaded England, Anglo-Saxon or Old English was spoken there.
- William, Duke of Normandy, invaded England and conquered the Anglo-Saxons.
- Today, Latin and Greek roots are used to develop words like radioactive.
- Anglo-Saxon and Old French (Norman) combined to make Middle English.
- In the beginning, Celtic was the only language spoken in the land now called England.
- The printing press standardized English.

1. _____

2. After the Germanic tribes invaded England, Anglo-Saxon or Old English was spoken there.

3. _____

4. Anglo-Saxon and Old French (Norman) combined to make Middle English.

5. _____

6. _____

Exercise 4-15 Map Check

Use the maps in the reading or in the Appendix to find the places listed below. Then use the information you have learned to answer the following questions. You may also need a collegiate dictionary, an atlas, or the Internet. An answer may be used more than once.

England	Atlantic	English Channel	Canada	New Mexico
Scotland	Germany	Ireland	Mississippi	California
Wales	France	Mexico	Texas	Normandy

1. What body of water separates France from Great Britain?

   _____

2. What other two countries share the island with England?

   _____   _____

3. What large island is west (to the left) of England?

   _____

4. Normandy is now part of what country?

   _____

5. The original 13 English colonies all had a shoreline on what ocean?

   _____

6. Louisiana is at the mouth of what river?

   _____

7. Name three U.S. states that were once Spanish-held land.

   _____   _____   _____

Exercise 4-16   Writing About What You've Read

Today, the computer revolution is causing major changes in the English language. On your own paper, write a paragraph about these changes. You might start by thinking about all the new vocabulary words used when discussing computer technology.

Going Beyond

Words can come from the oddest places. Some words actually started out as the name brand of a product. Did you know zipper was the name of the company that made the first slide fastener, the zipper? When you ask for a Band-Aid, are you upset when someone gives you another brand of adhesive bandage? When some people ask for a Coke, they mean any drink that is brown and fizzy. Even Ping-Pong is named after a company that made table-tennis balls.

Find a partner or a team and see how many trademark words you can think of. Use the Internet to help you with your search. _____

_____

_____

Just for Fun

Finding Facts Fast

Here's a challenge that will let you use both your dictionary and sequencing skills. If you want an added challenge, compete with others in your classroom or team. The one who can correctly complete the exercise fastest is the winner.

Exercise 4-17 **Dictionary Races—American Presidents**

In the exercises below, place the American presidents in the correct chronological sequence using only your dictionary. Number them in order, starting with number 1 as the earliest president.

Race 1

____ Andrew Jackson

____ Woodrow Wilson

____ Martin Van Buren

____ Warren Harding

____ Andrew Johnson

Race 2

____ James K. Polk

____ Thomas Jefferson

____ Benjamin Harrison

____ Rutherford B. Hayes

____ Bill Clinton

Race 3

____ Theodore Roosevelt

____ Dwight D. Eisenhower

____ William Howard Taft

____ Chester Alan Arthur

____ John F. Kennedy

____ Calvin Coolidge

____ Richard M. Nixon

____ Jimmy Carter

Race 4

____ Gerald Ford

____ John Adams

____ Lyndon B. Johnson

____ Franklin D. Roosevelt

____ George W. Bush

____ John Quincy Adams

____ James A. Garfield

____ George Washington

CHAPTER 4 REVIEW

■ **Asking the Right Questions**

To find the answers you need for comprehension you need to ask the right questions. Some questions have simple answers like who? where? and when? Other questions have more complex answers like how? what? and why?

■ **Finding the Facts You Need for Comprehension**

There are several strategies for finding the facts you need for comprehension:

Start by accessing your background information about the topic you are reading.

Use key words to scan the text for important information or answers to questions.

Use other resources such as the Internet and library. A quality college-level dictionary can be used as a mini-encyclopedia.

■ **Noting Sequence of Events**

You need to learn to note the sequence of events or chronological order of what is happening in particular readings.

Finding Context Clues

Once a detective has an overview of the mystery to be solved, he or she is ready to start collecting clues. The first place to find clues to the meaning of what you've read is in the text itself.

Looking for Context Clues

When Detective Lee first came to Mrs. Jones' house in "The Case of the Missing Necklace" (Chapter 1), she did a quick overview of the grounds and house before coming back to do a thorough investigation of the crime. As a reading detective, you want to do a first reading without stopping—not even to look up a word you don't know.

Why? You do a first reading because the clues you need for understanding both new words and even the meaning of the reading can often be found in the reading itself. These clues are called **context clues**.

Think of context clues as **hints** to the meaning. Some clues are weak. The speck of mud Detective Lee found on the fire escape was not a strong clue. Anyone could have had muddy shoes. Finding the gardener's fingerprint in the bedroom, however, was very strong evidence.

In this chapter, you will not only learn how to find context clues but also to judge whether they are weak or strong. You will then make **deductions** (conclusions drawn from the clues). Listed below are the types of clues discussed in this chapter.

CONTEXT CLUES

Context Clues to Understanding New Vocabulary
- Definition or Information Clues
- Synonym Clues
- Antonym Clues
- Example Clues
- Clues from Your Background Knowledge

Other Context Clues
- Grammar Clues
- Punctuation Clues

Context Clues to Understanding New Vocabulary

Definition or Information Clues

There are several ways to look for meaning in words.

- Often the meaning of a new or difficult word will be stated immediately *after* the word.
- Other helpful information might also be found *close* to the word.
- Watch for a set of commas, parentheses, or dashes that *sets off* this information.

In the examples below, the new word has been *italicized* and the clues underlined.

> *Linguists*, people who study languages, were very interested in the Rosetta Stone.

> Early humans created *ideographs* (picture symbols for ideas) to write about their feelings or thoughts.

> *World War II*—fought by the United States from 1941–1945—caused hardship for the people of the entire world.

Exercise 5-1 Using Definition/Information Clues

Use the clues to find the definition of the italicized word. Underline *the definition of that word.*

1. Sheri wants to be a *pediatrician*, a baby doctor, because she loves children.

2. Amelia Earhart was an *aviatrix*, a woman pilot.

3. In Arizona, *monsoons*—seasonal heavy rain storms—usually occur in the summer.

4. *Archeologists* (people who study ancient cultures) were excited by the discovery of the Mayan ruins.

5. The first step in reading is to *decipher* (figure out) the meaning of the symbols.

6. Hieroglyphs were often written on *papyrus*, an earlier form of paper.

7. A true *alphabet*, which is a group of symbols that stand for sound, was first invented by the Phoenicians.

8. A *collegiate*—college-level—dictionary can often be used as a mini-encyclopedia.

9. There are over 800 Mayan *glyphs* (symbols that stand for sound).

10. A dollar sign is an example of a *logograph*, a symbol that represents an idea.

Synonym Clues

A **synonym** is a word that has a similar meaning to another word.

For example, *large* is a synonym for *big*, and *tiny* is a synonym for *small*. There are several ways to look for synonym clues.

- The synonym clue is often in the <u>same sentence</u> as the unknown word.
- It can come <u>before</u> or <u>after</u> the word.
- Sometimes the clue is in the <u>next sentence</u> or even the <u>one before</u>.

In the sentences below, the word to be defined is *italicized* and the synonym clue <u>underlined</u>.

The treasurer of the club takes care of *fiscal* (money) matters.

You think my sister is <u>stubborn</u>. I am even more *obstinate* than she is.

The dentist decided to tell all his patients about *gingivitis* because <u>gum disease</u> is a very common problem.

Exercise 5-2   Using Synonym Clues

Use the clues to find the synonym that defines the italicized word. (This may be more than one word). <u>*Underline*</u> *the synonym.*

1. Jorge has been the *proprietor* of the store for thirty years. His father was the owner before that.

2. When Lara woke in the morning, the pain was still *acute*. It had been very sharp now for two days, and she was worried.

3. Arthur rented the most *remote* cabin he could find. He wanted to be as far away from people as possible.

4. Suzanna loved the *emerald* because the dark green gemstone matched her eyes perfectly.

5. I thought I was interested in *ichthyology* until I spent a week on a boat. After being seasick for seven days, I knew I didn't want to study fish after all.

Antonym Clues

Antonyms are words with opposite meanings like big and small.

Watch for the following words that **signal** antonyms:

but however yet on the other hand in contrast

These words tell you to watch for an antonym clue. Here are some examples of antonym clues.

I would like to be *affluent*, <u>but</u> I guess I will always be <u>poor</u>.

My best friend Susan is very <u>shy</u>. Her husband, <u>on the other hand</u>, is *gregarious*.

Exercise 5-3 Using Antonym Clues

Use the clues to find the definition of the italicized *word.* <u>Underline</u> *the clue(s), then write your definition of that word on the line below.*

Example: I thought all dinosaurs were *carnivores*, <u>but</u> in fact some <u>ate plants not meat</u>.

  Dinosaurs that ate meat. _____

1. The tiny dog looked *innocuous*, but in fact he was very dangerous.

   _____

2. Taylor was never very hungry, but after going without food for three days he was so *ravenous* he ate like a starving dog.

   _____

3. Lela is usually very *verbose* in class. Today, however, she didn't talk at all, not even to her friends.

   _____

4. I thought a run through the park would *rejuvenate* me, but now I am feeling older and even more tired and weak than I did before I ran.

   _____

5. The swinging bridge looked *precarious*, but our tour guide told us it was very safe.

   _____

Example Clues

In example clues, the author helps you understand a new or difficult word by giving you **examples**. Whether the clues are helpful or not depends on how much you know about the examples given. For example:

Mathematics courses such as geometry, algebra, and calculus can be difficult.

Kitchen *utensils* (knives, forks, and spoons) should be rinsed in weak bleach water to kill germs.

Rodents—rats, mice, and guinea pigs—can make good pets.

Many *celestial* objects like stars, galaxies, and nebulas are hard to see without a telescope.

Los Angeles, New York, Chicago, and Miami are all examples of the growing number of *megalopolises* in this country.

Exercise 5-4   **Using Example Clues**

From the example clues above and from your own knowledge, write the best definition you can for each word. Note: Try not to use the examples in your definition.

1. mathematics _____

2. utensil _____

3. rodent _____

4. celestial _____

5. megalopolis _____

Was one definition easier to write than the others? Why? Do you know what a guinea pig is? Are the words galaxy and nebula in your vocabulary? Finding a definition using only your background knowledge is impossible if you aren't familiar with the examples.

For Your Information

IMPORTANCE OF BACKGROUND KNOWLEDGE

How well you understand example clues will depend on your background knowledge about the subject plus your ability to use resources to find information.

Clues from Your Background Knowledge

Have you heard of the famous detective Sherlock Holmes? He could solve almost any case because he was an expert on almost every subject.

Of course, Sherlock Holmes was a fictional character. Obviously, no one can be an expert of every subject.

If you are reading about a subject you know, you will find the clues more easily. If you are reading about a subject that is completely new to you, expect to miss some of the clues. You should also realize that you will have to use more tools such as dictionaries, maps, or other aids to help you understand what you are reading when the subject is new to you.

As you read, you should always be looking for clues. The information in the sentence where you find a new word often will give you a general idea about the word's definition. Again, your background knowledge of that subject might make the clue either strong or weak. Here is an example:

> My 75-year-old mother and my 93-year-old grandmother are both in the same *geriatric* care home.

Without using your dictionary, what do you think *geriatric* means?

_____

What were the clues? _____

_____

Here's another example:

> Trying to win the game in the last minute of play is *futile* when your team is losing 45 to 92.

What do you think *futile* means? _____

How do you know? _____

Exercise 5-5   Using Your Background Knowledge

*Use context clues and your own background knowledge to **deduce** (guess from the clues) the best definition of the italicized word. Write the letter of the best answer on the line. Be ready to discuss where you found the clue and whether that clue was strong or weak.*

_____ 1. The girl was obviously a *novice* at skating. She was down on the ice more than she was on her feet.
      a. expert   b. teacher   c. beginner

_____ 2. Five $20 bills are *equivalent* to one $100 bill.
      a. more than   b. equal to   c. less than

_____ 3. Eating oranges and getting lots of sleep can be *beneficial* if you don't want to catch cold.
      a. good   b. harmful   c. careful

_____ 4. Tom wouldn't be so *fatigued* every day if he went to bed before midnight.

a. happy   b. tired   c. hard

_____ 5. Children *thrive* when they are given lots of attention and loving care.

a. grow well   b. become weak   c. need help

For Your Information

CONTEXT CLUES IN OTHER SENTENCES

One reason it is important to continue to read without stopping is that context clues are often found in other sentences near the unknown vocabulary word.

Exercise 5-6   Using Context Clues to Understand New Vocabulary

In the sentences below, use the context clues and your own background knowledge to deduce the best definition for the italicized word. Check your answer by substituting your choice for the italicized word.

_____ 1. The explosion of the fireworks factory was *audible* for miles. Even I heard it in the next county.

a. able to be seen   b. able to be felt   c. able to be heard

_____ 2. Mice, skunks, and squirrels are often *prey* of the hawk, though this bird sometimes also hunts for fish.

a. friends   b. hunted food   c. enemy

_____ 3. *Descending* the mountain was much more difficult than climbing up.

a. hiking   b. going down   c. going up

_____ 4. Magellan was the first man to *circumnavigate* the world. He sailed west from Europe and went all the way around the world in a wooden sailing ship.

a. travel in a circle around   b. go across   c. visit

_____ 5. Some people really enjoy the *rural* life, but I personally would rather live in the city.

a. factory   b. city   c. country

Challenge 5-6

____ 6. Jerrod had never been *candid* with his wife about her weight. Now, however, he knew it that it was time to speak honestly with her about the health risks of being overweight.

   a. mean   b. honest   c. curious

____ 7. There is a lot of *controversy* about whether the town should spend $5 million to build a new school. Some people say the school is necessary because of overcrowding; others say the cost is too high.

   a. cause of disagreement   b. expense   c. interest

____ 8. The little boy's appetite was *insatiable*. He could eat everything in the refrigerator and still want more.

   a. hungry   b. never satisfied   c. unpredictable

Mastery 5-6

____ 9. I would be very *leery* of buying stock in a computer company, especially after what happened with Silicon Valley.

   a. pleased to   b. suspicious of   c. anxious about

____ 10. My aunt is as *stingy* as King Midas.

   a. royal   b. happy   c. tight with money

Secrets to Success

CHECKING YOUR ANSWERS

Once you have used the context clues to deduce the meaning of a new word, check to see if the meaning makes sense. For example:

> My 75-year-old mother and my 93-year-old grandmother are both in the same *geriatric* care home.

If you think *geriatric* means something to do with *the elderly*, substitute that definition for the word in the sentence.

> My 75-year-old mother and my 93-year-old grandmother are both in the same *elderly* care home.

Other Context Clues

Grammar and Punctuation

Reading is finding meaning from the text, but the words themselves are not the only place you find meaning. Grammar and punctuation also provide clues to meaning. Spelling too can give valuable clues. Spelling clues will be discussed in a later chapter.

Read the two sentences below and think about how a single capital letter and a **pronoun** (noun substitute) can change meaning.

1. I invited Brother John to have dinner with us tonight.

2. I invited my brother John to have dinner with us tonight.

In which sentence is a monk or priest coming to dinner? _____

In sentence 1, the fact that the b in Brother is capitalized should tell you that the word Brother is a title. You may or may not know that the title is used for a priest or monk. In sentence 2, the fact that the b in brother is not capitalized should tell you that you are reading about a relative.

In the following sentences, look at the punctuation to decide how many dogs there are in each sentence.

The roof on the dog's house is leaking. _____ dog(s)

The roof on the dogs' house is leaking. _____ dog(s)

In the first, there is only one dog. In the second, there is more than one. You only know that if you understand how apostrophes work.

Look at one more pair of sentences. In which one is little Timmy never sick?

Timmy is always good.

Timmy is always well.

If you picked the second sentence, you were right. Well when used as an **adjective** (a word that describes a noun) means "healthy." Good in this sentence is an adjective that means "well-behaved."

For Your Information

GRAMMAR AND PUNCTUATION RULES

Don't worry if you're not an expert at grammar or punctuation! You can still read and comprehend without knowing all the rules. You will just miss some of the clues that others with a better understanding might find.

Exercise 5-7 Using Grammar and Punctuation Clues

_____ 1. In which sentence below are there four people on the team?
   a. Sarah Jane, Ann, and Norma bowled in the tournament.
   b. Sarah, Jane, Ann, and Norma bowled in the tournament.

_____ 2. In which sentence below was the archer (person who shoots arrows) careless?
   a. The archer was about to loose an arrow.
   b. The archer was about to lose an arrow.

_____ 3. In which sentence below does the soldier have a hollow leg?

   a. The soldier dropped, a bullet in his leg.
   b. The soldier dropped a bullet in his leg.

_____ 4. In which sentence below would you probably have an easy climb?

   a. You will find the mountain trail easy.
   b. You will find the mountain trail easily.

_____ 5. Which of these two advertisements found on a large sign outside a convenience store would probably have people standing in line?

   a. Free ice! Cold beer here.
   b. Free ice cold beer here.

Beware the Red Herring!—Idioms

Do you know what *Beware the red herring* means?

- ■ Beware means be careful .
- ■ You probably know the color red.
- ■ Use your dictionary to look up the definition of herring.

   herring—_____

Do you know what *Beware the red herring* means now? Obviously, *Beware the red herring* does not mean "Be careful of the tiny fish."

When groups of words have meaning completely different from the words used, they are called **idioms**. There are thousands of idioms in the English language.

A *red herring* is, in fact, a suspect or a clue in a mystery novel that is meant to confuse the reader. This idiom came from the fact that criminals at one time used the tiny red fish, which are very smelly, to confuse the police dogs that were following them.

Idioms can certainly confuse a reader. Fortunately, context clues will often help you understand the meaning of a red herring. For example:

   I'm sure if I *keep my nose to the grindstone* I will get a raise. I work hard every day, so I deserve the extra $50 a week.

Did you guess *keeping your nose to the grindstone* means to keep working without rest? The clue was "work hard every day."

   Here's another.

   Sally is living *high on the hog* now that she won $3 million in the lottery.

This clue is not as strong. First, you must know what the lottery is. Next, you must have a good idea how someone might suddenly live once they've won $3 million. *High on the hog* means "very well" or "very extravagantly."

Now it is your time *to test your wings*. Try using the context clues in the sentences below to **detect** the meaning of the italicized idiom.

Exercise 5-8 Understanding Idioms

Write the letter of the best definition of each idiom on the line.

_____ 1. The new salesperson is such an *eager beaver*. She is at the store by 7:00 a.m., works through her lunch hour, and doesn't leave until 6:00 p.m.

a. animal lover   b. overly hard worker   c. beginner

_____ 2. Mr. Thompson is so *tight-fisted* he would rather starve than spend $2 for a bowl of soup.

a. cheap   b. hungry   c. angry

_____ 3. You should *hit the books* if you plan to pass the math test tomorrow.

a. rest   b. go to the library   c. study

_____ 4. Don't *pull my leg*. I know that Martians didn't land in your backyard.

a. knock me down   b. lie to me   c. hurt my feelings

_____ 5. "You don't need to worry about Joey, Mrs. Smith. Most twenty-year-olds are still *wet behind the ears*. He'll start acting like an adult before you know it."

a. not yet mature   b. spoiled   c. stubborn

_____ 6. Liam *put the cart before the horse* when he set a wedding date before he asked Marilyn if she would marry him.

a. proposed   b. worked for the farmer   c. acted too soon

_____ 7. Leah must have gone *into the red* when she bought that sports car. She surely can't afford it on a secretary's salary.

a. into debt   b. into a store   c. into the bank

_____ 8. Our teacher is *under the weather* today. He has the flu, as do so many of his students.

a. late   b. sick   c. busy

_____ 9. I've read this story five times, and I just can't *make heads or tails of* it. It's just too difficult.

a. remember   b. understand   c. tell it correctly

_____10. Clyde is such a *couch potato*. His sister says the only time he gets up from watching TV is to go to the bathroom.

a. lazy person   b. active person   c. vegetable

For Your Information

DICTIONARY OF AMERICAN IDIOMS

Many idioms are not listed in a regular dictionary. If you have difficulty understanding idioms or are not a native American speaker, you may want to buy a dictionary of American idioms.

Making Deductions

In one of the Sherlock Holmes' novels, the famous detective said to his friend and assistant Dr. Watson, "It is a capital mistake to theorize before you have all the evidence." Or, as a common idiom goes, *Don't jump to conclusions!* Gather all the evidence you can before you decide that you understand what you've read.

Using Context Clues to Make Deductions

Context clues are not only useful for understanding new vocabulary, but they are also very important for comprehension. Use your new detective skills to find the clues that will give you meaning as you read.

Below is the same basic sentence with more and more clues added. Look for the clues, then circle *all* the answers that might be true for each sentence based on those clues.

1. Sam loves to bark.

   Sam is: a. a dog   b. a seal   c. a man   d. a girl

   Did you circle *a*? A dog certainly can bark, but so can a seal, a man, and a girl. You should have circled all the answers. Be sure to think carefully when you do number 2.

2. Sam loves to bark out the car window at people .

   Sam is: a. a dog   b. a seal   c. a man   d. a girl

   Did you circle *a*, *c*, and *d*? All three could easily bark out a window, though a dog would be the most likely answer. A seal could also be in a car, though that seems unusual. For that reason, you cannot completely eliminate the seal as a possibility. Think very carefully when you do number 3.

3. Sam loves to bark and wave a hand out the car window at people.

   Sam is: a. a dog   b. a seal   c. a man   d. a girl

   Did you circle circle *c* and *d*? It can't be *a* or *b* because dogs have paws and seals have flippers, not hands.

4. Sam loves to bark and wave her hand out the car window at people.

Sam is: a. a dog   b. a seal   c. a man   d. a girl

You should now have solved the mystery. Sam is a girl!

For Your Information

GATHERING ALL THE EVIDENCE

Remember, as a reading detective you need all the clues you can find to solve the mystery of what you are reading. These include vocabulary, grammar, punctuation, and background knowledge.

Exercise 5-9 Using Context Clues to Solve the Mystery

Use the context clues to solve the following reading mysteries.

_____ 1.   His nails dripped with blood. With his long, raspy tongue, he licked the sticky redness from them, one after another. A hunk of fur stuck to a tooth. A swipe of a giant, golden paw quickly removed it. His stomach full, the contented *feline* stretched out under the warm African sun and fell asleep still purring.

Who or what is this *feline*?
a. a housecat   b. a mountain lion   c. a lion   d. a bear

What were the clues? _____

_____

_____ 2.   Eighty-year-old Mrs. Wilkerson was a *philanthropist*. She went to the hospital twice a week. On Tuesdays, she brought toys and balloons to the young patients. On Fridays, she gave magazines and books to the elderly.

Who or what is a *philanthropist*?
a. an old woman   b. a sick woman   c. a generous person
d. a salesperson

What were the clues? _____

_____

_____ 3.   The *filly* ran through the meadow. The grass of her first spring was thick beneath her hooves. The April sun warmed her back. She neighed in joy as she ran across the broad field toward her mother.

Who or what is a *filly* in this paragraph?
a. a happy young girl   b. a stallion
c. an elderly horse   d. a young female horse

What were the clues? _____

_____

____ 4. "I bought a *settee* today," Mrs. Jones told her husband.

"Where are you going to put it? The house is already too crowded," Dr. Jones replied.

"Oh, it's not for the house. There are never enough chairs in your waiting room. Now there'll be a comfortable place for a couple more people to sit."

Who or what is a *settee*?
a. a wooden bench   b. a place to wait
c. a small, soft couch   d. an operating table

What were the clues? _____

_____

____ 5.   Terry was in a very *jovial* mood. Even though he had failed his math test that morning, wrecked his car during the lunch break, and broken up with his girlfriend after school, a glance at the afternoon paper had given him a great surprise. He had won $150,000 in the lottery.

What kind of mood is Terry in?
a. depressed   b. angry   c. satisfied   d. very happy

What were the clues? _____

_____

Challenge 5-9

____ 6. "I'm not going to the *podiatrist*!"

"But, Cary, that plantar wart is horrible," his mother argued.

"I'll keep using that medicine. I know it kills a lot of healthy skin too, but eventually it will get rid of the wart."

"No arguing, young man. I know you hate doctors, but you can't even walk, that thing has gotten so big. You're going tomorrow."

What is a <u>podiatrist</u>?

a. a skin doctor   b. a foot doctor   c. an athletic trainer
d. a pharmacist

What were the clues? _____

_____

_____ 7.   It was a bitterly cold night—too cold to be out—but Houston had to find the *maverick*. Nothing, especially such a young thing, could live through this snowstorm on its own. Remembering the desperate mother bellowing for her offspring, the tired cowboy kicked his horse gently to urge her on through the snow. This was the third time in a week the ornery thing had run off. Next time, if there was a next time, he'd let the stubborn thing take its chances.

Who or what is a *maverick*?
a. a young boy   b. a lost cow   c. a lost calf
d. a calf who has strayed

What were the clues? _____

_____

_____ 8. "*Run!*"

"I can't."

"You have to *run*. What will this race be without you?"

"I told you I can't. I just don't have the money for the campaign."

What does *run* mean in this reading?
a. to move quickly by foot   c. to compete for an elected office
b. to race in a competition   d. to fight in a battle

What were the clues? _____

_____

Mastery 5-9

_____ 9. "Did you hear? Darth got *black-balled* by the honor society."

"No way! He's the smartest dude in this school."

"It's the hair. The ponytail just don't go over well with the powers that be."

"Like, ain't that discrimination or something?"

"Think he cares? Darth is too cool to hang with that bunch anyway."

What does it mean to be *black-balled* by someone or something?

a. kept from joining a group   b. thrown out of a group

c. painted a dark color   d. ignored by a group

What were the clues? _____

_____

_____10.   The revolver lay on the table, loaded with a single silver bullet. Outside, the sun sank toward the horizon. The <u>lycanthrope</u> paced up and down by the window. He was terrified of what was coming with the night. Soon, the full moon would rise. Then he would have to make the choice—kill again or kill himself.

Who or what is a <u>lycanthrope</u>?

a. a vampire   b. a werewolf   c. a police officer   d. a terrorist

What were the clues? _____

_____

In this chapter, you have learned to use context clues to find the meaning of new vocabulary words. For this reading, only words that cannot be defined by context will be given in the vocabulary list. You as a reading detective must deduce the meaning of the others from the clues in the sentence or surrounding sentences. Do not use your dictionary.

This reading is a bit different from the ones you have read before. Part I is written in **academic** style, the style you usually find in textbooks. Part II is written in a more informal style and uses idioms. Note as you read Part II whether or not the idioms make comprehension difficult for you.

Did the Anasazi Really Vanish?

1   Long before the Navajo Indians settled the area of the **American Southwest** called **Four Corners**, there was a more **ancient** people living there. The evidence of this Native American people, the **Anasazi** (ä´ nə sä´ zē), is found everywhere in the region. There are petroglyphs carved on rocks in Utah. In Arizona and Colorado, there are incredible towns built high above the canyon floor on cliff faces and in caves. In New Mexico, bits of ancient **pottery** and baskets tell of the people's talents. Archeologists have learned much from all this evidence. The most surprising thing they have learned is that for some reason, after thriving for more than a thousand years, this ancient people simply **vanished**. Or did they?

PART I

WHO WERE THE ANASAZI?

Four Corners Region
of Southwest U.S.

UTAH   COLORADO

Navajo Lands

ARIZONA   NEW MEXICO

2   The true name of this ancient **culture** has vanished. Today, the name used for these long-gone people is the Anasazi. Anasazi is a Navajo Indian word. At first, linguists **translated** this word to mean "the ancient ones." These language experts, however, have discovered recently that a closer translation of Anasazi is actually "ancient enemy." The Pueblo Indians, who believe they are **descendants** of the Anasazi, do not like the name Anasazi because they think it insults their distant relatives. Instead of Anasazi, the Pueblos use the Indian word meaning "Pueblo ancestors."

3   The **evolution** of the Anasazi **civilization** was much the same as the long, slow process that changed the wandering **nomads** of ancient Europe into the **citizens** of Rome. For thousands of years, people in the Americas, like those in Europe, were hunter-gatherers. To find their food, the people moved with the **migrating** herds of wild game animals like deer, elk, and bison. Like the animals, the people were always moving with the changing seasons. Such nomads did not have **permanent** villages.

4   Eventually, both the early American and European nomads started to **supplement** their diet by growing **grain** crops, such as corn, wheat, or rice. To grow this additional food, some of the tribe had to stay with the crops, at least during the growing season. This was the beginning of farming. The Anasazi grew **maize**—a kind of early corn—squash, and eventually beans. They also **domesticated** the wild turkey.

5   These farmers needed something to store their crops in, so the people began making woven baskets. The early Anasazi people are sometimes called the **Basketmakers**. The Basketmakers dug round pits in the dry ground and lined them with rocks. They would store their baskets of maize and squash in these round holes covered with sticks, rocks, or mud. They also lived in similar pit houses.

6   By around the time of the birth of Jesus, 1 CE, the Anasazi were no longer nomads. They had settled into an organized group of people. Archeologists use this date to mark the beginning of the Anasazi culture. Over the centuries that followed, this culture **evolved**. As their numbers grew, Anasazi farmers gathered into small villages. These villages grew into towns. Roads were built to connect towns and religious sites. **Politics**, the organization of power in a community, also developed. Baskets were eventually replaced by beautiful pottery. The tiny pit houses of the Anasazi had evolved into elaborate cliff dwellings near the end of the civilization.

7   By 1200 CE, a true civilization had developed, a complex culture of towns and villages with roadways connecting them. By 1300 CE, the Anasazi civilization had vanished. The towns and villages stood empty, the beautiful pots and baskets left behind. What happened to the Anasazi? That is the mystery archeologists hope to solve.

Exercise 5-10   Decoding

Write the correct pronunciation for each word below.

1. ancient _____

2. maize _____

3. evolve _____

4. domesticate _____

5. descendant _____

Exercise 5-11   Finding Vocabulary from Context

Below are two paragraphs from the reading. Reread them carefully. <u>Underline</u> any clues you find to help you define the bold-faced words. Then match each word and its definition based on context clues. Do not use your dictionary.

The **evolution** of the Anasazi **civilization** was much the same as the long, slow process that changed the wandering **nomads** of ancient Europe into the **citizens** of Rome. For thousands of years, people in the Americas, like those in Europe, were **hunter-gatherers**. To find their food, the people moved with the **migrating** herds of wild game animals like deer, elk, and bison. Like the animals, the people were always moving with the changing seasons. Such nomads did not have **permanent** villages.

Eventually, both the early American and European nomads started to **supplement** their diet with **grain** crops such as corn, wheat, or rice. To grow this additional food, some of the tribe had to stay with the crops, at least during the growing season. This was the beginning of farming. The Anasazi grew **maize**—a kind of early corn—squash, and eventually beans. They also **domesticated** the wild turkey.

_____ 1. migrate   a. "corn, wheat, [and] rice"

_____ 2. evolution   b. "additional"

_____ 3. maize   c. "people [who] moved with the . . . herds"

_____ 4. nomads   d. "a kind of early corn"

_____ 5. permanent   e. not always on the move

_____ 6. supplement   f. moving "with the seasons"

_____ 7. citizens   g. "long, slow process [of] change"

_____ 8. grain   h. no longer "wild"

_____ 9. domesticated   i. "deer, elk, and bison"

_____ 10. game   j. the people of a country or city

Exercise 5-12 Finding Facts

Answer the following questions in complete sentences.

1. Who are the modern-day descendants of the Anasazi? _____

   _____

2. In what area of the world did the Anasazi live? _____

   _____

3. What date do archeologists use to mark the beginning of the Anasazi culture?

   _____

4. Why did the first Anasazi people start making baskets?_____

   _____

5. Why do the Pueblos dislike the name Anasazi? _____

   _____

Challenge 5-12

6. In what kind of dwelling did the Anasazi live near the end of that civilization? _____

   _____

7. Define politics according to this reading. _____

   _____

Mastery 5-12

8. Explain why you think the Anasazi people developed politics.

   _____

   _____

   _____

   _____

Exercise 5-13 Map Check

Label the map below by writing the number of the state or area on the line provided.

1. Arizona

2. Colorado

3. Four Corners

4. New Mexico

5. Utah

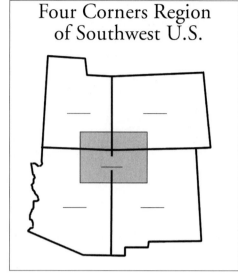

Four Corners Region
of Southwest U.S.

Remember that Part II of the reading will have idioms. Informal language can be very hard to read sometimes. If this is too difficult for you, you might want to work with a partner or a team.

WHAT REALLY HAPPENED TO THE ANASAZI?   PART II

8   Making *heads or tails out of* any ancient culture can be difficult when the only clues archeologists have are bits of pottery, baskets, ancient ruins, and other pieces of some ancient **lifestyle**. Solving the mystery of why a **flourishing** civilization like the Anasazi would suddenly vanish has been an especially *tough nut to crack*. After *putting their heads together*, archeologists have finally decided that there was probably not one but several reasons for the Anasazi's disappearance.

9   One reason may have been the **arid** climate of the Four Corners area. There is very little rain during most of the year, and summers are very hot. Luckily, most summers have heavy **monsoon** rains. Anasazi farmers depended on these **brief** *gully-washers* plus the **run-off** from the melting mountain snows to provide the water they needed to grow their crops. What, however, would have happened if these rains didn't come? Researchers studying the growth rings of trees from the Four Corners region have *brought to light* some amazing information.

10   When a tree is cut down, you can see its **annual** growth rings. The thickness of each growth ring shows you how much a tree has grown each year. A tree's yearly growth depends on rain and growing conditions. With plenty of rain mixed with periods of sun, a tree grows rapidly. When it is too dry or cold, there may be very little growth.

11   Tree ring research proves that in the early 1200s there was a period of 30 years when there was little or no rain. That's about the time the Anasazi civilization began to **decline**. Since that discovery, most archeologists were *willing to bet the farm* that this **drought** was the main reason for the Anasazi's problems. Not having enough rain would have meant there would not have been enough food. If the people didn't or couldn't move in search of food, then they would have starved.

12   New research, however, shows those archeologists using the old-growth-ring studies were *barking up the wrong tree*. This new research shows that there was, in fact, a very dry period but not dry enough that the people couldn't have grown crops. Besides, studies of Anasazi villages show that not all the people *took off* at this time. They moved out little by little—sometimes village by village, town by town.

13   There is another piece to this puzzle. Like all people, the Anasazi *put a big dent in* the land on which they lived. They hunted the animals and used the resources of the desert to survive. As the population grew, there were more and more *hungry mouths to feed*. A need for more food meant more and more hunting. Over the years, the animals became harder and harder to find. Trees for building timbers and firewood were *few and far between*. More farmers also meant a growing thirst for water. In the end, there may have simply been too many people for the environment to support.

14   Studies of human bones found at several of the ruins show that this theory probably *hits the nail on the head. The wolf was at the door* even before the Great Drought began. There were simply too many people and not enough to eat. Then of course drought *goes hand in hand* with **famine**. Throughout the 1200s, the Anasazi people were starving more and more with each passing year.

15   There is yet another *piece to the puzzle*. Whenever a people's *back is against the wall*, there is bound to be **conflict**. People argue. People fight. When their children are *nothing but skin and bones*, parents will do whatever it takes to feed them, including raiding the next village for food. In **revenge**, that village will probably attack back. The Anasazi were at war with themselves.

16   Research shows it was about this time period that many of the Anasazi left the valley floor and moved into cliff dwellings high on the canyon walls. Some archeologists say that the cliff dwellings are proof that the people were trying to defend themselves from their neighbors. There is a chance too that other tribes such as the Utes and the ancestors of the Navajos were also starting to move into the area. These *new kids on the block* would have been hungry and looking for whatever they could take. The cliff dwellings would have offered the Anasazi protection from these invaders as well. In the end, however, even the cliff dwellings would not have been enough to save the Anasazi.

17   Overpopulation, drought, famine, warfare—no wonder the once-mighty civilization *fell like a house of cards*. But did the Anasazi people themselves *disappear from the face of the earth* as well? No! Those who still survived *went off in search of greener pastures*. Some went deeper into Arizona and New Mexico; others went to Mexico.

18   No, the Anasazi did not vanish. They deserted their homeland because they had to in order to survive. And survive they did. Even today there are still descendants of the Anasazi—the Hopis in Arizona and the Zunis, Acomas, and Pueblos in New Mexico.

Exercise 5-14 Deducing Idioms from Context

Use the context clues in Part II to see if you can match its meaning to each idiom.

_____ 1. tough nut to crack

_____ 2. disappear from the face of the Earth

_____ 3. few and far between

_____ 4. new kids on the block

_____ 5. nothing but skin and bones

_____ 6. goes hand and hand with

a. go together with

b. starving, very thin

c. newcomers

d. difficult

e. vanish, become extinct

f. not many, rare

Challenge 5-14

_____ 1. barking up the wrong tree

_____ 2. hit the nail on the head

_____ 3. willing to bet the farm

_____ 4. make heads or tails out of it

_____ 5. put their heads together

_____ 6. put a dent in

a. were right, correct

b. were very sure, certain

c. talked, communicated

d. damage something

e. understand/make sense of something

f. were wrong

Mastery 5-14

_____ 1. gully-washer

_____ 2. the wolf was at the door

_____ 3. back is against the wall

_____ 4. fell like a house of cards

_____ 5. took off for greener pastures

_____ 6. brought to light

a. no opportunities left

b. left for better opportunities

c. danger/death was waiting

d. very heavy rain

e. showed, revealed, discovered

f. collapsed

Exercise 5-15 Vocabulary Check

Use context clues from Part II, your background knowledge, and the vocabulary list to choose the word from the Answer Box that makes the sentence correct. <u>Underlining</u> the context clues might help you find the answer.

ANSWER BOX

flourishing	brief	run-off	drought
decline	arid	environment	annual
monsoon	theory	famine	conflict

1. There has been so little rain during the last two years, the mayor says that no one is allowed to water their lawn until the

   _____ ends.

2. The school talent contest is an _____ event. Every year the students compete for the grand prize of $250.

3. In Arizona, people wait for the summer _____ rains to cool down the heat for a few hours each day.

4. The Four Corners area has a very _____ climate. There is very little rain during most of the year.

5. Children who grow up in homes with a lot of arguing and fighting often find they do not like _____ when they are adults. They hate disagreement.

6. After floods or droughts, there are often periods of

   _____ when thousands of people starve.

7. A monsoon rain might be _____, but even though it does not last long there can be flooding in the desert.

8. At one time the Anasazi had a _____ civilization with cities, busy roadways, and art and other culture.

9. The first _____ that archeologists had to ex-
plain the disappearance of the Anasazi was the 30-year drought that
occurred in the early 1200s.

10. If people today are not careful to protect the _____,
this civilization might end up like the Anasazi.

Exercise 5-16   Events in Sequence

*Put the sentences in the Answer Box in the correct chronological order to
show the evolution of the Anasazi civilization.*

ANSWER BOX

To protect themselves, the Anasazi became cliff dwellers.
Today's Pueblo Indians are the descendants of the Anasazi.
Eventually, the Anasazi became farmers.
In the beginning, the ancestors of the Anasazi were nomads.
As the Anasazi population grew, farmers became villagers.

1. _____

2. _____

3. _____

4. _____

5. _____

Exercise 5-17   Checking the Facts

*Read the following sentences and decide if they are true (T) or false (F).
Write your answer on the first line. On the second line, write whether you
found your answer in Part I or Part II.*

____ _____ 1. The great drought lasted 30 years.

____ _____ 2. Anasazi is a Zuni word for "ancient ones."

____ _____ 3. As the Anasazi population grew, the game animals
like deer became harder to find because there were
too many people hunting them.

_____ _____ 4. The early nomadic ancestors of the Anasazi were hunter-gatherers.

_____ _____ 5. The Anasazi had roads to travel from town to town.

Challenge 5-17

_____ _____ 6. Annual growth rings of trees from the Four Corners area show that there was a drought from 1 CE to 1300 CE.

_____ _____ 7. The Anasazi's overuse of the environment may have been one reason they were forced to leave the Four Corners region.

_____ _____ 8. It has been easy for archeologists to discover what happened to the Anasazi.

Mastery 5-17

_____ _____ 9. All the Anasazi died because of a famine caused by the drought.

_____ _____ 10. Both early American and European hunter-gatherers evolved into complex civilizations with cities, governments, and religions.

Exercise 5-18 **Writing About What You've Read**

If there were a terrible drought where you live, so that there would not be enough food or water for everyone, what would you do? Write a response on your own paper.

Going Beyond

Research

Go to the Internet or your local library. Find at least four different Anasazi sites and list in which state they are located.

1. _____

2. _____

3. _____

4. _____

Recommended

If you are interested in the Anasazi, you might want to read the novel *A Thief of Time* by Tony Hillerman. There is also a television movie based on the book.

Enhancing Your Thinking

Proverbs

A **proverb** is a short saying that expresses some basic truth. Proverbs may almost seem like a mystery until you think about them carefully. Here are a few examples:

Two heads are better than one.

A penny saved is a penny earned.

A stitch in time saves nine.

Did you understand what each of these proverbs means?

Two heads are better than one means that two people trying to solve a problem are better than just one person trying to solve a problem.

A penny saved is a penny earned suggests that it is better to save than spend, even if you have just a small amount of money.

A stitch in time saves nine is saying that it is better to solve a problem while it is small; then you won't have a big problem.

Exercise 5-19

Try to match the ending of each of the proverbs below with its beginning. When you are done, try to explain them.

_____ 1. Many hands make . . .   a. by its cover.

_____ 2. Don't judge a book . . .   b. when he's down.

_____ 3. A rolling stone . . .   c. the forest for the trees.

_____ 4. Don't kick a man . . .   d. light work.

_____ 5. You can't see . . .   e. gathers no moss.

Challenge 5-19

Match them, then be ready to explain their meanings.

_____ 6. A watched pot . . .   a. run deep.

_____ 7. A fool and his money . . .   b. lie.

_____ 8. Still waters . . .   c. are soon parted.

_____ 9. Let sleeping dogs . . .   d. never boils.

_____ 10. Beauty . . .   e. is only skin deep.

Mastery 5-19

Complete the following proverbs by using a word from the Answer Box. Use each word only once. When you have completed the proverbs, try to explain them to your partner or group.

ANSWER BOX

race	wash	stone
brave	lemonade	horse
tricks	bath water	storm

1. When life gives you lemons, make _____.

2. Don't throw the baby out with the _____.

3. Leave no _____ unturned.

4. Dirty water will never _____ clean.

5. You can lead a _____ to water but you can't make it drink.

6. Fortune favors the _____.

7. You can't teach an old dog new _____.

8. After a _____ comes a calm.

9. Slow and steady wins the _____.

CHAPTER 5 REVIEW

- **Looking for Context Clues**
  Context clues are any clues in the text—vocabulary, punctuation, grammar—that give you a hint to the meaning of a word, a sentence, or a paragraph.

- **Context Clues to Understanding New Vocabulary**
  Within the same sentence as a new vocabulary word or in surrounding sentences, you may find clues to the meaning of that word. There are four common kinds of vocabulary context clues:

  Definition or Information Clues—stated definition or information

  Synonym Clues—words nearby with similar meaning

  Antonym Clues—words nearby with opposite meanings

  Example Clues—a listing of examples to help reader find meaning

  Other clues come from the reader's background knowledge. That is why the more you know, the easier it is to read.

- **Other Context Clues: Grammar and Punctuation Clues**
  A knowledge of grammar and punctuation gives the reader more understanding.

- **Beware the Red Herring!—Idioms**
  Some writing includes idioms. An idiom is a group of words that has a completely different meaning than the words themselves.

- **Making Deductions**
  It is important to gather as many clues as you can before you decide you understand what you've read.

CHAPTER 6

Solving the Mysteries of Your Dictionary

Getting to Know Your Dictionary

You have already been using your dictionary to find the correct pronunciation of new words. You may also have used it to check for definitions. As with any tool, there are many skill levels of use possible. If you want to be a successful reading detective, you need to master your dictionary.

A quality dictionary is filled with resources. Those resources, however, are only valuable if you know they are there and understand how to use them. In this chapter, you will discover the many resources available in your dictionary. You will also learn how to master the use of those resources. The first step before using your dictionary should be a **preview**.

Exercise 6-1 Dictionary Preview

1. Flip through your dictionary to get a general idea how the book is organized and what different **features** are in your dictionary.

2. Put a check mark next to any of the following features it has.

   _____ bold-faced **entry words** (the word you are looking up)

   _____ two **guide words** at the top of each page

   _____ a guide to how to use the dictionary

   _____ a list of the abbreviations and symbols used

   _____ a pronunciation key

   _____ photographs or illustrations

   _____ maps

   _____ charts of special information

   _____ others: _____

Abbreviations and Symbols

All dictionaries use abbreviations and symbols to shorten the length of the dictionary entries. Be sure to find the page in your dictionary that lists these abbreviations and symbols. Here are a few of the more common ones.

inf. = informal   *n.* = noun   *pl.* = plural   *pr.* = pronoun   *v.* = verb

Finding an Entry Word Quickly

According to *The American Heritage English as a Second Language Dictionary*, a dictionary is "a reference book containing an **alphabetical** list of words with information given for each word." To use your dictionary effectively, you need to know the alphabet.

If your dictionary does not already have **notches** or markings that show where each letter of the alphabet begins, you can do one of several things to speed up the process of finding a word.

1. On the outside of the dictionary, mark the place where several of the more common letters begin. If you know your alphabet well, you can then make a quick, educated guess where the letters in between would begin.

2. If you do not want to write on your dictionary, use small sticky tabs with each letter written on the end, and attach each tab to the first page of words where the matching letter begins. The letter should show on the outside of the book. You might also want to write the alphabet in large letters on a $3\frac{1}{2}$" × 5" note card that you keep in your dictionary. This will help you find the word you are looking for more easily.

Exercise 6-2 Alphabetizing

Check your alphabetizing skills by rewriting the words below in alphabetical order on the lines provided.

A. 1. tent _____

   2. mouse _____

   3. spin _____

   4. quit _____

   5. lamp _____

B. 1. broom _____

   2. distant _____

   3. break _____

   4. garden _____

   5. heart _____

C. 1. carpet _____   D. 1. street _____

    2. carrot _____   2. stutter _____

    3. car _____   3. strange _____

    4. cap _____   4. stamp _____

    5. cartoon _____   5. stretch _____

Guide Words

If you are using a dictionary, encyclopedia, phone book, or other re-source to look for information, make use of the **guide words** to find what you are looking for quickly and easily. Guide words are the pair of words at the top of the page that indicate the first and last word on the page.

For example, in the phone book, you might find a page with the guide words Jenks/Jotter. The word on the left of the pair is the first word or name on the page. The word or name on the right of the pair is the last word or name on the page. If the word or name you are looking for is listed **alphabetically** between those two words, it should be on the page.

Would Janet Jones be listed on the page with the guide words Jenks/Jotter? _____ Here's such a page with alphabetical listings. Check to see if you were right.

			JENKS/JOTTER
Jenks, C.	555-1098	Johns, Bill	555-9086
Jern, Dick	555-3714	Johns, Bob	555-5534
Jess, Rob	555-9753	Johns, James	555-6807
Jess, Tom	555-1328	Joh, Juan	555-1712
Jesse, Ben	555-2020	Joley, Sue	555-7772
Jesse, Kay	555-8887	Jones, D.	555-0907
Jiang, Li	555-5766	Jones, Janet	555-1031
Jinda, B	555-4360	Jones, Tom	555-0515
Job, Lyle	555-9119	Jose, Dean	555-5462
Jodi, K.	555-0039	Joss, Bridget	555-8360
Joffe, Ole	555-7311	Jotter, Kevin	555-8777

Exercise 6-3 Using Guide Words

*Four words will be listed after each pair of guide words below. Put an **X** on the line next to each word that would appear alphabetically on the page of that pair of guide words. An alphabet has been provided to help you.*

Example:

rabbit/target   <u>X</u> star   <u>X</u> run   ___ umbrella ___ tarp

drawer/dresser <u>X</u> dream ___ drink <u>X</u> dress   ___ down

button/calcium ___ carton <u>X</u> by   <u>X</u> buy   <u>X</u> cab

A B C D E F G H I J K L M N O P Q R S T U V W X Y Z

A. 1. flop/fluff   ___ flood   ___ flow   ___ flour   ___ flub

    2. ride/right   ___ ridden ___ rig   ___ rise   ___ rift

    3. entry/episode   ___ envy   ___ epic   ___ entire ___ eon

    4. steer/stew   ___ steeple ___ stick   ___ stern   ___ stem

    5. cab/carpool   ___ cable   ___ call   ___ cage   ___ can

B. 1. order/orient   ___ organ   ___ orderly ___ outside ___ ore

    2. upbeat/upswing ___ update ___ upward   ___ upon   ___ up

    3. polka/pop   ___ popcorn ___ pony   ___ polo   ___ pool

    4. ground/grub   ___ group   ___ gun   ___ grow   ___ gourd

    5. day/dear   ___ date   ___ daydream ___ deaf   ___ deal

Finding the Correct Entry Word

When you look up a word in the dictionary, that word is called the **entry word.** As you have already learned, you use the guide words to find the entry word quickly. Before you can do that, however, you must decide what form of the word to look up.

Words come in many forms. Not all of them are shown as entry words. To find most words, you must be aware of the different forms they can take. Understanding the parts of speech—noun, verb, adjective, adverb, and so on—can help you. Nouns can be plural. Verbs have many different forms. Most adverbs are not even listed as entry words. You must know the adjective form of most adverbs to find them in the dictionary. If you are not familiar with parts of speech, the table below will give you a basic description of the four with which you will most commonly be working.

Common Parts of Speech

Noun	a thing, person, or idea	pencil, teacher, education
Verb	shows action;	run, study, laugh, work
	shows state of being	is, was, can, will, had
Adjective	describes a noun	happy, brave, easy, worried
Adverb	describes verb, adjective, or other adverb	sadly, carefully, very, hardly

Nouns

Nouns can be singular or plural. Most noun plurals are **regular**. A regular plural is the word + s, such as cat + s = cats. Nouns are usually listed in the dictionary in their singular (*s.*) form. The dictionary does not list all the regular plural nouns.

Irregular plural nouns (*pl.*), such as geese, should be listed in your dictionary. An entry for any irregular plural noun should look something like this: mice (mīs) *n. pl.* of mouse. If the irregular plural is not an entry word, you may have to look up the singular form.

Exercise 6-4 Finding the Correct Entry Word—Nouns

Write the entry word you will have to use to find the definition of the following nouns. Example: mice _____ mouse _____

1. nomads _____
2. dishes _____
3. cries _____
4. wives _____
5. enemies _____

Verbs

Verb entries can also be very difficult to find because verbs come in many tenses. The main entry word for a verb is usually given in the first-person present tense form. For example, I run. I talk. I study. Verbs often add an -s, -ed, or -ing to this form of the verb—He runs. We talked. They were studying. These forms of the verb will not be shown as entry words. You must remove these endings and look up the base word to find the entry word.

Many verbs, like the word drink, also have irregular forms (drink, drank, drunk). Most dictionaries will list an irregular form as an entry form that will look something like this:

drank (drăngk) *v.* Past tense of drink.

You must then look up the main entry word (drink) to find the correct definition.

The main entry word will also list several different forms of the verb if the verb is irregular. The forms will be listed in this order:

entry word *v.* past tense, past participle, present participle, and third-person singular.

fly (flī) *v.* flew (flo͞o), flown (flōn), fly·ing (flī´ĭng), flies (flīz).

Secrets to Success

FINDING THE DEFINITION OF AN IRREGULAR VERB FORM

Some irregular verb forms will be listed in your dictionary. However, the easiest way to find a verb definition is to look for the first-person singular form of the verb. For example, to find the definition of **swam**, look up the word **swim**, as in **I swim**.

Exercise 6-5 **Finding the Correct Entry Word—Verbs**

Write the entry word you will have to use to find the definition of the following verbs. Example: flown _____fly_____

1. adapts _____

2. decoding _____

3. wandered _____

4. deducing _____

5. classified _____

6. evolving _____

7. strode _____

8. caught _____

9. crept _____

10. deciphered _____

Adjectives

Adjectives too can come in several forms, for example tall, taller, tallest. When two things are compared (He is taller than you), that is called the comparative form of the adjective. When more than two things are compared (He is the tallest in the room), that is called the superlative form.

Some adjectives are irregular, like good, better, best. The dictionary should give you these irregular forms. Most dictionaries will list the base adjective form so you can look up that entry word. The definition may be listed with some irregular adjectives.

Exercise 6-6 Finding the Correct Entry Word—Adjectives

Write the entry word you will have to use to find the definition of the following adjectives. Example: biggest _____ big _____

1. harder _____

2. craziest _____

3. quicker _____

4. pinkest _____

5. lazier _____

6. best _____

7. hardest _____

8. dirtier _____

9. least _____

10. most _____

For Your Information

NOUNS USED AS ADJECTIVES

Sometimes a word such as mountain that is usually used as a noun does the job of an adjective. Here are several examples:

Finn has gone to his mountain home for the summer.

Susan is a carpet layer.

Yesterday, I went for a long bike ride.

In these cases, even though the word is doing the job of an adjective (describing a noun), you would look up the noun definition of the word to find the correct meaning.

Adverbs

Adverbs are usually made by adding an -ly to an adjective, such as sad + -ly = sadly. There may be a spelling change such as pretty + -ly = prettily. To find the meaning of most adverbs, you must look up the base adjective. Other irregular adverbs like backward will be shown as entry words.

Exercise 6-7 Finding the Correct Entry Word—Adverbs

Write the entry word you will have to use to find the definition of the following adverbs. Example: crazily _____*crazy*_____

1. safely   _____

2. fortunately   _____

3. happily   _____

4. momentarily   _____

5. daringly   _____

6. very   _____

7. intelligently _____

8. carefully   _____

9. courageously _____

10. up   _____

Understanding a Dictionary Entry

A **dictionary entry** is the word to be defined, its definition(s), and all other information about that word. To use a dictionary well, you not only have to know how to find the correct entry word, but you must also learn how to use the information provided in the entry.

Sample Dictionary Entry

Here is a sample entry from *The American Heritage Dictionary* for you to study. This entry may be slightly different from the entry for this word in your dictionary.

> **cart** (kärt) *n.* 1. a small wheeled vehicle usually pushed by hand: *a shopping cart.* 2. a two-wheeled vehicle drawn by an animal. 3. a light motorized vehicle: *a golf cart.* —*v.* 1. to convey in a cart or truck: *cart away garbage.* 2. To convey laboriously or remove unceremoniously: *carted the whole gang off to jail.* [< OE *cræt* and < ON *kartr,* wagon.] **cart'er** *n.*

Every dictionary entry is filled with information. Here is a list of all the information the reader should be able to gather from this short entry.

■ The word cart can be used as both a noun (*n.*) and a verb (*v.*).

■ There are three different noun definitions and two verb definitions for this word.

- The words in *italics* give an example of each of those definitions.
- The pronunciation of the word cart (kärt) rhymes with the word heart (härt).
- The word cart has one syllable.
- The plural of cart must be carts because there is no *pl.* (plural) symbol to show that the word cart has an irregular plural.
- The word cart originally came from the Old English (OE) word cræt and from the Old Norse word kartr, which meant wagon.
- Cart has a related noun—cart´er—which is a two-syllable word with an accent on the first syllable. Since the ending -er often means a person, a carter must be a person who uses a cart.

Exercise 6-8   **Understanding a Dictionary Entry**

Study the dictionary entries below, then answer the questions using the information you find there.

> **grain** (grān) *n.* 1. A small one-seeded fruit of a cereal grass. 2. Cereal grasses collectively. 3. A small amount. 4. The pattern of the fibrous tissue in wood. 5. Texture. 6. Basic temperament. —idiom. **with a grain of salt**. With reservations; skeptically. [< Lat. *grānum.*]—**graininess** *n.,*—**grainy** *adj.*

A. 1. What part(s) of speech (noun, verb, adjective, adverb, etc.) is the

    word grain? _____

    2. How many different noun definitions does the word grain have?

    _____

    3. What does the idiom with a grain of salt mean? _____

    _____

    4. From what language does the word grain come? _____

    5. The word grain has another noun form. What is it? _____

    6. What is the adjective form of the word grain? _____

> **shave** (shāv) *v.* **shaved, shaved** or **shav·en** (shāv´ən), **shav·ing.** 1. To remove the beard or body hair with a razor. 2. To remove thin slices of or from. 3. To come close to or graze in passing. See *Syns* at **brush**. —*n.* 1. The act or result of shaving. [< OE *sceafan.*]

B. 1. As what part(s) of speech can the word shave be used? _____

_____

2. What is the past tense of the word shave? _____

3. What is the past participle of the word shave? _____

4. Where would you look to find synonyms of shave? _____

_____

5. From what language did the word shave evolve? _____

---

calm (käm) *adj.* **-er, -est.** 1. Nearly completely motionless, undis-
turbed. 2. Not excited or agitated. —*n.* 1. An absence of motion;
stillness. 2. Serenity, peace. —*v.* 1. To make or become calm. [< Lat.
cauma].—**calm·ly** *adv.,*—**calm·ness** *n.*

C. 1. As what part(s) of speech can the word calm be used? _____

_____

2. What is the superlative form of the adjective calm? _____

3. How many syllables does the adverb form of calm have? _____

4. How many noun definitions does calm have? _____

5. What is an alternate noun form of the word calm? _____

---

cul·ture (kŭl′ chər) *n.* 1. The behavior patterns, arts, beliefs and
other products of human work or thought of a community. 2. In-
tellectual and artistic activity and the works produced. 3. Development of intellect through training or education. 4. The breed-
ing of animals or plants to improve stock. 5. *Biol.* The growing of
microorganisms in a specially prepared nutrient medium.—*v.*—
cultured, culturing. 1. To grow microorganisms in a nutrient
medium. [< Lat. *cultūra* < *colere,* cultivate]—**cultural** *adj.,*
—**culturally** *adv.,*—**cultured** *adj.*

D. 1. How many syllables does the word culture have? _____

2. How many noun definitions does culture have? _____

3. How many verb definitions does culture have? _____

4. Which definition of culture is used only in biology? _____

_____

5. What are the past and present participle forms of the word culture?

_____   _____

6. From what language does the word culture come? _____

7. What is the adverb form of culture? _____

8. What are the two adjective forms of culture? _____

_____

Finding the Correct Definition

A reading detective looks first for clues in the context to give meaning to unknown vocabulary words. If the clues are not there or are weak, the reader must then use the dictionary to look for the correct meaning.

For some words, that is very simple. For example, the definition of the word hart is "a male red deer." Of course, there may be words even in a simple definition that you do not understand. In that case, you will have to use your dictionary again to clarify the definition.

Words with Multiple Meanings

Many words actually have more than one definition. Take for example the word run. *The American Heritage Dictionary* has more than 50 definitions for the word run. Compare the following sentences.

I run every morning before work.

Georgio can run to the store for milk later.

The salmon run starts next week.

Suzette, you have a run in your pantyhose.

The gambler was having a run of good luck.

Their team is only one run ahead of ours.

The governor says he will not run for office again.

I think you should run along now. It's getting late.

Obviously a salmon run is very different from a run of good luck or a run in a pair of pantyhose. All three are very different from the most common definition of run as it is used in I run every morning before work: "to move on foot at a pace faster than a walk." When a word has **multiple** definitions, you will have to use context and grammar clues to find the correct definition.

Using Context Clues to Find the Correct Meaning

Context clues should help you find the definition you need if the word has several meanings. Look for the context clues in the following sentence:

Their team is only one run ahead of ours.

What do you think the definition of run is in this sentence? _____

_____

What were the clues that led you to that deduction? _____

_____

The clue here was the word team. If you are familiar with sports, you might know that a run is a word in baseball. Even if you didn't know baseball, you could scan over the definitions of run until you found one related to sports. In this case, the definition actually has a **label** *Baseball*, then the definition: "A point scored by reaching home plate safely."

Exercise 6-9   Using Context Clues to Choose the Correct Definition

Use the dictionary entry below to decide which definition is correct. Put the number of that definition next to the sentence.

> **dis·or·der** (dĭs ôrʹ dər) *n.* 1. Lack of order or regular arrangement. 2. A public argument or fight. 3. A sickness of the body or mind.

A. _____ 1. My brother is not able to work because he suffers from a nervous disorder.

_____ 2. Quinten was fined by the police for "inciting public disorder."

_____ 3. If your house is in disorder, why don't you hire a maid to clean it for you?

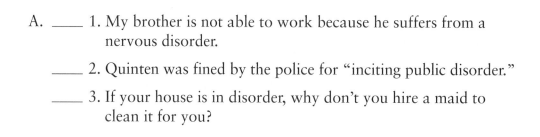

> **heart** (härt) *n.* 1. The muscular organ in the chest that pumps blood. 2. The vital center and source of one's emotion: *I loved him with all my heart.* 3. The ability to feel sympathy, kindness, or concern: *Doesn't your heart go out to these starving people?* 4. Courage, determination: *The young soldier had the heart of a lion.* 5. The center or central portion: heart of the matter. 6. A figure that represents the heart, often colored red or pink. 7. A playing card resembling this figure.

B. ＿＿ 1. On Valentine's Day, each child in the class colored a bright red heart.

＿＿ 2. My friend is in the hospital because he had a heart attack.

＿＿ 3. It broke Rafael's heart when his wife died.

＿＿ 4. I only need the queen of hearts to win this game of cards.

＿＿ 5. It takes a lot of heart to finish college when you are also working full time.

＿＿ 6. The Eiffel Tower is in the heart of Paris.

＿＿ 7. That man has no heart if he can let his own children starve to death when he has money in the bank.

Using Grammar Clues to Find the Correct Definition

A knowledge of grammar can also help you find the right definition. Remember the word run. According to *The American Heritage Dictionary*, the word has 29 verb definitions, 21 noun definitions, several idiomatic definitions, and several other phrasal definitions.

If you can identify the different parts of speech (noun, verb, adjective, adverb, preposition, conjunction, and others), finding the correct definition is a bit easier. Here are some clues to help you identify nouns and verbs.

- The following words often **precede** (come before) **nouns:** a, an, the, his, her, my, your, its, their, that, this, and others.

- **Verbs** may have the following endings: -s, -ed, -ing, -en, and others. The main verb may also have **helpers** like is, can, will, has, had, would, could, should, may, and others.

Exercise 6-10 Noting Parts of Speech

First underline the clues *then write an* **N** *on the line if the word run is used as a noun or a* **V** *if run is used as a verb.*

＿＿ 1. He had a run of bad luck.

＿＿ 2. I can run to the store to buy some bread.

＿＿ 3. Please put the dog in the run.

＿＿ 4. If you clean the air filter, your car will run much better.

_____ 5. The governor says he will not run for office again.

_____ 6. The falling stock prices caused a run on the bank.

_____ 7. Kim will run in tomorrow's 10-mile race.

_____ 8. Did you know the curtains on the front window have a bad run in them?

_____ 9. That little boy has run away from home five times.

_____10. I run into my sister at the grocery store every Monday.

Secrets to Success

WATCH THE NUMBERS!

In a dictionary entry, if a word is most often used as a verb, all the verb definitions will be listed first. The numbering will start at 1 and continue from the most common definition used to the least common definition. When the numbers start back at 1, you are beginning a new part of speech.

Exercise 6-11   **Dictionary Entries with Multiple Parts of Speech**

Use the dictionary entry below to decide which definition is correct for each sentence. First note the part of speech, and then the number for that part of speech. Example: <u>v.-3</u>

---

cart (kärt) _n._ 1. a small wheeled vehicle usually pushed by hand: _a shopping cart._ 2. a two-wheeled vehicle drawn by an animal. 3. a light motorized vehicle: _a golf cart._ —_v._ 1. to convey in a cart or truck: _cart away garbage._ 2. To convey laboriously or remove unceremoniously: _carted the whole gang off to jail._ [< OE _cræt_ and < ON _kartr_, wagon.] **cart´er** _n._

A. _____ 1. When I was a child, my German Shepherd used to pull me around in a dog cart.

_____ 2. You should rent a truck to cart off all that trash at the construction site.

_____ 3. After my sister was arrested for drunk driving, the police carted her off to the station to wait for my parents.

_____ 4. Instead of a wheelchair, my aunt used an electric cart to get around town.

_____ 5. The grocery cart crashed into the side of my car.

---

nose (nōz) *n.* 1. The part of the human or animal face that contains the nostrils and is used for smelling and breathing. 2. The sense of smell. 3. The ability to detect things as if by smell. 4. The forward part of an airplane, rocket, etc. —*v.* 1. To touch with the nose; nuzzle. 2. To move or push with the nose. 3. To steer (a vehicle) ahead carefully. 4. To move forward cautiously.

B. _____ 1. My nose always stuffs up when I have allergies.

_____ 2. Sam nosed the car out into the heavy traffic.

_____ 3. The paint on the nose of the old plane was peeling.

_____ 4. The cow nosed her calf away from the edge of the cliff.

_____ 5. Sally really has a nose for the news.

---

ferry (fĕr' ē) *v.* **ferried, ferrying**. 1. To carry by boat across water. 2. To cross by a ferry. 3. To transport from one point to another.— *n., pl.* **ferries** 1. a ferry boat. 2. A place where a ferry boat embarks. 3. A service for delivering an aircraft under its own power to its eventual owner. [< OE, *ferian*.]

C. _____ 1. The ferry tipped back and forth wildly in the stormy sea.

_____ 2. Marta has to ferry all the neighborhood children to school and back every day.

_____ 3. Katrin runs a ferry taking planes to their new owners.

_____ 4. There were over a hundred cars waiting at the ferry for the boat to come.

_____ 5. The refugees were ferried across the river by canoe.

Finding Idioms, Phrasals, and Compound Words

Idioms

Remember the red herring. You already know to be alert for idioms, certain word combinations that have their own meanings. Many words have one or more idiomatic definitions as well as their single-word definitions. The idiomatic definitions are usually listed near the end of the entry.

> **Exercise 6-12**   Finding Idiomatic Definitions

Use your dictionary to find the correct definition for each of these idiomatic definitions of the word run. You may need a college-level dictionary for this exercise.

1. a run for one's money _____

2. in the long run _____

3. in the short run _____

4. on the run _____

5. run out of _____

6. run for one's life _____

7. run up against _____

8. run off at the mouth _____

9. run a temperature _____

10. run in one's family _____

Phrasal Words

You should also be aware of **phrasal words**. A phrase, as you know, is a group of words that has its own meaning. Noting phrasal uses of a word is very important!

Look at the two sentences below. They look like they say exactly the same thing, but in fact have two very different meanings.

1. Turn right here!

2. Turn right here!

In sentence 1, you are being told to make a turn to the right (the opposite of left). In sentence 2, you are being told to turn right here or exactly at this point. You do not know what direction. Right here is a **phrasal word** because the phrase right here has its own very different meaning. Phrasal words are very common, especially combinations of verbs and prepositions.

Exercise 6-13 Finding the Definition of Phrasal Words

In the Answer Box below are six phrasal words using run. Phrasal words are found under the main entry word. Use the context clues in the sentences that follow to complete the sentences.

ANSWER BOX

run along	run out of	run over
run through	run off with	run down

1. Please go to the grocery and buy some more Cheerios. I've completely _____ cereal.

2. I think you should start taking vitamins. You look really

   _____ .

3. Please _____ . We're too busy to play with you today.

4. The antelope was _____ by the hunter's six-foot spear.

5. It's so sad. Susan's kitten got _____ by a car yesterday.

6. Some thief will _____ your bike if you don't lock it.

Compound Words

As you learned earlier, a reader also has to be alert for compound words. The word run is also part of several compound words—some regular, some hyphenated.

Exercise 6-14 Finding the Definition of a Compound Word

Use your dictionary to match the correct definition with each of these compound words. Remember that compound words are usually found as ***entry words.***

_____ 1. rundown   a. a complete but rapid review or rehearsal

_____ 2. runaround   b. a point-by-point summary

_____ 3. runaway   c. water that is not taken in by the soil

_____ 4. run-through   d. a strip of level land on which a plane lands

_____ 5. runway   e. a quarrel or argument

_____ 6. run-in   f. deception, usually in form of false excuses

_____ 7. runoff   g. not special; average

_____ 8. run-of-the-mill   h. one who has escaped or run away

Finding Homographs

The active reader must also be alert for **homographs.** Homographs are words that are spelled the same but have different meanings. They may also have different pronunciations. Compare the following sentences.

We saw your bow.

We saw your bow.

The two sentences look exactly the same, but the letters b-o-w have two very different meanings and pronunciations. One word rhymes with cow (kou). The other rhymes with so (sō). Without context clues, you cannot tell the difference.

Now compare the homographs in sentences that have context clues.

We saw your deep bow before the queen.

We saw your bow and arrows.

Can you understand the meaning of these homographs now?

You bow (bou) before a queen.

You shoot arrows from a bow (bō).

Secrets to Success

HOMOGRAPHS

In your dictionary, homographs will be noted with a **superscript** beside the entry word, for example: light[1], light[2]. Homographs are spelled with the same letters, but they are completely different because they have different **origins**. That is why their meanings are different.

Sample Dictionary Entries of Homograph

> **port**[1] *n.* 1. a city, town, or other place on a waterway with facilities for loading or unloading ships. 2. A place that gives shelter for ships.
> **port**[2] *n.* The left side of a ship or aircraft facing forward.
> **port**[3] *n.* A sweet, strong wine.

As always, context clues will lead you to the correct definition of an unknown homograph. Look for the context clues in the following sentences. See if you can choose the correct homograph definition for each.

_____ 1. Sometimes, I want a nice dry white wine, but today I want a port.

_____ 2. With the news that a hurricane was coming, all small ships headed to port.

_____ 3. The captain told the crew to paint the port side of the ship first.

Did you guess 1. port[3], 2. port[1], 3. port[2]? Then you were correct!

Exercise 6-15   Finding the Correct Definition of Homographs

On the line, write the homograph with superscript that correctly defines the homograph as it is used in each sentence, for example: sole[2]. *You should be ready to defend your answer using context clues.*

> **sole**[1] (sōl) *n.* The bottom surface of your foot or shoe.
> **sole**[2] (sōl) *adj.* Being the only one.
> **sole**[3] (sōl) *n.* A fish related to the flounder, used for food.

_____ 1. Ted Carter is the sole owner of this business.

_____ 2. The nail went right through the sole of my shoe and into my foot.

_____ 3. I think I will have a fillet of sole for dinner tonight.

Challenge 6-15

Put the number of the homograph on the line, then decide whether the correct definition is a noun, verb, idiom, or phrasal. Also, write the number of the definition if there is more than one.

Example: _palm² n._ or _palm¹ idiom_

---

palm¹ (päm) *n.* 1. The inside surface of the hand between the wrist and the base of the fingers. *v.* 1. to hide (an object) in the palm of the hand. *Idiom.* **in the palm of (one's) hand.** Under one's control or influence. *Phrasal.* **palm off.** To get somebody to buy or accept something through deception.
palm² (päm) *n.* 1. A tree of tropical and subtropical regions, usually with a branchless trunk and a crown of large leaves shaped like feathers or fans.

_____ 1. The large palm in their frontyard gave plenty of shade.

_____ 2. The magician palmed the coin then pretended to pull it out from behind the little boy's ear.

_____ 3. Don't try to palm off your old car on me. I know it needs new brakes.

_____ 4. I'll have my boss in the palm of my hand by next payday.

_____ 5. Please put some hand cream on my palm.

Mastery 6-15

Put the number of the homograph on the line and the number of the best definition if there is more than one definition. Several answers may fit, but try to choose the best answer based on the context clues.

Example: _grave²_ _adj.-3_

---

grave¹ (grāv) *n.* 1. A hole dug in the ground for the burial of a dead body. 2. A place of burial: *The ocean is the grave of many sailors.* 3. Death or extinction. *The pioneers went to their graves centuries ago.* [< OE *graef*]
grave² (grāv) *adj.* **graver, gravest** 1. Requiring serious thought. 2. Filled with danger or harm. 3. Dignified or serious in behavior or character. —**gravely** *adv.* [< Lat. *gravis*, heavy]
grave³ (grāv) *v.* **graved, graven** 1. To engrave. [< OE *grafan*]
graver *n.*

_____ 1. Most judges are very grave. I would be too if I had to decide whether someone lived or died.

_____ 2. Outer space will probably be the grave of many future astronauts.

_____ 3. The letters were graved deeply into the stone.

_____ 4. Be careful! You are in grave danger.

_____ 5. Digging the grave was very difficult in the rocky soil.

How to Make a Personal Dictionary

If you find that it is hard to remember the meaning of new words, you may want to make your own personal dictionary. It is very easy. Here's how. On a $3\frac{1}{2}$" × 5" note card, write:

- the word and its pronunciation in the upper-right-hand corner of the card,
- the word's definition—in your own words, and
- a sample sentence of related words that you want to remember.

---

code (kōd)

Definition: *a special language made up so other people can't understand the words*

Sentence: *The Japanese could not break the Navajo code.*

Related words: *encode, decode*

For Your Information

VOCABULARY CARDS

To keep from losing your vocabulary cards, buy a round metal key ring at the hardware store. Punch a hole in the upper-left-hand corner of each card, then place them on the ring in alphabetical order. Having your cards on the ring will make finding a word easier and help you keep the cards in order.

Other Dictionary Uses

For a reader, a dictionary is absolutely necessary to find meaning, information, and pronunciation. There are other uses for your dictionary that might be helpful when it is time to write about what you have read. These are a few of them:

- Use it as a spellchecker; look especially for homophones such as miner and minor.
- Use it to find the correct plural of a noun.
- Use it to check the correct past participle of an irregular verb.
- Use it to find synonyms and antonyms.
- Use it to check whether a word is acceptable for your use of it. Words labeled slang, informal, or offensive would not be used in school writing.
- Use it to find specialized uses. Words with labels such as biology or math have very specific uses.

Since you now know how to find the correct meaning of new vocabulary words, a vocabulary list will no longer be provided. Remember not to stop at words you do not know. You might want to underline or circle them, so you can look them up later. If you continue to read without stopping, you may find the meaning in the context.

Is There Life on Mars?

1   From the heavens, a ball of fire fell toward Earth. Deep in **Antarctica,** at the very bottom of the world where there was no one to see, this **extraterrestrial** crashed into the deep snow. The first Martians had landed!

2   Who were these visitors from outer space? Were they little green men or tall, ghostly white figures like those **portrayed** in so many popular movies? No! Was their spacecraft a huge silver saucer or perhaps a long shiny cylinder as science fiction writers like to suggest? No again! In fact, these Martian visitors were nothing more than **microscopic** bacteria—or rather, the remains of those tiny living **organisms**—and their spaceship a rock the size of a potato.

3   Fifteen million years ago, a gigantic **asteroid** slammed into Mars. The impact was so powerful that chunks of the Martian surface were thrown into outer space. Eventually, some of these Martian rocks were captured by our planet's **gravity.** Thirteen thousand years ago, several of these extraterrestrial chunks fell to Earth near the South Pole.

4   In 1984, a team of scientists from **NASA** (National Aeronautics and Space Administration) discovered several of these rocks during a research expedition to Antarctica. Scientists around the world became very excited when NASA announced that these rocks had come from Mars and immediately began to study them for traces of life.

5   Mars is the fourth planet from the sun and one of Earth's nearest neighbors. If you see a "star" in the night sky that looks red, you are probably looking at the planet Mars. Because of its blood-red color, the Romans

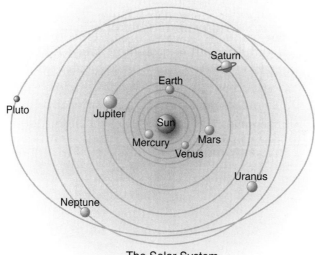

The Solar System

named the planet after Mars, the Roman god of war. Mars is a little smaller than Earth and farther from the sun, so the planet is much colder.

6   For a long time, people believed that there was life on Mars. Even with poor-quality **telescopes**, scientists could see that there were polar ice caps on Mars just like the ones here on Earth. These polar ice caps would grow larger during the Martian winter and smaller during the summer. People were certain that ice meant water, and where there is water there is usually life.

7   There also seemed to be an **atmosphere** that might be much like Earth's. If there was oxygen in the air, creatures like those on Earth might have developed. Another thing that suggested life was the "red bloom." During certain times of the year, this red coloring would spread across the planet as if there was something growing there.

8   One early **astronomer** also noted a series of **channels** across the surface of Mars. Some people thought that these were canals that had been dug by Martians to take water to their cities and fields. The existence of canals seemed to prove that there had been, and might still be, some kind of people living on Mars.

9   As the quality of telescopes improved, scientists began to have some doubts. In the 1960s, NASA sent several **unmanned** missions to fly by Mars and other planets. These crewless spacecraft were called the Mariners.

10   Photographs sent back to Earth by the Mariners showed a very different Mars than the planet scientists expected to find. First, there was very little atmosphere around the planet, only about 1 percent of what we have on Earth. The planet's surface also looked more like the moon than the Earth. It was covered by thousands of craters. There were also huge volcanoes and deep canyons. The photographs did show possible evidence that there may have once been running water on the planet. Sadly, however, the "red bloom" was not living growth but rather blowing red dust. And the ice at the poles, as well as the atmosphere, was not made of water as scientists had hoped but of carbon dioxide. Mars' atmosphere also proved to be too thin to hold in the heat necessary for most life. The average temperature on Mars is around 58 degrees below zero. Even the canals that Martians had supposedly built to carry water across the planet are nothing more than natural channels. All these newly discovered facts seemed to prove that Mars today is, in fact, a dead planet.

11   Still, scientists did not want to give up on the idea of life on Mars, even if that life was in the distant past. Studies over the last few decades suggest that Mars may once have had a very different climate. About 3.5 million years ago, Mars may have been much more like Earth with running water, a thicker atmosphere, and slightly warmer temperature. Though this early Mars would have still been an extremely cold and **inhospitable** place, scientists believe it might have been possible for some simple form of life to have developed there.

12   Research here on Earth supports that theory. Simple **lifeforms** like bacteria and viruses can survive in even the harshest conditions. Tiny, one-celled bacteria have been found living in boiling hot springs and in the deepest depths of the sea. In **Siberia**, the cold northern portion of **Russia** where the ground is permanently frozen, scientists have also discovered microscopic life living in the **permafrost**. Some viruses, at least in their spore form, are also believed to be able to travel unharmed through the freezing **vacuum** (absence of air) of outer space. If that is true, the existence of life on Mars, sometime in its past, seems at least possible.

13   **Exobiologists**, scientists who search for life from outside the Earth, believe that very simple life forms probably did exist on Mars during that early time period. Inside ALH 84001, one of the Martian rocks that landed on Earth, some scientists believe they have found the proof they had been looking for. Sealed inside tiny air bubbles inside ALH 84001, they discovered what they think is **organic** material. Organic material is what makes up the **complex** building blocks of life.

14   Scientists studying ALH 84001 also found what they believe are microscopic fossils of a very special bacterium. This bacterium, like a similar one found on Earth, is **magnetic**. The bacterium uses the magnetic **crystals** in its body to help it find food and energy. "This [the microscopic fossils] is *the smoking gun* for life on Mars," said chemist Ian Wright. Other scientists think that the so-called **fossilized** bacteria are as ridiculous as little green men.

15   What is the truth? Was there life on Mars in the past? Does life still exist on the Red Planet today? *Viking I* and *II* and the *Mars Pathfinder* spacecraft have already landed on the Martian surface, but the information they sent back was **inconclusive.** They simply did not collect enough information to prove whether or not life exists on the Red Planet. In 2003 and 2004, the U.S. land-roving *Spirit* and *Opportunity* landed on opposite sides of Mars to collect data. Future fly-by and orbiting satellites will continue to collect data about the red planet. Perhaps one day, from the information they gather, scientists will be able to solve one of the biggest mysteries of all: Are we alone in the universe?

Exercise 6-16   **Using Your Dictionary to Find the Correct Meaning**

On the line, write the number of the correct definition for each italicized word as it is used in a sentence. Be sure to indicate the correct part of speech, if that is necessary. Example: __v. 2__ *.*

_____ 1. The *gravity* on the Moon is only one-fifth what it is on Earth.

> **grav·i·ty** (grăv´ ĭ tē) *n.* 1. The natural force that causes objects to move or tend to move toward the center of the earth as a result of gravitation. 2. Seriousness; importance: *The students realized the gravity of the test and its effect on their grades.*

_____ 2. Movies often *portray* Martians as little green men.

> **por·tray** (pôr trā´) *v.* 1. to describe or picture (somebody/something) through the use of words. 2. To show (somebody/something) by means of a picture or film. 3. To play someone on the stage or screen.

_____ 3. An astronomer with an old-fashioned *telescope* first discovered the canals of Mars.

> **tel·e·scope** (tĕl′ ə skōp′) *n.* 1. A device that uses an arrangement of lenses, mirrors, or both to observe or photograph distant objects. —*v.* **telescoped, telescoping, telescopes.** 1. To cause something to slide inward or outward in overlapping sections, as the tube sections of a small hand telescope. 2. To make something briefer; condense. —**telescopic,** adj.

_____ 4. Scientists once thought that nothing could live in the *vacuum* of outer space.

> **vac·uum** (văk′ yōōm) *n.* 1. a space from which everything, including air, has been removed. 2. total emptiness. 3. a vacuum cleaner. —*v.* 1. To clean with or use a vacuum cleaner.

_____ 5. Some scientists want more *proof* before they will believe there is life on Mars.

> **proof** (prōōf) *n.* 1. Evidence or demonstration of truth. 2. The demonstration of truth of a mathematical equation. 3. The act of testing the truth by an experiment. 4. A trial copy of something, such as printed material. 5. The alcohol content of liquor. —*v.* 1. To read and mark corrections in printed material.

_____ 6. Researchers believe they found evidence of *organic* matter inside ALH 84001.

> **or·gan·ic** (ôr găn′ ĭk) *adj.* 1. Relating to living things. 2. Relating to fertilizers of animal or vegetable matter and not artificial fertilizers or pesticides: organic gardening. 3. Relating to compounds containing carbon. —**organically** *adv.*

_____ 7. Some bacteria have tiny *magnets* inside to help them find their food or direction.

---

magnet (măg′ nĭt) *n.* 1. A person or place that has a powerful attraction: *Our mulberry tree is a magnet for birds.* 2. A stone, piece of metal, or other object that attracts iron or steel through natural or electrical power. 3. An electromagnet. —**magnetic** *adj.*

_____ 8. Astronomers were disappointed that Mars' *atmosphere* was so thin it could not support life.

---

atmosphere (ăt′ mə sphîr′) *n.* 1. The air that surrounds the Earth or other celestial bodies. 2. A unit of pressure equal to the pressure of air at sea level. 3. The air or climate of a place. 4. A general feeling or mood. —**atmospheric** *adj.*, **atmospherically** *adv.*

_____ 9. Scientists now doubt that they will ever find *complex* lifeforms on Mars.

---

complex (kŏm′ plĕks′) *adj.* 1. Difficult to understand. 2. Consisting of many connecting parts. *n.* 1. A system or unit consisting of a large number of parts. 2. A group of related ideas, wishes, emotions that influences a person's behavior and personality. —**complexly** *adv.*

_____ 10. The *crystals* in the rock caught the sunlight.

---

crys·tal (krĭs′ təl) *n.* 1. A regular geometric shape formed by some substance like salt or sugar. 2. A clear colorless glass of high quality. 3. A transparent cover that protects the face of a watch. *adj.* 1. clear, transparent.

Exercise 6-17 Finding the Facts

Use the reading to answer the following questions:

1. On what continent did the first "Martians" land? _____

2. Who or what was this first Martian? _____

3. When did a gigantic asteroid hit Mars? _____

4. When did chunks of Martian rocks fall to Earth? _____

5. What did scientists name this first Martian rock? _____

6. Mars was named after the Roman god of what? _____

7. List three things that made people think there was life on Mars.

   a. _____

   b. _____

   c. _____

8. What is the average temperature on Mars? _____

9. Name two simple lifeforms that can live in very harsh places.

   a. _____

   b. _____

10. When did the U.S. Mars' rovers *Spirit* and *Opportunity* land on Mars? _____

Challenge 6-17

On the line provided, write the letter of the answer that best completes the sentence.

____ 1. The "smoking gun" that Ian Wright believes proves that there is

   life on Mars is _____.
   a. dust
   b. smoke
   c. microscopic fossils
   d. little green men

____ 2. The red color on Mars is actually _____.
   a. blood
   b. growing bacteria
   c. blowing dust
   d. red oceans

_____ 3. Early astronomers believed that the lines or channels that criss-

crossed Mars were _____.
a. irrigation canals
b. rivers
c. earthquake faults
d. mountain ranges

_____ 4. Mars is a _____.
a. moon
b. planet
c. sun
d. star

_____ 5. The polar Martian ice caps are made of frozen _____.
a. water
b. carbon dioxide
c. oxygen
d. hydrogen

Mastery 6-17

_____ 1. Inside ALH 84001, scientists discovered _____.
a. organic material
b. fossilized bacteria
c. magnetic bacteria
d. all of these

_____ 2. Ian Wright is a(n) _____.
a. astronomer
b. physicist
c. exobiologist
d. chemist

_____ 3. Mars is between _____.
a. the sun and Mercury
b. Mercury and Venus
c. Earth and Jupiter
d. Earth and the moon

_____ 4. Exobiologists would probably study which of the following?
a. Antarctica
b. deep sea animals
c. viruses from outer space
d. the atmosphere

_____ 5. Which of the following is *not* a reason humans would find Mars
    inhospitable?
    a. no oxygen to breathe
    b. very cold temperatures
    c. plants are poisonous
    d. frequent meteorite impacts

Exercise 6-18 Vocabulary in Context

Choose a word from the Answer Box to complete the sentences below.
Look carefully for the context clues that will help you find the correct
answer.

> ANSWER BOX
>
> | | | | |
> |---|---|---|---|
> | extraterrestrials | microscopic | asteroid | channels |
> | inhospitable | permafrost | lifeform | fly-by |
> | fossilized | exobiologists | vacuum | unmanned |

1. Mars' lack of atmosphere and very cold temperatures make the

   planet very _____ for human beings.

2. Within ALH 84001, scientists think they have found microscopic

   _____ bacteria. These tiny organisms were

   turned to stone millions of years ago on Mars.

3. What early astronomers thought were canals built by Martians are in

   fact nothing more than _____ through the

   planet's surface.

4. Surprisingly, bacteria can survive in Russia's _____.

   It is hard to believe that anything can live in this permanently frozen

   ground.

5. The *Mariner* spacecraft were _____. These

   crewless space explorers were sent looking for life on Mars.

6. Bacteria and viruses are _____ lifeforms.

   They are too tiny to see without a microscope.

7. Nothing living can survive in the freezing, airless _____ of space.

8. Scientists who search for life from outside the Earth are called

_____.

9. There are many movies about _____ even though no lifeforms from beyond the Earth have ever been found.

10. A space mission where the spacecraft does not land on the planet is called a _____ because the craft continues on into other parts of space.

Exercise 6-19 Sequencing

Write the events in the Answer Box in the correct chronological order.

> ANSWER BOX
>
> Thousands of years ago, a Martian rock (now named ALH 84001) fell to Earth.
> Soon after its discovery, scientists decided that ALH 84001 is from Mars.
> Millions of years ago, a huge asteroid slammed into Mars, sending debris into outer space.
> Scientists believe they have found traces of Martian life inside ALH 84001.
> NASA scientists found ALH 84001 in Antarctica in 1984.

1. _____
2. _____
3. _____
4. _____
5. _____

Exercise 6-20 Graphics Check

Use the reading, Appendix, maps, and your dictionary to answer the following questions.

1. What is the sixth planet from the sun? _____

2. What planet is just beyond Jupiter? _____

3. What planet is closest to the sun? _____

4. Is Antarctica part of the North Pole or the South Pole? _____

Challenge 6-20

5. What two planets are probably the hottest? _____

   _____

6. What planet is the probably the coldest? _____

Mastery 6-20

7. In what country is Siberia? _____

8. Would you find permafrost in Alaska? _____ Explain your answer.

   _____

Exercise 6-21 Writing About What You've Read

On your own paper, write a paragraph about how you would feel if life were to be discovered on Mars.

Going Beyond

Research

To discover more about this topic, check out any of the following key words at your local library or on the Internet.

Mars	space exploration	ALH 84001
exobiology	Mars missions	*Mars Pathfinder*

Recommended

If you are interested in the search for life on Mars, visit NASA's fascinating Center for Mars Exploration website at: cmex-www.arc.nasa.gov/CMEX/index.html.

Just for Fun

Dictionary Races

Challenge your classmates, friends, or even yourself to a dictionary race. Below are lists of words. The goal is to look up each word as quickly as possible. Write the *guide words from the page where you found the word* on the line provided. The first one finished is the winner. If you are competing against yourself, record your time and try to beat it on the next round.

Race 1

giraffe _____

tap _____

cargo _____

fraternity _____

zoology _____

Race 2

fun _____

target _____

quiet _____

lamb _____

marble _____

Race 3

mission _____

ridicule _____

infantry _____

apple _____

statue _____

route _____

Race 4

quick _____

eclipse _____

asteroid _____

opal _____

cupcake _____

map _____

Race 5

vain _____

carpet _____

umbrella _____

marsh _____

tardy _____

balance _____

garden _____

rabbit _____

aimless _____

x-ray _____

Race 6

celery _____

hymn _____

zipper _____

gnat _____

utter _____

ache _____

vision _____

flash _____

notion _____

bounce _____

Race 7

quit _____

flexible _____

yellow _____

key _____

barber _____

fluff _____

savage _____

particle _____

vintage _____

create _____

invent _____

solve _____

zeal _____

Race 8

stun _____

dainty _____

jam _____

cap _____

fish _____

radio _____

excel _____

water _____

traditional _____

active _____

locate _____

mystery _____

gnu _____

Race 9

knuckle _____

talent _____

ginger _____

yellow _____

energy _____

nut _____

ratio _____

sharp _____

dollar _____

mission _____

halo _____

bait _____

harp _____

violet _____

Race 10

barbeque _____

quarter _____

jumble _____

yeast _____

murmur _____

cat _____

salad _____

pumpkin _____

karat _____

zipper _____

quick _____

organic _____

review _____

arch _____

C H A P T E R   6   R E V I E W

■ **Getting to Know Your Dictionary**
Every dictionary is different. You must get to know yours.

■ **Finding an Entry Word Quickly**
Get to know the alphabet and practice looking up words alphabetically.
Learn to use guide words to help you find entry words more quickly.

■ **Finding the Correct Entry Word**
To find the correct entry word, you must have an understanding of the
different forms of parts of speech—nouns, verbs, adjectives, and
adverbs.

■ **Understanding a Dictionary Entry**
Get to know all the different kinds of information that can be found in
a dictionary entry—syllables, pronunciation, parts of speech, various
meanings, irregular forms, word origin, and more.

■ **Finding the Correct Definition**
To find the correct definition of a word, use context and grammar
clues.

■ **Finding Idioms, Phrasals, and Compound Words**
Readers should be very watchful for these particular word uses and
look carefully when finding their definitions.

■ **Finding Homographs**
Homographs are words that are spelled the same but are of different
origins and have completely different definitions. They are marked by
superscripts such as grave^1 and grave^2. Use context and grammar clues
to deduce the correct definition of homographs.

■ **How to Make a Personal Dictionary**
To keep an easy-to-use personal dictionary, make vocabulary note
cards, hole-punch each card, and place them in alphabetical order on a
metal ring.

■ **Other Dictionary Uses**
To use as a spellchecker, especially for homophones.
To find the correct plural of a noun.
To check the correct past participle of an irregular verb.
To find synonyms and antonyms.
To check whether a word is acceptable for your use of it.
To find specialized uses such as biology or math.

Word Parts: Clues to Meaning

Another Strategy for Understanding New Vocabulary

As a reading detective, you know that the first place to look for clues to the meaning of a new word is in the context. Grammar, punctuation, and spelling might also give you clues to a word's meaning. If these are not enough, you may need your dictionary to find the definition. There is, however, one more strategy you can try before you take out your dictionary: Use word parts to check meaning.

Roots and Affixes

Every word has a **root**, from which it takes its basic meaning. Let's use the root word code as an example. Beginnings and endings can be **fixed** (attached) to the root as in the word <u>decoder</u>. Word parts that are attached to a root are called **affixes**. There are two kinds of affixes: prefixes and suffixes. **Prefixes** are attached to the *beginning* of a root. **Suffixes** are attached to the *end*.

Roots and affixes are powerful tools for the reading detective because they carry meaning. For example, in the word decoder, the de- means "to remove something" and the -er at the end means "a person." Consider this sentence: "Even the best decoder could not decipher Egyptian hieroglyphs before the Rosetta Stone was found."

If you did not know the word decoder, you could follow these steps:

1. Use context clues plus your background knowledge to make an educated guess about the definition.

2. Then use your knowledge of word parts to check that guess. If you knew what the root code meant and the meaning of the affixes de- and -er, you could guess that a decoder was "a person who removes (breaks) codes."

3. If the word parts don't support what you can deduce from the context clues, then you should use your dictionary to find the correct definition.

Caution

BE VERY CAREFUL USING ROOTS AND AFFIXES

You must be very careful when using roots and affixes to check the meaning of a new word. One root or affix may have the same or part of the same letter combination as another root or affix but have a very different meaning. Only use word parts as clues if you can clearly see the root and know that the prefix or suffix has been attached to that root. And then only use word parts to check the clues you found in the context.

Seeing the Root Word

Remember that the **root** of the word is the main part onto which you may attach (affix) prefixes and suffixes. The first step in using roots is to note the root or root word(s) in complex words. For example, in the word ir-regular, the root word is regular. If regular means "usual or normal" and the prefix ir- means "not," then irregular means "not regular."

Exercise 7-1   Seeing the Root Word

Underline the root in each of the words below.

1. reality	5. illegal	9. attendant	13. sadly
2. collection	6. childhood	10. confession	14. impossible
3. inactive	7. posttest	11. recycle	15. preview
4. buyer	8. employer	12. touchable	16. crusty

For Your Information

THE ROOT WORD

If you are a beginner at using this strategy, it is enough to see a root word rather than all the word parts. Later, when you become more knowledgeable about word parts, you will see that often the root word itself is made up of word parts. For example: in the word biolo-gist, you might see biology + -ist. You could use that information to define the word as "a person who studies biology."

Once you know more word parts, you might see that the root word can be broken down even more. bio- (life) + -ology (study of) + ist = "a person who studies life or living things."

Noting Spelling Changes

Sometimes, when a root word adds a prefix or suffix, there is a slight spelling change as there was in bicyclist. These changes may be similar to the changes when a verb adds an -s, -ed, or -ing or an adjective becomes an adverb by adding an -ly.

Exercise 7-2 **Noting Spelling Changes**

Find the root word and spell it correctly. Use your dictionary for help if necessary. Example: bicyclist ____cycle____

1. confusion _____   6. evolution _____

2. captivity _____   7. energize _____

3. argument _____   8. completion _____

4. invasion _____   9. idiomatic _____

5. sincerity _____   10. descendant _____

Using Roots and Affixes

As a reading detective, you can use roots and affixes in several ways. You can:

- Deduce the meaning of new words using word parts you already know.
- Memorize some of the more common roots and affixes and use these to help check word meanings you have deduced from context clues.
- Use word parts to help build families of words rather than learning a new word.

Deducing the Meaning of Roots and Affixes

Here are three words that have a different prefix attached to the same root. See if you can match each picture with the word it matches.

_____ 1. unicycle   _____ 2. bicycle   _____ 3. tricycle

A.   B.   C.

What root word do unicycle, bicycle, and tricycle have in common?
_____

Can you think of any other words with this root? _____
Can you deduce the meaning of this root? _____

If you said that the root cycle means wheel or circle, your deduction was correct. You can always check your definition of a root or affix by seeing if you know another word that fits the pattern. For example, the word motorcycle is indeed a wheeled vehicle with a motor. Once you start to become familiar with the Greek and Latin roots and affixes, start to notice related words, or word families.

Common Roots

You probably already know the meaning of some of the more common roots. Below are three sets of common roots. Look them over carefully and see which you recognize, then use these roots to do the exercises that follow.

COMMON ROOTS: SET 1

Root	Meaning	Sample Word
aud	hear, listen	auditorium, audio-visual
dict	speak, words	dictation, dictionary
gen	create	generator, Genesis
meter	to measure	thermometer, metric
mit, miss	send	missile, transmit
nom, non, nym	name	synonym, anonymous
phon	sound	homophone, telephone
port	carry	import, transport
script, scribe	to write	prescription, transcribe
vid, vis	see	video, vision

Exercise 7-3 Using Common Roots

The root in each word in the left column (1–10) has been underlined for you, as well as the clue in the definition in the right column (a–j). Use this information to match the word with its definition.

_____ 1. anto<u>nym</u>   a. a person <u>sent</u> to another place to teach religion

_____ 2. <u>dict</u>ator   b. something <u>written</u> on paper, leather, or stone

_____ 3. <u>aud</u>itory   c. the book of <u>Creation</u> in the Bible

_____ 4. ex<u>port</u>   d. a word that has the opposite meaning (<u>name</u>)

_____ 5. <u>vis</u>or   e. the <u>sounds</u> of a language

_____ 6. in<u>scrip</u>tion   f. a protective covering for the <u>eyes</u>

_____ 7. <u>Gen</u>esis   g. having to do with the ears or <u>hearing</u>

_____ 8. baro<u>meter</u>   h. a ruler whose "words" (<u>speech</u>) are law

_____ 9. <u>phon</u>ics   i. an instrument <u>to measure</u> air pressure

_____ 10. <u>miss</u>ionary   j. <u>to carry</u> products out of the country

COMMON ROOTS: SET 2		
Root	**Meaning**	**Sample Words**
auto	self	automatic, automobile
capt, capit	head	captain, decapitate
cide	to kill	pesticide, homicide
crat, cracy	to rule	bureaucrat, democracy
graph	to write, draw	telegraph, phonograph
log, ology	study of	geology, psychology
matri	mother	matriarch, maternal
patri	father	patriarch, paternal
phobia	fear	claustrophia, arachnophobia
tract	to pull	traction, tractor, attract

Challenge 7-3

This time, underline the root(s) in each word in the left column, then use the root to match the word with its definition in the right column. The clues in the definitions have been underlined for you.

_____ 1. autobiography   a. <u>afraid</u> of <u>light</u>

_____ 2. decapitate   b. <u>kills mice, rats, spiders</u>, etc.

_____ 3. patricide   c. related to your <u>mother</u>

_____ 4. pesticide   d. the story of a person's life she <u>writes herself</u>

_____ 5. geology   e. <u>the study of</u> rocks

_____ 6. maternal   f. <u>killing</u> your <u>father</u>

_____ 7. photophobic   g. a ruler who <u>rules</u> by <u>himself</u>

_____ 8. telegraph   h. <u>pull back</u>, or pull back again

_____ 9. autocrat   i. to remove <u>the head</u>; beheading

_____ 10. retract   j. machine that sends <u>written</u> messages from a <u>distance</u>

COMMON ROOTS: SET 3

Root	Meaning	Sample Words
bio	life	biology, antibiotic
chron	time	chronology, chronicle
micro	very small	microscope, microbe
ped, pod	foot	pedal, tripod
photo	light	photograph, photosynthesis
scope	to look at	telescope, microscope
tele	distance	television, telephone
terri/a	land, earth	territory, terrier
therm	heat	thermometer, thermos
trans	across	transport, transcontinental

Mastery 7-3

This time, find the clues for yourself, then match the definition to its word.

_____ 1. podiatrist

_____ 2. antibiotic

_____ 3. micrometer

_____ 4. photosensitive

_____ 5. stereoscopic

_____ 6. teleprompter

_____ 7. terrarium

_____ 8. transcribe

_____ 9. thermostat

_____ 10. chronograph

a. bothered by light

b. an instrument that regulates temperature

c. being able to see with both eyes

d. an aquarium filled with dirt rather than water

e. a tool that measures very small sizes

f. a foot doctor

g. to rewrite (across) from one set of paper to another

h. a medicine that kills bacteria (tiny life) in your body

i. a machine that records time

j. a machine that gives a performer his lines from a distance

Using Roots to Understand New Vocabulary

These are only a few of the many roots used to create words in the English language. You don't need to memorize them all now. With practice and effort, you will start to remember more and more. Until then, you can use context clues and words that you already know that have the same root to help you remember. The following exercises will help you practice your deduction skills.

For Your Information

WORD PARTS AND YOUR DICTIONARY

Be aware that some words with certain prefixes and suffixes are not listed in the dictionary. It is assumed you know these affixes and can deduce the meaning from the word parts.

Exercise 7-4 Using Root Clues

Choose a word from the Answer Box below to complete each of the sentences. The root has been italicized for you.

1. If you have a *port*able radio, you are able _____ it with you wherever you go.

2. Egyptian priests wrote in hieroglyphs. The common _____ wrote in a form called *demo*tic.

3. You might lose your *vis*ion if your _____ are injured.

4. The farmer used the *tract*or _____ the plow.

5. The spy had been _____ on a secret *miss*ion.

6. Hieroglyphs are based on pictures and *phon*ics, which are the _____ of language.

ANSWER BOX
people
to pull
sounds
to carry
eyes
sent

Challenge 7-4

See if you can discover the missing words or answer the questions, based on the clues in the sentences. You may want to work with a partner or team.

1. The U. S. imports bananas, but we _____ corn to other countries.

2. A television lets us watch shows from far away; a _____ allows us to hear distant sound.

3. What does the thermostat in your house control? _____

4. Rockets that are sent to destroy the enemy are also called _____.

5. Where in the body would you find the auditory canal?

   _____

6. What do you lose if you are decapitated? _____

7. If a clam is a pseudopod, what part of the clam's body is not "real"?

   _____

8. If a patriarch is the male leader of a family, what do you call a female
   leader? _____

9. If a telescope is used to look at stars, what is used to look at very tiny
   objects? _____

10. What do you think a terrier would rather do: hunt birds, dig in the
    earth, or swim? _____

Mastery 7-4

1. If the root -cracy means "ruled by," what is the name of the government in which the people choose their leaders? _____

2. One spy said to the other, "We should synchronize our watches."
   What does synchronize mean? _____

3. If extra- means from "beyond or outside" and terra- means "earth,"
   what would you call someone from Mars? _____

4. In photosynthesis, what is necessary to make the plants produce (syn-
   thesize) their food? _____

5. If something that goes underground is called a subterranean, what do
   you call a vessel that goes under the ocean? _____

For Your Information

MULTIPLE ROOTS OR AFFIXES

As you probably noticed, some words have several affixes attached to
a root. Some even have more than one root. For example, the word
autobiographical can be broken into several parts: auto = self, bio =
life, graph = to write; -ic and -al are adjective endings.

Prefixes

Common Number Prefixes

Prefixes that represent numbers are some of the most common. Test your background knowledge and detective skills on Exercise 7-5.

Exercise 7-5 Deducing Number Clues

Match the definition with the correct word. Try to do this without your dictionary.

_____ 1. tripod   a. a period of ten years

_____ 2. unicorn   b. glasses with split lenses for two types of vision

_____ 3. octopus   c. a period of a thousand years

_____ 4. decade   d. a sea animal with eight legs

_____ 5. duet   e. a mythical animal with one horn

_____ 6. century   f. half of the earth

_____ 7. millennium   g. a period of one hundred years

_____ 8. quadruped   h. two people singing together

_____ 9. bifocals   i. an animal with four legs

_____ 10. hemisphere   j. a stand with three feet

Now check your answers for Exercise 7-5 using the following chart of common number prefixes.

COMMON NUMBER PREFIXES

Prefix	Meaning	Sample Words
uni-	one	union, unite, unique
mono-	one	monorail, monogram
bi-	two	bilingual, biceps
du-	two	duo, duel, duet
tri-	three	trio, trifocals, triceps
quad-/quart-	four	quadruplets, quarter
oct-	eight	octagon, October, octopus
dec-	ten	decimal, decimate, decade
cent-	hundred	cent, centipede, century
milli-	thousand	millennium, millipede
poly-	many	polygamy, polygon
multi-	many	multicolored, multiply
hemi-/semi-	half or part	hemisphere, semicircle

Challenge 7-5   Using Number Clues

In the left column, <u>underline</u> any word parts you see. In the right column, <u>underline</u> the context clue(s) in each definition. Then using your knowledge of number prefixes, match the definition to its word. One pair has been done as an example.

_____ 1. duel

_____ 2. bilateral

_____ 3. monologue

_a_   4. <u>tri</u>angle

_____ 5. polygon

_____ 6. universe

_____ 7. centipede

_____ 8. millipede

_____ 9. quadrangle

_____ 10. centimeter

a. a shape with <u>three</u> angles (and sides)

b. a shape with four angles (and sides)

c. figure with many sides

d. a wormlike animal with 100 legs/feet

e. one person giving a speech

f. $\frac{1}{100}$ of a meter

g. the great "oneness"

h. two-sided

i. a wormlike animal with 1,000 legs/feet

j. a formal fight between two people

Mastery 7-5   Using Number Clues

Use your knowledge of the number prefixes and the prefix chart above to answer the following questions.

1. If a monogamist has one wife and a polygamist has many wives, what do you call a man with two wives? _____

2. Is a human a quadruped or a biped? _____

3. If a person who speaks two languages is called bilingual and a person who speaks three languages is called trilingual, how many languages does someone who is multilingual speak? _____

4. Which has more legs, a millipede or a centipede? _____

5. Which is longer, a decade or a millennium? _____

Common Negative and Opposite Prefixes

Another common group of prefixes are those that make words **negative**, or opposite. Look at the prefixes below and some of the words that use those prefixes. Can you think of other examples for each prefix?

When you do Exercise 7-6, be certain you check to see that the prefix is attached to a root and not just the same combination of letters. For example, unlock = un + lock is an example of a prefix + a root. The word uncle, however, can not be broken down into un + cle because cle is not a root word.

Exercise 7-6   Negative/Opposite Prefixes

Underline the root word of each of the sample words.

COMMON NEGATIVE/OPPOSITE PREFIXES

Prefix	Meaning	Sample Words
a- (an-)	without, not	amoral, anaerobic, atheist
de-	remove or reverse	defuse, decode, dehumidify
mis-	wrong	mistake, misspell, misuse
non-	not or won't	nonstick, nontaxable, nonrefundable
un-	not	unlikely, unnecessary, unfriendly
in-, im-, ir-, il-	not	incomplete, inactive, inadequate

Exercise 7-7   Negative/Opposite Prefix Clues

Use prefix clues and your background knowledge to match the following words to their definitions.

_____ 1. mispronounce   a. having no sense of right and wrong

_____ 2. atheist   b. not a make-believe story; real

_____ 3. illegal   c. not able to tell what will happen in the future

_____ 4. inequality   d. to remove the water from something

_____ 5. unemotional   e. a person "without" a god

_____ 6. nonfiction   f. to say a word incorrectly

_____ 7. anaerobic   g. without air

_____ 8. immoral   h. not allowed by law

_____ 9. unpredictable   i. a condition where things are not the same

_____ 10. dehydrate   j. having no feelings

Spelling Changes of the Prefix in-

The prefix in- has several different spellings depending on the root word it is attached to. Use your dictionary to check for the correct spelling, if necessary.

- in- + m-word becomes im- immoveable, immature
- in- + p-word becomes im- impossible, improbable
- in- + l-word becomes il- illegal, illegible
- in- + r-word becomes ir- irregular, irresponsible

Caution

BEWARE THE PREFIX IN-!

Beware! Besides the meaning "not," the prefix in- can also have the meaning "in" or "inside," like interior. Its opposite is ex-, which means "out" or "outside," like exterior. The spelling changes (il-, im-, or ir-) are used for this definition as well, such as in the word import or immigration.

Other Common Prefixes

In the box below are some other common prefixes with sample words. Study these before you complete Exercise 7-8.

OTHER COMMON PREFIXES

Prefix	Meaning	Sample Words
ant(i)-	against	antiwar, antibiotic, anti-venom
auto-	self	automatic, automobile, autograph
bene-, bon-	good	benefit, benevolent, benefactor
circum-	around	circumference, circumnavigate
ex-	out, outside	export, exterior, expel
en-, in-, im-	in, inside	encode, import, inhale
mal-	bad, evil	malfunction, malaria, malevolent
mid-	middle	midmorning, mid-Atlantic, midriff
pre-	before	preview, pretest, prenatal
post-	after	postpone, posttest, postgame
re-	do again	reuse, redo, recycle
sol(i)-	one, alone	solo, solitary, solitude
sub-	under	submarine, sub-Sahara, subway
super, supr-	above, over, more	supervisor, superman, supreme
sym-, syn-	similar	sympathy, synonym, synchronize
trans-	across	transport, transcontinental, transmit

Exercise 7-8   Using Prefixes to Find Meaning

*Use the words in the Answer Box to complete the following sentences. Context and prefix clues should help you find the correct answer without using your dictionary. Clues have been **bold-faced** for you.*

ANSWER BOX

antacid	implant	revive	exorcism
autobiography	malnutrition	subsoil	postgame
benefactor	midair	superior	transport
circumsolar	prenatal	synchronize	pregame

1. **Before** a baby is born, the mother should have excellent ____ care.

2. His art is ____ to everyone else's in the class. He doesn't work harder. He just has a talent that is far **above** the other students.

3. **After** watching football all day, my dad watches the ____ show.

4. If you have too much **digestive acid** in your stomach, you take an ____ to work **against** it.

5. Many children in Africa are so poor they suffer from ____ because there is often little or only **bad** food **to eat**.

6. If you need to ____ yourself while studying, take a cold shower. That should **bring you back to life again**.

7. The priest said he performed the ____ to drive the demon **out** of the girl.

8. My ____ is such a **good** person. She pays all my college expenses.

9. If you need a pacemaker **put in** your heart, a doctor must ____ it.

10. Directly **below** the rich black **dirt** is a rocky ____.

11. The two planes were so close **in the sky** they almost had a ____ collision.

12. Please ____ your watches. We want to arrive at exactly the **same time**.

13. Hillary Clinton wrote an ____. She wanted to tell **her own story about her life** in the White House.

14. The earth has a _____ orbit. It travels **all the way around the sun.**

15. The fruit company used a refrigerated truck to _____ the strawberries from California to Ohio.

Suffixes

Suffixes are endings added to a root. They do not usually carry as much meaning as prefixes and roots. They do, however, have an important job. Suffixes often tell us the part of speech of a word. Some endings show that the word is a noun. Some show verbs, and others show that the word is an adjective or adverb.

Exercise 7-9 Suffixes

Here are several lists of suffixes. See if you can identify the root word in each of the example words.

SUFFIXES THAT NAME PEOPLE

-ist	cyclist, geologist, artist
-er	teacher, writer, invader
-or	actor, director, contractor
-eer	engineer, volunteer, auctioneer
-ant, -ent	assistant, attendant, resident
-cian	physician, beautician, musician

SUFFIXES FOR NOUNS

-ness	sadness, happiness, tiredness
-ment	government, contentment, refreshment
-tion, -sion	education, television, comprehension
-ship	friendship, penmanship, hardship
-hood	childhood, adulthood, priesthood
-ism	socialism, alcoholism, communism
-ity	complexity, simplicity, rigidity
-dom	boredom, freedom, kingdom
-ance, -ence	resistance, preference, existence

SUFFIXES FOR VERBS

-ize	terrorize, modernize, sympathize
-fy	simplify, beautify, glorify
-ate	originate, domesticate, communicate
-en	shorten, tighten, frighten

SUFFIX THAT NAMES ADVERBS

adjective + -ly	simply, happily, hardly

Caution

WATCH OUT FOR SPELLING CHANGES IN ADVERBS

Watch out for spelling changes when an -ly is added to an adjective to make an adverb.

- Adjectives like happy that end in -y, change the y to i in front of the -ly suffix—happily. Here are a few other common examples: crazily, busily, hastily.

- Adjectives like able that end in a silent –e often drop the e before adding the –ly suffix—ably. Use your dictionary to check if unsure, because there are exceptions to this rule.

SUFFIXES FOR ADJECTIVES

-able, -ible	portable, incredible, capable
-y	shaky, creepy, inky, dusty
-ful	joyful, thankful, peaceful
-less	joyless, careless, fruitless
-ive	destructive, expensive, defective
-al	natural, mechanical, sensational
-ous	joyous, adventurous, rebellious
-ish	childish, Irish, boyish

Exercise 7-10   **Using Suffixes to Determine Part of Speech**

Use the ending of each word below to determine if it is a noun, verb, adjective, or adverb. Write the correct part of speech on the line provided.

_____ 1. criticize   _____ 6. gratefully

_____ 2. carefully   _____ 7. domesticate

_____ 3. recreation   _____ 8. adorable

_____ 4. piggish   _____ 9. containment

_____ 5. occupational   _____ 10. heighten

Using Roots and Affixes to Build Word Families

Words are like people. They have histories, and they have families. If you want your vocabulary to increase quickly, don't learn just one word at a time. Notice words that are related to the word you are learning and add them to your growing vocabulary as well.

Using Roots

Once you start to learn the Greek and Latin roots, you can start to learn entire groups of words. For example the words thermal, thermos, geothermal, thermometer, and thermostat all have the same root. If you know the root thermo means "temperature" or "heat," you can make an educated guess at the meaning of those words.

Exercise 7-11   **Using Word Parts to Build Word Families**

Use your knowledge of word parts and your personal vocabulary to match the definition to each word. Use your dictionary only if you cannot deduce an answer.

_____ 1. matricide   a. killing your father

_____ 2. homicide   b. killing ants, crickets, etc.

_____ 3. infanticide   c. microscopic, disease-producing life forms

_____ 4. larvicide   d. killing an oppressive or cruel king or queen

_____ 5. genocide   e. killing the environment

_____ 6. patricide   f. killing a human being (Homo sapien)

_____ 7. insecticide   g. killing your mother

_____ 8. tyrannicide   h. killing insects in their wingless, wormlike stage

_____ 9. germicide   i. killing newborn children

_____ 10. ecocide   j. killing an entire race (all generations of people)

Using Affixes to Expand Vocabulary

Many words are created by simply adding a prefix or suffix or other ending to a root word. For example, take the word code.

- By adding *verb endings*, you get codes, coded, and coding.
- By adding *prefixes*, you can get encode and decode.

Though not dictionary entries, you might also think of recode and precode.

New vocabulary words are created as needed by using existing roots and affixes.

- By adding a *suffix*, you can get encoder and decoder.
- By adding the *suffix* -fy, you get codify, and turn the noun code into a verb.

If you were really interested, you could also check your dictionary for other related words. One you might find is codex, which has the same Latin root as code. A codex is a book of ancient (difficult to read) text.

Exercise 7-12   Building a Word Family

Start with the root word educate *and find other words in this family by following the instructions. (Watch your spelling!)*

1. Add the suffix -ing to educate. _____

2. Add the suffix -ion to educate. _____

3. Add the suffix -or to educate. _____

4. Add the prefix re- to educate. _____

5. Add the suffix -ed to educate. _____

6. Add the prefix un- to Number 5's answer. _____

Some readings, particularly those about the sciences, are often full of long and difficult words. Many of these words have word parts that may help you decipher the word's meaning. If you don't know the word parts, try to figure them out so they can help you remember the new word. Reading 7 is a difficult scientific reading that will take time and effort.

Into the Abyss

1   One mile down! Two miles! The tiny **submersible** *Alvin* descends into the **abyss** of the deep sea. Few humans have visited this place. Here, the sun never shines. The water outside the three-manned craft is black and **frigid**, on the very edge of freezing. Here, beneath thousands of feet of water, the pressure is so great it would crush even a steel-walled submarine. The specially designed *Alvin*, however, has to dive still deeper. Another mile down lies the submersible's final destination: a **hydrothermal** vent and the incredible, recently discovered **ecosystem** of plants and animals that live there.

2   Until 1977, when life was first discovered at the deep-sea vents, scientists believed that the deep ocean was a dead wasteland because the sun could not reach so deeply below the surface. Scientists agreed that all life known on Earth needs sunshine. Plants have to have the sun for **photosynthesis**, the process that changes sunlight into the sugar a plant needs to grow. Many animals depend on plants as their food source. Other animals eat those plant-eaters. Even animals living in totally dark caves depend on plants and animals from sunlit areas for their food. For that reason, scientists assumed nothing could live in the deep-sea abyss. They assumed wrong.

3   Like a seam running across a baseball, the Mid-Oceanic Ridge is a volcanic, undersea mountain range that wraps around the earth for 46,000 miles. Here, fiery **magma** is constantly forced upward from deep in the earth. This is one of the most hostile places on the planet. Besides the darkness and crushing pressure of the deep sea, in some places there are fields of hydrothermal vents, underwater

geysers that spew scalding water filled with poisonous chemicals. There seemed no place more unlikely to find life. It was, however, at one of these deep-sea hydrothermal vents that *Alvin's* crew made a discovery that changed the way scientists think about life itself. Here, in the crushing darkness, clustered around the hydrothermal vents, were colonies of gigantic red tube worms.

4   In the more than 20 years since the crew of *Alvin* first discovered these hot-water vents and the strange gigantic tube worms, deep-sea explorers have discovered hundreds of fields of hydrothermal vents. They have given these places curious names like Rose Garden, Clam Acres, The Garden of Eden, and Lucky Strike. Around these areas of hot-water vents, scientists have discovered not only the giant tube worms but also an entire ecosystem of plants and animals.

5   In this undersea world of frigid darkness and **toxic** water live communities of shrimp, crabs, lobsters, sea anemone, clams and mussels, octopuses, and clouds of tiny flealike crustaceans called **amphipods**. There are no plants in the abyss. Without sunlight, they cannot survive. Animals, however, seem to thrive in the darkness. In the last two decades, scientists who have ventured into the deep have discovered more than 500 new species of animals, from tiny microscopic bacteria to the giant squid of sailors' legends. According to one scientist, a new species is being discovered every week and a half, and that is "only the tip of the iceberg." Some scientists believe that 94 percent of all life on Earth lives in the oceans, and only 2 percent of that has ever been seen.

6   How is it possible? How can life survive, let alone flourish, without sunlight, especially in such a hostile environment? The secret is the hydrothermal vents themselves. These "black smokers," as the vents are sometimes called, are formed by superhot water welling up from deep in the earth. Tiny cracks in the earth's crust allow the ocean water to seep deep into the seafloor. As it does, the water draws **minerals** like sodium, potassium, and calcium from the rock. Nearby magma heats the water to temperatures up to 760 degrees Fahrenheit. This superheated water dissolves other chemicals like sulfur, iron, copper, and zinc from the earth as it boils upward. The mineral-rich water is then spit out into the sea through a crack or vent.

7   When the hot water from deep in the earth hits the icy cold water of the sea, the minerals fall out or mix with other chemicals to form chimneylike black smokers. In these chemical-filled waters around the smokers lives a unique bacterium. This bacterium can create food not from sunlight but from sulfur. This process is called **chemosynthesis**. Just as plants are the beginning of all life on the surface, this bacterium is the beginning of an entire food chain in the abyss.

8   The giant tube worms are a perfect example of how **alien** this deep-sea world is from life on the surface. The giant tube worm has no mouth, no digestive tract. The tube worm depends completely on the sulfur-eating bacteria for its nutrition. The insides of the tube worm are packed with billions of bacteria. The feathery red plumes that wave at the top of the worm contain **hemoglobin**, like that found in human blood. The hemoglobin captures and carries hydrogen sulfide, a bad-smelling chemical

How a Black Smoker Forms

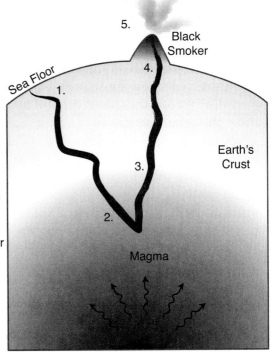

5.

Black
Smoker

4.

Sea Floor

1.

Earth's
Crust

3.

2.

Magma

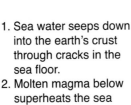

1. Sea water seeps down into the earth's crust through cracks in the sea floor.
2. Molten magma below superheats the sea water.
3. The superheated water dissolves chemicals from the crust.
4. The chemical-rich water boils back up into the sea.
5. The cold sea water causes the chemicals to fall out (precipitate); the chemicals build up as a black smoker.

compound often called rotten egg gas, to the bacteria. The bacteria use the hydrogen sulfide to make the carbon compounds that feed the worm.

9   Study of this new ecosystem is very hard. The animals that live there are used to the darkness. To study an animal's behavior, researchers need to use bright lights. Unfortunately, the lights themselves can change the animal's behavior. Capturing animals for study has not been successful either. These animals have bodies designed to withstand pressures up to 16,000 pounds per square inch. When taken to the surface where there is little pressure, their bodies either explode or disintegrate, so they are of no use for study.

10   Reaching these depths to study the animals is a problem in itself. Deep-sea submersibles are very expensive to build because they must be able to withstand the immense pressures in the abyss. At these depths, a malfunction or flaw in the craft could mean death for the crew. At present, there are only a handful of submersibles in the world that can dive to these depths. For this reason, research expeditions to the submarine vents are very expensive and limited.

11   The Mid-Oceanic Ridge, where most hydrothermal vents are found, makes up only a tiny portion of the ocean left to explore. The tops of this underwater mountain range lie around three miles below the surface. In other places, the sea is even deeper. In the **trenches**, the deep valleys or canyons of the sea floor, ocean depths reach more than seven miles.

12   *Alvin* can only dive to depths of around three miles. A Japanese submersible, the *Shinkai 6500*, was built in 1989 to reach depths closer to four miles. Japan and the United States are also now developing research submersibles able to reach Challenger Deep, the deepest point in the ocean.

Challenger Deep is at the southern end of the Marianas Trench of the Marianas Islands in the South Pacific. For safety, at least in the beginning of this exploration, unmanned probes will be sent into the deeper regions of the abyss. What incredible wonders will be discovered there, only time will tell.

13   Discovery of the new and incredible life forms in the abyss also has scientists asking questions about the very beginnings of life. Did all life on Earth begin here at the deep-sea vents? And if life can thrive in the extremely harsh environment, then is there a possibility that life might exist, or at least have existed at one time, on Mars or perhaps one of Jupiter's volcanically active moons?

14   So many questions! Perhaps future explorations to the abyss will find the answers to these questions and more.

Exercise 7-13   Pronouncing New Words

Look up the correct pronunciation of the following words and write them on the line provided.

abyss _____

geyser _____

toxic _____

frigid _____

magma _____

Exercise 7-14   Understanding Pronunciation

Use the pronunciation of the words in Exercise 7-13 to answer the following questions.

1. Does the y in abyss have the same sound as the y in the word geyser or the i in the word frigid? _____

2. List the word(s) that has (have) the schwa (ə) sound. _____
   _____

3. Do both of the a's in the word magma have the same sound? _____

4. What consonant does the g in frigid sound like—a j or a g? _____

5. Is abyss accented on the first syllable or the second? _____

Exercise 7-15 Defining Difficult Vocabulary

Use context clues and word parts to help you match each word to its correct definition. Write the letter of the correct definition on the line beside the vocabulary word.

_____ 1. ecosystem	a. a craft built to "go under" the water
_____ 2. hydrothermal	b. making food from chemicals
_____ 3. photosynthesis	c. to work incorrectly or poorly
_____ 4. chemosynthesis	d. no human in craft
_____ 5. amphipod	e. an area with little or no life
_____ 6. wasteland	f. making food from light
_____ 7. malfunction	g. breaking up into pieces
_____ 8. submersible	h. heated water
_____ 9. disintegrate	i. an organized group of plants and animals living in a particular environment
_____ 10. unmanned	j. a tiny shelled sea animal whose name means "both feet"

Exercise 7-16 Finding the Correct Definition

Write the part of speech and number of the correct definition of the italicized word as it is used in each sentence. Example: <u>n. 3</u>

_____ 1. Deep-sea vessels must be carefully built because a malfunction in the *craft* could mean sudden death to the crew.

> **craft** (krăft) *n.* 1. Skill in doing something. 2. Skill in deception. 3. A trade. 4. A boat, ship, or airplane—*v.* 1. To make or devise with great care.

_____ 2. Giant tube worms are an example of how *alien* deep-sea dwellers are to life on the surface.

> **alien** (ā′ lē ən) *adj.* 1. Owing political allegiance to another country. 2. Belonging to a very different place. 3. Opposed to something —*n.* 1. A person from a different country. 2. An outsider. 3. A person from outer space.

_____ 3. No submersibles have yet been built that can go into the deepest *trenches* of the ocean.

---

trench (trĕnch) *n.* 1. A deep ditch, such as used as protection for soldiers in warfare. 2. A long, deep valley on the ocean floor. *Idiom.* **in the trenches.** The place in a game, war, or daily life where the most intense action takes place. —*v.* 1. To cut a trench in. 2. To fortify with trenches. [< OFr. *trenchier,* cut]

Exercise 7-17   **Using New Vocabulary Words**

Use Reading 7 plus your dictionary to define the new vocabulary words in the Answer Box. Then use those definitions along with context clues in the sentence to find the word that best completes the sentence. Write it on the line.

ANSWER BOX			
destination	spew	nutrition	venture
frigid	unique	cluster	toxic
trenches	abyss	minerals	alien

1. Scalding, mineral-rich waters _____ out into the colder seawater at the hydrothermal vents.

2. The *Alvin*'s final _____ was the hot-water vents three miles down.

3. The gigantic tube worms are _____ to the deep-sea vents. That is the only place in the world they are found.

4. Many chemicals like carbon monoxide and chlorine are _____ to a human being. They are so poisonous that even a short exposure can be deadly.

5. Thousands of giant tube worms might _____ around a single black smoker. They are gathered so tightly it is hard to tell one from another.

6. Sodium, potassium, and calcium are several of the _____ the superheated water dissolves from the rock.

7. Until the 1970s, scientist believed the _____ was desolate, with little or no life possible. Without sunlight, nothing could grow at this depth.

8. Life in the abyss is so _____ that it seems like something from a science fiction movie, not a place that would be found on Earth.

9. The giant tube worm receives its _____ from chemo-synthesis. Without the food provided by the bacteria, the worm would starve.

10. Humans cannot yet _____ into the deepest places in the sea, because the technology is not yet perfected that would safely allow people to go to those depths.

Exercise 7-18 Finding the Facts

Write the correct answer to each question on the line provided.

1. What percent of the living things on Earth do scientists believe live in the sea? _____

2. Where is the deepest spot on Earth? _____

3. Which animal is the beginning of the food chain in the hydrothermal ecosystem? _____

4. Why don't plants grow in the abyss? _____

   _____

5. Why is it difficult to study animals in the abyss? _____

   _____

6. Who first told stories about giant squids? _____

7. What is *Alvin*? _____

8. When were the undersea vents first discovered? _____

9. Where are most of these hydrothermal vents located in the abyss?

_____

10. What were the first animals discovered at the deep-sea vents?

_____

Exercise 7-19   Sequencing

Reread this portion of Reading 7, then based on what you read, put the events listed in the Answer Box in the correct chronological order on the lines below.

The insides of the tube worm are packed with billions of bacteria. The feathery red plumes that wave at the top of the worm contain **hemoglobin**, like that found in human blood. The hemoglobin captures and carries hydrogen sulfide, a bad-smelling chemical compound often called rotten egg gas, to the bacteria. The bacteria uses the hydrogen sulfide to make the carbon compounds that feed the worm.

> ### ANSWER BOX
> Bacteria converts hydrogen sulfide into carbon compounds.
> The plume of the tube worm collects hydrogen sulfide.
> Tube worm receives nutrition from the carbon compounds.
> Hemoglobin carries hydrogen sulfide to bacteria in the tube worm's body.

1. _____
2. _____
3. _____
4. _____

Exercise 7-20   Writing About What You've Read

On your own paper, write a paragraph about why the discovery of the ecosystems around the hydrothermal vents is so exciting to scientists.

Going Beyond

Research

Check your local library or the Internet for any of these key words:

Alvin	*Shinkai 6500*	tube worms
black smokers	hydrothermal vents	Challenger Deep

Recommended

If you'd like an interesting book about the abyss, try reading *The Octopus's Garden: Hydrothermal Vents and Other Mysteries of the Deep Sea* (1996) by Cindy Lee Van Dover.

Just for Fun

Word-Building Dominoes

Here is a game you can play by yourself, with a friend, or in teams. The goal of the game is to use as many words as possible until you can no longer play or have reached a set time. If you know how to play the game dominoes, you already have the general idea how to play. These are the specific instructions for Word-Building Dominoes:

1. Start with a word that has a root and at least one affix. For an example, start with the word television.

2. The next word (chosen by you if you are playing alone or your **opponent** if you are playing against someone) must contain one of the word parts from the original word, for example: telephone.

3. The next word must play off the parts of telephone. For example, you could choose telegraph or microphone or even phonics. Spelling changes are OK as long as you are using the same root or affix. For example, let's choose microphone.

4. The game continues until someone cannot find a word to play or your set time has run out. Here is an example game.

television	thermal
telephone	sensual
microphone	sensory
microscope	dormitory
periscope	dormant
perimeter	etc.
thermometer	

WATCH THOSE RULES

Remember, you must use *word parts*, not just combinations of letters that look the same as a word part. Also, be careful with similar roots and affixes. For example, the prefix anti- means "against," but the prefix ante- means "before."

Play the Game

Now, it's your turn to play. You can challenge yourself, find a classmate to play with or against, or have teams play each other. It is helpful too if you have one person who is the judge. This person decides whether or not a word is acceptable. Below are some possible game starters, or you can make up one of your own.

bicycle	petroglyph	auditorium	photograph	electrical
transport	chronological	autonomic	demotic	fortify
geologist	domesticate	prescription	generator	synonym

Good luck and have fun learning!

CHAPTER 7 REVIEW

- **Another Strategy for Understanding New Vocabulary**

  A knowledge of word parts can be used to check the understanding of a new word gained from context clues. Using a dictionary is only necessary if the word parts do not support the context clues.

  - The root carries the basic meaning of the word.
  - Affixes—prefixes (attached before the root) and suffixes (attached at the end) add meaning to the root.
  - Seeing the root is the first step in finding meaning.
  - Remember that the spelling of a root may be changed by the addition of affixes.

- **Using Roots and Affixes**

  There are three ways to use roots and affixes:

  - Deduce the meaning of new words using word parts you already know.
  - Memorize some of the common ones and use these to help check word meaning you have deduced from context clues.
  - Use word parts to help you build a family of new words

- Prefixes

  Like roots, prefixes carry meaning.

- Suffixes

  Suffixes most often indicate that a word is a particular part of speech. Several suffixes also denote a person such as in the words actor, employee, or artist.

- **Using Roots and Affixes to Build Word Families**

  A knowledge of roots and affixes will allow you to learn not just one new word at a time but a whole family of related words. Building word families can help improve comprehension.

Solving the Mystery of Organization

Thinking Like a Writer

To become a better reader, it might help to understand the writing process. Most good writers don't just sit down and start to write. Before the first word is on the page, a writer gathers information then organizes the facts. Some of the material may be very **general**. A general thought often becomes the **main idea** of a paragraph. More **specific** ideas explain or describe the general thoughts. These specific ideas become the **supporting details** of the paragraph.

For example, a student's assignment is to write a paragraph about the animals found on a farm.

- First, she thinks of as many animals as she can and writes them down.

  horses, cows, chickens, dogs, cats, mice, rats, hawks, snakes, pigs, foxes

- Next, she organizes them into categories.

Farm Animals	Pets	Wild Animals
horses	dogs	mice
cows	cats	rats
chickens		hawks
pigs		snakes
		foxes

- Finally, she is ready to write the paragraph.

  A farm is the place to be if you like animals. Of course there are the usual farm animals such as horses, cows, chickens, and pigs. There are also animals like dogs and cats that help out around the farm. And don't forget about all the wild animals like mice, rats, hawks, foxes, and snakes who find an easy meal around the barnyard.

She has a main idea: "A farm is the place to be if you like animals." She then uses the specific animals to support her main idea.

Secrets to Success

THE SECRET TO UNDERSTANDING WHAT YOU READ

If you want to be a better reader, think like a writer. Pay close attention to the organization of what you read. Previewing before you read is one of the best ways to discover the organization.

Understanding Organization: General and Specific

Your job as a reader is to notice the general or main idea. You must also find the specific details in the paragraph that support that main idea. Unfortunately, noticing the main ideas and supporting details in paragraphs may be very difficult for some people. Before you attempt this strategy in a paragraph, practice seeing the difference between general and specific words. Think about these five words. Put an X on the line by the most general.

pound _____

ton _____

weight _____

ounce _____

gram _____

How are they related to each other? Is one word broader than the others?

In this example, the word weight is broader, more general, than the other four words. In fact, pound, ton, ounce, and gram are all specific kinds of weight.

WEIGHT			
pound	ton	ounce	gram

Exercise 8-1   Seeing General and Specific

Consider the following lists of words. Put an X or check mark on the line next to the word that is the most general. Use your dictionary if necessary.

A. 1. cotton   _____

   2. silk   _____

   3. rayon   _____

   4. cloth   _____

   5. satin   _____

B. 1. carnation _____

   2. daisy   _____

   3. flower   _____

   4. rose   _____

   5. pansy   _____

C. 1. happiness _____

   2. sadness _____

   3. bitterness _____

   4. emotion _____

   5. anxiety _____

D. 1. trout   _____

   2. fish   _____

   3. salmon _____

   4. sunfish _____

   5. bass   _____

E. 1. orange   _____

   2. red   _____

   3. violet   _____

   4. color   _____

   5. blue   _____

F. 1. checkers _____

   2. chess   _____

   3. games   _____

   4. bingo   _____

   5. cribbage _____

G. 1. canoe   _____

   2. raft   _____

   3. kayak   _____

   4. boats   _____

   5. rowboat _____

H. 1. tiger   _____

   2. jaguar   _____

   3. big cat   _____

   4. lion   _____

   5. leopard _____

I. 1. flavor   _____

   2. vanilla   _____

   3. strawberry_____

   4. chocolate _____

   5. cherry   _____

J. 1. carrot   _____

   2. squash   _____

   3. lettuce   _____

   4. cabbage _____

   5. vegetable _____

K. 1. shirt   _____

   2. clothing _____

   3. pants   _____

   4. dress   _____

   5. blouse   _____

L. 1. maples   _____

   2. elms   _____

   3. trees   _____

   4. pines   _____

   5. oaks   _____

M. 1. aluminum _____   N. 1. artists _____

   2. copper _____   2. jobs _____

   3. gold _____   3. linguists _____

   4. metal _____   4. plumbers _____

   5. silver _____   5. geologists _____

Main Idea and Supporting Details

In some paragraphs, the writer has so much information that the supporting details themselves have ideas that support *them*. The ideas that support the *main* idea are called **major** supporting details. The details that support the major *supporting* details are called **minor** supporting details. In some longer readings, you may find that even minor supporting details have supporting details.

As an example, think about a writer who wants to write a paper about different kinds of dogs. As you probably know, there are hundreds. The writer knows he can't possibly write about all of these, so he decides his first step is to break dogs into categories. The broadest categories he can think of are purebred and mixed breed.

The writer decides he only wants to write about purebred dogs, but there are still hundreds of different kinds, so again he looks for a more specific category that interests him. Under the purebred category, he finds several supporting categories, working dogs, herding dogs, companion dogs, and others.

He decides he wants to write about herding dogs, but again there are specific categories: sheep herders (**shepherds**) or cattle dogs. Finally, he decides he will write about shepherds. Under this category, he finds collies, Old English sheepdogs, and Shetland sheepdogs.

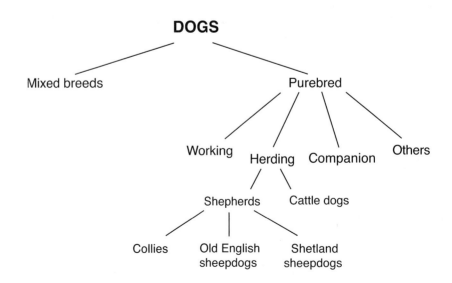

As you can see in this illustration, each category of detail supports the one above it. As a reader, your job is to see this organization. Noting what is the main idea, what is major supporting detail, and what is minor supporting detail will help you see what is important in what you are reading.

Seeing this complex organization may be very difficult in a paragraph, so again practice this strategy on groups of words.

Exercise 8-2   Noting Major and Minor Supporting Details

Study each group of words. Find the main idea, major supporting detail, and minor supporting details, then rewrite them as shown in the example:

> coffee table, couch, furniture, entertainment center, living room furniture, recliner, chair

I. main idea	I. furniture
A. major supporting detail	A. living room furniture
1. minor supporting detail	1. coffee table
2. minor supporting detail	2. couch
3. minor supporting detail	3. chair
4. minor supporting detail	4. recliner
5. minor supporting detail	5. entertainment center

1.

> saws, hammers, tools, drills, levels, screwdrivers, carpenter's tools

I. _____

  A. _____

    1. _____

    2. _____

    3. _____

    4. _____

    5. _____

2.

> Coke, Pepsi, soft drink, Sprite, beverage, Dr Pepper, 7-Up

I. _____

  A. _____

    1. _____

    2. _____

    3. _____

    4. _____

    5. _____

3.

> ears, head, nose, body,
> mouth, eyes, hair

I. _____

    A. _____

        1. _____

        2. _____

        3. _____

        4. _____

        5. _____

4.

> strawberry pie, fruit pie, apple
> pie, pie, lemon meringue pie,
> peach pie, cherry pie

I. _____

    A. _____

        1. _____

        2. _____

        3. _____

        4. _____

        5. _____

5.

> K, letters, R, B, consonants,
> Z, Q

I. _____

    A. _____

        1. _____

        2. _____

        3. _____

        4. _____

        5. _____

6.

> tornado, hurricane, typhoon,
> weather, thunderstorm,
> storm, cyclone

I. _____

    A. _____

        1. _____

        2. _____

        3. _____

        4. _____

        5. _____

7.

> peanuts, snacks, pretzels,
> corn chips, salty snacks,
> potato chips, popcorn

8.

> spatulas, sieves, utensils, stir-
> ring spoons, kitchen utensils,
> carving knives, electric mixers

I. _____   I. _____

   A. _____   A. _____

      1. _____   1. _____

      2. _____   2. _____

      3. _____   3. _____

      4. _____   4. _____

      5. _____   5. _____

9.   10.

media, comedy, movies, drama, science fiction, action, horror

burgundy, colors, reds, scarlet, cranberry, magenta, fuchsia

I. _____   I. _____

   A. _____   A. _____

      1. _____   1. _____

      2. _____   2. _____

      3. _____   3. _____

      4. _____   4. _____

      5. _____   5. _____

Implied Main Idea

In most paragraphs, the main idea is stated. A stated main idea is often also called the "topic sentence." However, many times, especially in more difficult readings, the writer assumes the reader can figure out the main idea by seeing what the supporting details have in common. When the main idea is not stated, it is called an **implied** main idea. Can you guess the implied main idea in the following words?

lemonade, water, cola, juice

Actually, there are several answers that would be correct:

- beverages
- things you drink when you are thirsty
- liquids
- nonalcoholic drinks

Why would the answer sweet drinks not be correct? Did you notice that water is not sweet? When you are trying to find the implied main idea, all the supporting details must support the main idea. Before you try this difficult strategy in paragraphs, practice with groups of words.

Exercise 8-3   Implied Main Ideas

*Write an appropriate title for the missing main idea. Be as **specific** as possible. Exercise A has been done for you as an example.*

A.   things that are white

1. clean snow
2. the White House
3. fresh typing paper
4. milk

B.   _____

1. broom
2. dust rag
3. vacuum
4. mop

C.   _____

1. algebra
2. geometry
3. calculus
4. trigonometry

D.   _____

1. shells
2. sand
3. seagulls
4. sunbathers

E.   _____

1. pencils
2. markers
3. chalk
4. pens

F.   _____

1. elk
2. moose
3. deer
4. antelope

G.   _____

1. clouds
2. rainbows
3. birds
4. tornadoes

H.   _____

1. stove
2. refrigerator
3. microwave
4. oven

Challenge 8-3

I. _____

1. noun
2. verb
3. adjective
4. adverb

J. _____

1. Anasazi
2. Pueblo
3. Navajo
4. Apache

K. _____

1. lettuce
2. cheese
3. mustard
4. pickles

L. _____

1. Champollion
2. Kircher
3. Napoleon
4. Dr. Young

Mastery 8-3

M. _____

1. Celtic
2. Middle English
3. Old English
4. Modern English

N. _____

1. 4
2. 9
3. 16
4. 25

For Your Information

IMPLIED MAIN IDEAS

When working with implied main ideas, your answers may be different than someone else's but still be correct as long as the relationship you see between the supporting details is covered by your main idea.

Seeing Organization

A writer takes an organized outline or map and turns the words into sentences. Sentences are then combined into paragraphs. Paragraphs can be combined into essays or stories.

words → sentences → paragraphs → essays/stories

Secrets to Success

FIND THE TOPIC SENTENCE

Whether the main idea is stated or implied, you as the reader *must* note it. All else in the paragraph should support either that main idea or the major supporting details of that idea.

You will learn more about finding the main idea in paragraphs in the next chapter. Now, practice finding main idea in a group of sentences. See the example below.

1. Amelia liked to climb trees.

2. Amelia played baseball with her sister.

3. Amelia was an active and adventurous child.

4. Amelia wore trousers so she could play like the boys.

5. Amelia liked to go exploring in the woods.

Which of these five sentences is the broadest? Remember, if you have chosen the correct sentence, the other four will support the main idea.

Did you choose number 3? If so, you were correct. When the sentences are combined, they make a paragraph like the one below.

Amelia was an active and adventurous child. She loved to climb trees and play baseball with her sister. She also liked to go exploring in the woods. Her mother allowed her to wear trousers so that she could play rough-and-tumble games like the boys.

Exercise 8-4   Finding the Main Idea with Sentences

The groups of sentences below are actually paragraphs that have been separated to make it easier for you to find the main idea. Find the broadest statement that is supported by the others. Write the number of that sentence on the line.

A. ____

1. Detective Lee asked Mrs. Jones questions.

2. The detective did an overview of the property.

3. She carefully collected possible clues.

4. Detective Lee used many different strategies to solve "The Mystery of the Missing Necklace."

5. She used all her resources to find meaning in the clues.

B. ____

1. Originally the Anasazi people were hunter-gatherers.

2. The Anasazi civilization evolved slowly over time.

3. As they learned to domesticate corn and animals, the Anasazi became farmers.

4. These farms eventually grew into small villages.

5. Eventually, the Anasazi lived in pueblos joined by roads.

C. ____

1. The pyramids, altars, and most of the buildings had hieroglyphs inscribed on them.

2. These strange Mayan symbols were often also found painted on pottery.

3. Archaeologists have found Mayan hieroglyphs in many places.

4. Hieroglyphs were also carved into bones and shells.

5. Stelae, large free-standing stones, were covered with Mayan hieroglyphs.

D. ____

1. The first-known language spoken in England was Celtic.

2. The Anglo-Saxon invaders brought their own Germanic language with them to England.

3. After the Norman Conquest, many words of Latin origin came in from the Old French spoken by the new rulers of England.

4. American English has brought new words like tobacco and canoe into British English.

5. The language of England has changed over the centuries.

E. ____

1. Anthanasius Kircher tried to translate hieroglyphs in 1633.

2. Napoleon's scholars wanted to understand the mysterious Egyptian writing.

3. In 1814, Dr. Young proposed a new theory in an attempt to translate hieroglyphs.

4. Many people have tried to decode the ancient Egyptian writing called hieroglyphs.

5. For years Jean-Francoise Champollion studied the Rosetta Stone to decipher hieroglyphs.

F. _____

1. Early beliefs about Mars have been proved wrong.

2. The ice caps are not water but frozen carbon dioxide.

3. The canals thought to be manmade are in fact natural channels.

4. The "red bloom" is not living at all but blowing dust.

5. The atmosphere that was hoped to be like Earth's is almost nonexistent.

G. _____

1. Animals in the abyss depend on sulfur rather than carbon as a food source.

2. The animals in the abyss live in complete darkness.

3. Animals in the abyss must be able to withstand extreme pressure.

4. Animals in the abyss must survive in temperatures that are very hot near the hydrothermal vents and very cold away from the vents.

5. Animals living in the abyss are very different from those on the surface.

H. _____

1. The brain controls your blood pressure, heart rate, body temperature, and breathing.

2. Your brain receives input from your eyes, ears, nose, tongue, and skin.

3. You can think because your brain can process information.

4. Your brain does many incredible and important jobs.

5. Without your brain, you could not walk or talk.

Reading 8, "Who Killed the King?" is another scientific reading. It is dense with information, high-level vocabulary, and new concepts. Before you read, skim over the entire reading noting the titles of the major headings (they are **bold-faced**). Write them on the lines below. The first has been done for you.

1. _____ Dinosaur! _____

2. _____

3. _____

4. _____

5. _____

6. _____

7. _____

Remember to use these headings to help you find information when you are doing the exercises at the end of the reading.

Who Killed the King?: The Mysterious Disappearance of Dinosaurs

DINOSAUR!

1   Tyrannosaurus rex! Almost everyone knows about this "king" of the dinosaurs. However, this two-story-tall **carnivore** was not the biggest dinosaur. The allosaurus, another meat-eating dinosaur, was more than twice as big as a T. rex. Another dinosaur, the brachiosaurus, who was larger than 12 elephants, was actually an **herbivore**, a plant-eater. Many other dinosaurs ate plants as well.

2   Dinosaurs (which means "monstrous lizard" in Latin) came in all shapes and sizes. Like T. rex, many dinosaurs were huge. Some, however, were as small as rats. Some prowled the land, hunting in packs like wolves. Others lived in the sea. Still others flew through the air. For million of years, dinosaurs **dominated** the earth. Then suddenly they were gone.

THE END OF THE DINOSAUR'S REIGN

3   Scientists learn what happened in the far-distant past by studying both the **geology** of the earth and the **fossil** records they find in the rocks. Year after year, layers of dirt and **debris** pile up at the bottom of oceans, lakes, and ponds. If an animal or plant falls into this mud or sand, it can be covered over by more **sediment**. After millions of years, the sediment turns to stone. The plant or animal that was trapped is gone, but the fossil or **impression** left by that plant or animal remains. Scientists can then test the rock around the fossil to find the fossil's age.

4   From studying fossils, scientists know that the first dinosaur appeared on the planet about 225 million years ago. Humans only first appeared 2 million years ago. For more than 160 million years, dinosaurs roamed the earth. Then something happened!

5   The dinosaur's **reign** ended almost instantly. Fossil records show that 65 million years ago not only the dinosaurs, but 70 percent of all things living on the earth died—plants and animals—never to return again. For years, scientists puzzled over this unexplained **mass extinction**.

THE THEORIES

6   Scientists were certain that there had to have been a huge **natural catastrophe** to cause so much death so suddenly. Geological records show that this was a time period when the earth was very unstable. New mountains were being pushed upward. Volcanoes were **erupting**, and there were frequent earthquakes. Some scientists felt these harsh conditions were responsible for the die-off. Other scientists, however, felt that even the violence of earth building was not enough to cause the complete **extinction** of so many **species** so quickly.

7   Some scientists thought that perhaps a large **meteorite** had fallen from the sky. A meteorite is a meteor that actually hits the earth. The huge Barringer Meteor **Crater** in northern Arizona is an example of the damage a piece of rock falling from space can cause. This theory was not taken seriously, however, until photos taken from satellites revealed that there are about 150 large impact craters around the world.

8   In the late 1970s, Luis and Walter Alvarez, a father and son team, were working with scientists studying rocks in Italy, when they noticed something unusual. The rocks from the layer dated around the same time the dinosaurs disappeared had a very high level of a chemical called **iridium**. Iridium is a very rare chemical here on Earth. However, iridium is very common in **asteroids** and other space rocks. The amount of iridium that the scientists found in the Italian rock layer suggested that a meteorite at least six miles wide must have hit the earth. If it did, the scientists asked, where was the impact crater? None of the known craters on Earth were large enough.

FINDING THE EVIDENCE

9   In 1990, a scientist named Alan Hildebrand was looking through some old information made by **geophysicists** who had been looking for oil in the Yucatán **Peninsula** of Mexico. Near the northwest tip of the Mexican peninsula, he noticed something buried beneath layers and layers of sediment. The ring-shaped area was the right size and shape for an impact crater made by a gigantic meteorite.

10   An **international** team of scientists who went to the Yucatán to study the area decided that this was indeed a crater formed by a mountain-size piece of rock falling from the sky. The crater was named Chicxulub, after the Mayan village that sits atop the center of the crater. In the Mayan language, Chicxulub means "tail of the devil."

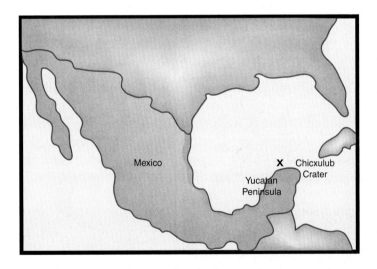

THE IMPACT

11   Scientists using **seismic** instruments similar to the ones used to study earthquakes have discovered some incredible facts about the damage caused by the impact of this gigantic meteorite. The force of the impact would have been equal to the explosion of millions of tons of **dynamite**. It punched a hole 22 miles deep into the earth.

12   At the same time, huge **shock waves** moving through the air at more than 500 miles per hour flattened anything in their path. The explosive force also started raging fires. Trillions of tons of earth, gases, and **water vapors** were blasted into the sky. Huge **tidal waves** spread out in all directions across the oceans destroying the **coastlines** of distant continents. The blow to the earth's crust also caused massive earthquakes and volcanic eruptions. In the days and weeks that followed the asteroid impact, the sky would have been so filled with debris that there would have been nothing but darkness. Some scientists say this period of little or no sunlight could have lasted as long as ten years.

THE SURVIVORS

13   With so little sunlight, nearly 25 percent of all the plants on Earth died. Many of the herbivores, especially the larger ones like the plant-eating dinosaurs, then died of **starvation**. That left the surviving carnivores like T. rex with little to eat. Only small animals that could eat a wide variety of foods had a chance for survival. **Scavengers**, which are animals that will eat anything they can find including decaying dead bodies, had an advantage because there was a constant supply of **carcasses**.

14   To make the disaster even worse, the area around the Yucatán where the meteorite hit is high in **sulfur**. This sulfur was thrown up into the atmosphere by the explosion. When the sulfur mixed with water, it became **sulfuric acid**, which then fell as **acid rain**. This deadly rain not only killed plants and animals on land but in the sea as well. The acid rain also lowered the level of oxygen in the water of the world's oceans. This meant a massive extinction of many **sea dwellers**.

THE LAST OF THE DINOSAURS

15   A few individual dinosaurs may have survived this natural disaster and even lived through the dark time that followed. Eventually, however, the once-mighty lizards were gone forever from this world. Or were they?

16   In **New Zealand**, an island country near Australia, lives a strange, miniature dinosaur called a **tuatara**. The tuatara has remained the same for the last 220 million years.

17   How did the tuatara survive when all the members of its family became extinct 65 million years ago? The answer may be its **lifestyle**. The tuatara needs very little food because it is very slow-moving. Unlike other

reptiles, particularly the dinosaurs, the tuatara lives well in cooler climates. During the sunless days that followed the meteorite impact, the ancestors of the present-day tuatara would have been better adapted to survive with limited food and cooler temperatures. The "king" and all the other dinosaurs died, but the lowly tuatara lives on today.

Exercise 8-5   Finding the Correct Pronunciation

Choose the pronunciation of the word that is correct.

_____ 1. reign   a. rān   b. rēn

_____ 2. fossil   a. fŏz´ əl   b. fŏs´ əl

_____ 3. herbivore   a. hûr´ bə vôr´   b. ûrb´ ĭ´ vôr

_____ 4. seismic   a. sīz´ mĭk   b. sēz´ mĭk

_____ 5. extinct   a. əg stĭnk´   b. ĭk stĭngkt´

Exercise 8-6   Understanding Compound Words

Define the following compound words. You should be able to use context clues in the reading to find the meaning. Use your dictionary only if necessary.

1. earthquake _____

2. coastline _____

3. tidal waves _____

4. shock waves _____

5. sea dweller _____

6. mass extinction _____

7. water vapor _____

8. acid rain _____

9. lifestyle _____

10. present-day _____

Exercise 8-7 Using Word Roots to Find Meaning

Use your knowledge of word parts to match the definition with the correct word. Write the letter of the correct definition on the line before the word.

_____ 1. geology

_____ 2. geophysicist

_____ 3. geologist

_____ 4. geochronology

_____ 5. geography

a. making maps and other writings about the earth

b. a scientist who studies rocks/earth

c. the study of rocks/earth

d. the study of earth's geological timeline

e. a person who studies the physics of the earth

All these words contain the root **geo-**, which means _____.

Exercise 8-8 Understanding Scientific Terms

Use the words in the Answer Box to complete the following sentences. Use context clues to find the correct answer.

ANSWER BOX				
sediment	fossil	extinct	species	meteor
seismic	sulfur	craters	carcass	vapor

1. All the dinosaurs except the tuatara have been _____ for millions of years.

2. Scientists believe that some animals can feel _____ waves before the actual earthquake happens.

3. A _____ is an impression of a plant or animal long dead that was left in rock.

4. After the explosion, _____ thrown into the air mixed with rain to make a deadly acid that killed all the plants for hundreds of miles.

5. Fog is nothing more than water _____

   hanging in the air.

6. Fortunately, the _____ burned up in the

   earth's atmosphere before it hit the ground.

7. There are more _____ of insects than there

   are of all the other kinds of animals on Earth.

8. The _____ of the dead whale washed up

   on the beach.

9. _____ from the eroding hillsides filled the

   old pond. Now instead of water, there is a swamp.

10. The moon is covered with _____ because it

    has no atmosphere to burn up the space debris that continually

    crashes to the surface.

Exercise 8-9   Finding the Facts

*Use the information from the reading to answer the following questions.
Write the letter of the correct answer on the line.*

_____ 1. Dinosaurs first appeared on Earth how long ago?
   a. 2 million years
   b. 65 million years
   c. 160 million years
   d. 225 million years

_____ 2. Who first suggested that a huge asteroid impact was responsible
   for the extinction of the dinosaurs?
   a. Barringer
   b. Hildebrand
   c. Alvarez
   d. Chicxulub

_____ 3. Which of the following is an ancient reptile that is still alive
   today?
   a. allosaurus
   b. brachiosaurus
   c. tuatara
   d. tyrannosaurus

_____ 4. What chemical did scientists discover in the rock layer from the time of the mass extinction 65 million years ago? This chemical hinted that an asteroid impact might have been the cause of this natural disaster.

a. sulfur

b. sulfuric acid

c. oxygen

d. iridium

_____ 5. Where did scientists find the impact crater that suggested the "killer asteroid" theory was probably true?

a. Arizona

b. Italy

c. Mexico

d. New Zealand

_____ 6. Of the following types of animals, which would eat decaying carcasses?

a. herbivores

b. carnivores

c. scavengers

d. dinosaurs

_____ 7. The chemical compound in acid rain is:

a. carbon

b. sulfuric acid

c. oxygen

d. iridium

_____ 8. The tuatara may have survived the mass extinction 65 million years ago because:

a. it can run very quickly.

b. it needs very little food.

c. it has very tough skin.

d. it likes heat.

Challenge 8-9

_____ 9. Which was _not_ a result of the impact of the huge asteroid?

a. Many plants died off.

b. Humans had to become scavengers to survive.

c. Many herbivores starved.

d. Most of the large carnivores died off.

Mastery 8-9

_____10. If a "killer asteroid" hit the earth today, which one of these animals would most likely survive?

    a. elephants

    b. rats

    c. whales

    d. tigers

Exercise 8-10   **Sequence of Events**

Place the following events in order from 1 to 6.

_____ 1. 70 percent of all life on Earth died.

_____ 2. Luis and Walter Alvarez suggested the possibility of a "killer asteroid."

_____ 3. Dinosaurs ruled the earth.

_____ 4. A huge crater was discovered beneath the ocean near the Yucatán Peninsula.

__3__ 5. A 6-mile-wide asteroid hits the earth.

_____ 6. Dinosaurs first appeared on Earth.

Exercise 8-11   **Finding the Main Idea with Words**

Use the words or phrases in the Answer Box below to complete the outlines in Exercise and Challenge 8-12.

ANSWER BOX		
chemicals	countries with coastlines	scavengers
scientists	things that fall from the sky	natural disasters
sea dwellers	compound words	dinosaurs
herbivores	carnivores	asteroids

A. _____

    1. allosaurus

    2. tyrannosaurus

    3. brachiosaurus

    4. triceratops

B. _____

    1. floods

    2. tidal waves

    3. earthquakes

    4. hurricanes

C. _____

1. sharks
2. whales
3. dolphins
4. crabs

D. _____

1. biologists
2. geologists
3. physicists
4. astronomers

E. _____

1. sulfur
2. oxygen
3. sulfuric acid
4. iridium

F. _____

1. France
2. Ireland
3. Japan
4. United States

G. _____

1. tidal waves
2. coastline
3. sea dwellers
4. mass extinction

H. _____

1. meteors
2. meteorites
3. asteroids
4. old satellites

Challenge 8-11

I. _____

1. cows
2. deer
3. rabbits
4. salad-eater

J. _____

1. tigers
2. great white sharks
3. Venus fly trap
4. steak-eater

Mastery 8-11

Use your dictionary and/or your background knowledge to make a title for each of the following sets of words.

K. _____

1. Neptune
2. Saturn
3. Pluto
4. Jupiter
5. Uranus

L. _____

1. Hawaii
2. New Zealand
3. Ireland
4. England
5. Puerto Rico

Exercise 8-12   Finding Main Ideas with Sentences

Write the number of the sentence that is the main idea on the line.

A. ____

  1. The tyrannosaurus rex was bigger than a two-story house.

  2. The allosaurus was twice as big as tyrannosaurus rex.

  3. Dinosaurs come in many different sizes.

  4. The brachiosaurus was larger than 12 elephants.

  5. Some dinosaurs were as small as rats.

B. ____

  1. Some dinosaurs swam in the ancient seas.

  2. Many of the carnivores like tyrannosaurus rex walked on two legs.

  3. Most of the plant-eating dinosaurs walked on four legs.

  4. Dinosaurs had many different ways of getting around.

  5. Some of the dinosaurs could even fly.

C. ____

  1. A plant or animal is washed into mud at the bottom of a body of water.

  2. It takes several steps to create a fossil.

  3. The plant or animal is covered by layers and layers of sediment.

  4. After millions of years, the mud is turned into rock.

  5. The plant or animal is gone, but its impression is called a fossil.

D. ____

  1. Luis and Walter Alvarez found iridium in the rock-level from 65 million years ago.

  2. This father and son said that the iridium was evidence that a gigantic meteor had hit Earth.

  3. It took several years and many people to discover the meteorite crater in the Yucatán.

  4. Alan Hildebrand accidentally discovered what might be a huge crater in Mexico.

  5. An international team of scientists who went to the Yucatán found the meteorite impact.

E. _____

   1. The impact of the 6-mile-wide asteroid was catastrophic.

   2. The meteorite punched a 22-mile hole in the earth.

   3. Shock waves from the huge explosion started fires for miles around.

   4. Tidal waves caused by the impact destroyed the coastlines half a world away.

   5. Huge clouds of dust, smoke, and water vapor darkened the earth.

F. _____

   1. The survivors needed to be scavengers in order to find enough food to eat.

   2. Those that lived were small in size and therefore needed less food.

   3. To find enough food, the animals had to be able to move from place to place.

   4. These animals had to be able to live in a cool, dark climate.

   5. The survivors of the mass extinction had several characteristics in common.

G. _____

   1. This animal lives in and on the small islands around New Zealand.

   2. The tuatara is a living dinosaur.

   3. There are many interesting facts about the tuatara.

   4. The tuatara is very tiny compared to the dinosaurs.

   5. Unlike most dinosaurs, the tuatara is slow-moving and needs little food.

Exercise 8-13   Writing About What You've Learned

On your own paper, write a letter to a friend explaining to her or him in detail what the earth was like after the asteroid hit our planet 65 million years ago.

Going Beyond

Research

Choose one of the following projects, do the research at your local library or on the Internet, then share your results with your partner, group, or class.

- Other Theories About the Extinction of Dinosaurs
- Other Mass Extinction Events
- Animals Facing Extinction Today
- Meteor Craters Around the World

Recommended

Worried another asteroid might hit the earth again? Check out NASA's Near Earth Project Program to check up on "potential future impact events" at neo.jpl.nasa.gov/risk.

Enhancing Your Thinking

Seeing Relationships

Remember the process you used to find an implied main idea? You had to find the relationship between words. Relationships are the connection between things. Relationships are rarely simple. A person, for example, has many relationships to other people. A woman may be a mother, sister, daughter, friend, tutor, and so on. Relationships between words and ideas can be just as complex. The deeper your background knowledge, the easier it is to see relationships. When a relationship is puzzling, you can always use resources to find the information you are missing.

Look at these five words: school, hospital, bus, store, gas station. Four of the words are related in some way. One is not! Can you decide which word is not related to the others? If you guessed bus, you were correct. A bus is a vehicle. The other four words are places.

How about these words?

rose, lilac, burgundy, daisy, daffodil

Which of the words is not related? This is more difficult. Several of the words have more than one meaning. Rose, lilac, and burgundy can be colors. A rose and a lilac, however, are also flowers. A daisy and a daffodil are flowers. Burgundy could be wine, or it could be a color. Since four of the five words are flowers, that must be the relationship. The word that does not belong is burgundy.

Exercise 8-14   Seeing Relationships

First, decide the relationship that connects four of the words and write it on the line provided. Next, decide which word does not belong to that relationship and cross it out. Use your dictionary or other resources if necessary.

1. dog, fish, cat, monkey, horse

   _____

2. honey, catsup, mustard, onion, relish

   _____

3. big, large, huge, small, gigantic

   _____

4. car, bus, boat, truck, van

   _____

5. circle, rectangle, square, triangle, sphere

   _____

6. happy, tall, short, fat, thin

   _____

7. rabbit, horse, dog, squirrel, person

   _____

8. France, Ireland, Scotland, England, Wales

   _____

9. Sahara, Nile, Napoleon, pyramid, pharaoh

   _____

10. astronomer, computer, actor, bishop, biographer

   _____

Challenge 8-14

11. weary, worn-out, excited, exhausted, fatigued

_____

12. four, ten, two, three, six

_____

13. steps, walls, floor, carpet, ceiling

_____

14. sprint, dash, scurry, toddle, gallop

_____

15. Mercury, Venus, Earth, Mars, Jupiter

_____

Mastery 8-14

16. Spanish, English, French, Italian, Portuguese

_____

17. siren, explosion, car backfire, alarm clock, fire

_____

18. hair, skin, lawn, losses, toenails

_____

19. four, twelve, one, sixteen, nine

_____

20. receipt, reindeer, sleigh, neighbor, feign

_____

CHAPTER 8 REVIEW

- **Thinking Like a Writer**

  To become a better reader, learn to think like a writer. Take notice of the organization of what you read.

- **Understanding Organization: General and Specific**

  A general statement is broad and covers a number of specifics.

- **Main Idea and Supporting Details**

  The general statement in a paragraph is the main idea. This is supported by major supporting details. Major supporting details may be supported by minor supporting details.

- **Implied Main Idea and Supporting Details**

  In some paragraphs, the main idea is not stated. The reader must infer the main idea from the supporting details.

- **Seeing Organization**

  To improve comprehension, the reader needs to notice how the paragraph is organized. Note how sentences relate to one another.

Finding the Elusive Main Idea

Topic and Main Idea

If asked to find the main idea of a paragraph or the central idea of an essay, many students would say something like,

"That paragraph is about motorcycles"

or

"That story is about earthquakes."

What the student has actually stated is the **topic** of the paragraph or essay. Topics can be things like: whales, ice cream, mathematics, cameras.

The **main idea** is *what the author is saying about that topic.* For example:

There are many varieties of whales.

To make ice cream, you need to follow several steps.

Mathematics is a universal language.

A main idea is a complete thought, so it should be written as a sentence. If you are taking a writing class, the stated main idea is called the **topic sentence.**

Topic Sentence = Stated Main Idea of a Paragraph

Where to Look for the Main Idea

The main idea of a paragraph can be stated anywhere in the paragraph or not given at all. Here are some places to look:

- in the first sentence
- near the first sentence, if there is a "hook," introduction, or definition
- in the middle of the paragraph
- at the end of the paragraph
- both at the beginning and end of the paragraph

Main Idea in the First Sentence

Here is an example of a paragraph where the first sentence is the stated main idea.

> <u>There are <u>several</u> ways to pronounce a new word</u>. First, you might try to sound out the letters. You might also try to rhyme the new word with a similar word that you already know how to say. Of course, if the word is difficult, you can always look it up in your dictionary.

In the paragraph above, the sentence that is underlined is the main idea. Did you notice several words were highlighted? Why do you think these words have been pointed out to you?

If you answered "because they give you clues," then you are right. The italicized words are **transition** clues. Transition clues tell you to watch for a change of some kind. There is also a clue in the first sentence: several. As you read the paragraph, you should be watching for "several ways to pronounce a new word." Watch for clues to organization in the following paragraphs.

Main Idea with "Hook," Introduction, or Definition

Hook

When you want to catch a fish, you don't just throw an empty line into the water. You put some bait on a hook to catch the fish's attention. If a writer has a paragraph that might not seem very exciting or interesting to a reader, she might add a hook to catch the reader's attention before she actually gives the main idea. Here's an example:

Paragraph A

> Yesterday, I saw a naked lady walking down the street. That was very surprising. In almost every culture in the world, people wear clothing. In the United States, that clothing might be anything from jeans and a T-shirt to a suit and tie. In Japan, some women still wear kimonos. In the hot, dry countries of the Middle East, people wear robes because it keeps them cooler, whereas, in the hot, wet places like the Amazon and Equatorial Africa, some natives still wear nothing but loincloths.

Do you see the **hook** in the paragraph? A "naked lady" is certain to catch the reader's attention. Now study the rest of the sentences. Pay close attention to the clue words to help you find the main idea in paragraph A. Can you find it?

Remember that the supporting details should support this main idea. If they do, you have chosen the correct sentence: "In almost every culture in the world, people wear clothing."

Introduction

When a writer thinks a subject might be new to his readers, he may give an **introduction** before stating the main idea to give the reader some helpful information. Here's an example:

Paragraph B

> Four states make up the Four Corners region of the American Southwest: Arizona, New Mexico, Colorado, and Utah. Here, in this hot and arid land, a civilization evolved and then vanished. Around the time of Christ, the nomadic ancestors of the Anasazi moved into this region. These hunter-gatherers eventually evolved into farmers. Later, they gathered in small villages that over the centuries grew into large pueblos. Unfortunately, as their natural resources became harder and harder to find, conflict between the people increased. To protect themselves, the Anasazi built cliff-dwellings high above the desert floor. Though scientists are still not certain why, these cliff-dwellers suddenly disappeared from the Four Corners area.

Can you tell the difference between the introduction and the stated main idea in this paragraph? The first sentence is introducing the reader to a new topic. Note that the transition words in this paragraph are organized by time. Does that help you find the main idea?

The main idea in paragraph B is: "Here, in this hot and arid land, a civilization evolved and then vanished."

Caution

WATCH FOR QUESTIONS!
Questions are almost never the topic sentence. Questions are usually a hook or some kind of introduction to the topic. The answer to the question, however, is often the main idea whether or not it is stated.

Definition

When a writer wants to introduce a word or concept, she might use a sentence or two to **define** the new word before stating the main idea. For example:

Paragraph C

> A mammal is a warm-blooded animal that has a backbone, hair or fur, and feeds its babies milk. Mammals are found all over the world. There are kangaroos in Australia and gorillas in Africa. There are tiny hedgehogs in England, and porcupines in Canada. Camels survive the scorching heat of the Egyptian desert while polar bears manage to live in the freezing Arctic. And of course there is one mammal you will find all over the planet—humans.

Can you find the **definition sentence** in paragraph C? Remember, the definition is not the main idea! Note in this paragraph that the transition clues revealing the supporting details are places. The stated main idea is: "Mammals are found all over the world."

Main Idea in the Middle of the Paragraph

Here's an example of a stated main idea in the middle of the paragraph. Watch the clue words to help you see the supporting details.

Paragraph D

> First, the plane's engine caught on fire and continued to burn. When Amelia flew to a higher altitude trying to put out the fire, ice began to build up on the plane's wings. From start to finish, Amelia Earhart's first solo transatlantic flight was filled with near disasters. The weight of the ice on the plane's wings finally forced her to come down. Because the clouds were so low and thick during her descent, she almost crashed into the ocean. By the time Amelia finally spotted the coast of Ireland, she was so far off course that her plane was nearly out of fuel.

After studying the clues, find the stated main idea in paragraph D. If you chose "From start to finish, Amelia Earhart's first solo transatlantic flight was filled with near disasters," then you were correct.

Main Idea at the End of the Paragraph

Often, the writer will give all the supporting details and then end the paragraph with the topic sentence, as in the example below.

Paragraph E

> First, set your oven at 400 degrees, then gather all your ingredients—flour, sugar, salt, spices, eggs, and milk. Next, mix together all the dry ingredients in a large bowl. Then in a small bowl, beat the eggs and milk together. Slowly pour this mixture into the dry ingredients. Mix thoroughly to make a thick batter. When all the lumps are gone, spoon the batter into a rectangular cake pan and bake in the preheated oven at 400 degrees for 45 minutes. Before removing your creation from the oven, touch the center of the cake with the tip of your finger. When it springs back from your touch, take it out of the oven and set on a cooling rack. If you follow these simple directions, you will have a delicious cake.

Paragraph E is a **process paragraph**. The transition clues make the steps easy to follow because they are written in chronological order. How many steps (directions) are listed? _____ Remember that there may not always be a transition clue with every supporting detail. Can you find any steps (supporting details) that do not have a clue? _____ Of course, the stated main idea is, "If you follow these simple directions, you will have a delicious cake."

Main Idea at the Beginning and End of the Paragraph

When a writer wants to emphasize the main idea, he states it near the beginning of the paragraph; then he repeats the main idea in slightly different words near the end.

Paragraph F

>   Learning to read is a complex process. First, a person must memorize the symbols of the language. In English that is the alphabet. The beginning reader must also learn the sounds that correspond to each symbol, so that she can sound out or correctly pronounce new words. After learning to decode words, this person must learn to read combined units of thought, such as sentences and paragraphs. Later, the reader must also learn to understand slang, idioms, and figurative language. Obviously, learning to read is not simple.

Read the first and last sentences in the paragraph above, then compare them. These are the stated main ideas. Do they say the same thing in slightly different words? How many supporting details do you see in this paragraph? _____

Main Idea Not Stated in the Paragraph: Implied Main Idea

Often the writer does not directly state the main idea in the paragraph. If the supporting details are strong, you as a reading detective should be able to solve the case of the missing main idea by using the clues. Also watch for repeated words, which are often the topic or part of the main idea. See if you can infer the main idea of the following paragraph:

Paragraph G

>   One way to relieve stress is to find a quiet, dark room and sit down for a few minutes and close your eyes. Another way is to go for a fast walk in the fresh air. Taking long, slow deep breaths will also help calm you if you are stressed. Some doctors suggest picturing your favorite place, a calm, beautiful spot like a beach or a mountain cabin. Perhaps the best way to relieve stress is to stop trying to do so many things at one time.

Study the clues and supporting details and decide what they have in common. Now, write your own main idea for paragraph G.

Secrets to Writing the Implied Main Idea

Use the vocabulary of the paragraph to help you write an implied main idea. Especially take notice of any repeated words or phrases. For example, in paragraph G, the phrases *one* way, *another* way, the *best* way are repetitious. The words stress and relieve are also mentioned several times. Using these clues, your topic sentence might be, There are several ways to relieve stress.

Using Transition Clues

Noting the transition clues in a paragraph is often the key to solving the mystery of its organization. Transition clues help you see the relationships between ideas.

Depending on the kind of paragraph you are reading, there are many different kinds of clues. Some of these clues might be single words like first or also. Others might be phrases like in the morning or in addition to. Often, these words or phrases are signals that additional information, perhaps major or minor supporting details, is being given. As mentioned before, not all supporting details have a clue. As a reading detective, you must use the clues that you can find to try to deduce the main idea by studying the supporting details.

There are hundreds of different clue words. Listed below are some of the more common ones that have been grouped by their common use.

Common Transition Clues

- **addition clues**—first (and consecutive numbers), also, another, in addition, last
- **time clues**—first (etc.), next, later, before, after, when, now, then, since, while
- **cause-and-effect clues**—because, as a result, so, consequently, thus, therefore
- **comparison clues**—similar, like, equally, the same as, just as, likewise
- **contrast clues**—even though, however, instead, but, in contrast to, although

There are many others, of course. And some words such as first and also can give you clues to several different types of paragraphs. You don't have to worry what kind of transition clue you have; just notice the job the transition clue is doing and remember that reading comprehension is 99 percent thinking. You have to do the work if you want to understand what you read.

Exercise 9-1 Noting Clues

Circle any clue words you can find in the following paragraph.

A. Addition Clues

Want to lose weight? There are several ways to lose those unwanted pounds. First, get rid of the "worthless" calories in your diet. Soft drinks, candy bars, and other snack foods give you lots of calories with no nutrition. Next, eliminate as much of the fat as you can from your meals. Bake or broil; don't fry your food. Last, get more exercise. Instead of taking the elevator, walk up the stairs. Play with your kids or take a hike instead of watching TV.

B. **Time Clues**

Ronald Reagan did many things before he became president of the United States. In high school and college, he was a football player. After graduation, he became a radio sportscaster. Five years later, he signed his first movie contract, and over the next few decades made many movies. During World War II, Reagan was a captain in the U.S. Air Force. In 1966, he ran for governor of California and won.

C. **Cause-and-Effect Clues**

As a result of a drunk driving arrest, a person may face serious consequences. Because of the arrest, the person may have to pay a large fine. The drunk driver might also be required to attend driver's school. Another consequence of being cited for driving under the influence of alcohol, especially for a second or third offense, may be the loss of that person's driver's license. The most drastic consequence for repeat offenders may be a jail sentence.

D. **Comparison Clues**

Though my father says I am crazy, I personally think there is little difference between a Ford truck and a Chevy truck. To me, both trucks look very much the same. Likewise, they are built to do exactly the same job. Both have similar options and color choices available. Their warranties are almost identical too, and there is almost no difference in cost between similar models. Studies also show that the resale values of both are almost the same. So what's the big difference, Dad?

E. **Contrast Clues**

Ivan and Ivor may be identical twins, but they are as different as day and night. Ivan is a night owl who will stay up until two or three in the morning, whereas Ivor is in bed by nine and up at dawn. Instead of partying to Ivan's rock and roll, Ivor would rather be relaxing to classical music. Food is another big difference between the two. Although Ivan is happy snacking away on junk food, Ivor is very particular and eats only organic food. Even their futures look to be very different. After graduation, Ivan wants to join the military. His brother, in contrast, wants to go to medical school to become a surgeon.

Exercise 9-2 Checking for the Main Idea

Now that you have carefully read paragraphs A–E, find the main idea for each. Write the topic sentence for each paragraph on the lines provided.

A. _____

B. _____

C. _____

D. _____

E. _____

A Strategy for Finding the Main Idea

Now that you are familiar with the organization of a paragraph—main idea and supporting details—and with transition clues, you should be able to find the stated or inferred main idea of a paragraph if you follow this basic strategy.

1. Watch for transition clues as you read.

2. Use these clues to identify the supporting details.

3. Consider what all the supporting details have in common (your main idea).

4. Note if there is a sentence that states this main idea. If there is not a stated main idea, you must determine the implied main idea yourself.

5. To double-check that you have found the main idea, make sure that the supporting details do indeed support that statement.

Exercise 9-3 Finding the Main Idea

Read each of the following paragraphs. Watch for and <u>underline</u> clues as you read. When you are done reading, look carefully at the organization of the paragraph. See if there is a sentence that clearly states the main idea. You may have to combine two sentences to completely state the main idea, especially if the paragraph begins with a question. If the topic sentence is repeated, write both sentences.

A. To improve your reading comprehension, follow these preview strategies. First, always read the first paragraph. Next, skim over the reading looking at the bold-faced words. Pay close attention to the headings, if there are any. These will tell you about the organization of what you are reading. Also, take a good look at any graphics such as maps, charts, cartoons, or photographs. Finally, read the very last paragraph. The last paragraph is often a summary of the essay.

_____

_____

B.   Sounding out a new word in English can be very difficult because spelling seems to have nothing to do with pronunciation. The word tough rhymes with the word cuff even though it looks like it should rhyme with the word bough. You shoot an arrow with a bow, which rhymes with sew but not cow, which is what you would expect. Even though it may seem hard to believe, the words sleigh, ray, quay, and fey all rhyme even though their spellings are very different. A desert is a hot and dry place, but when you desert the army the word sounds like the dessert you have when you have cake and ice cream.

_____

_____

C.   Are you always forgetting birthdays or important meetings? If you want to remember the important dates in your life, try the following time-management techniques. First, keep a monthly calendar where you will see it every day. On the refrigerator or next to the bathroom mirror would be a good place. Put all your important dates—birthdays, anniversaries, tests, doctors' appointments, and so on—on this calendar and glance at it frequently. Next, every morning when you get up, make a list of all the important things you need to do that day. Cross each thing off as you finish it. Third, make a long-range calendar. If you are a student, make one for the entire semester and check this at least once a week. If you do all these things, you shouldn't forget an important assignment or miss another doctor's appointment.

_____

_____

D.   *The American Heritage Dictionary* defines physics as "the study of matter and energy and the relationship between them." A physicist is a person who studies physics. Physicists do many types of research. Some study earthquakes. Others measure the movement of the stars and planets. Some physicists study sound or light waves. They also investigate everything from the inner workings of the tiniest atom to the ever-expanding universe.

_____

_____

E.   From the tiniest atom to the universe itself, all is in motion. Comets are drawn to the sun, circle it, then fly back to the dark reaches of space only to return again. The nine planets orbit around the sun. Moons orbit around their planets. Rings of rock and ice do a circular dance around Saturn. Even our solar system itself turns with the Milky Way across the vast expanses of space.

_____

_____

F.   During World War II, the Japanese tried desperately to break the Americans' secret communications code. There were several reasons, however, that the Japanese decoders could never break it. First, the code was based on the Navajo language. Other than a few non-Indians, none of whom were Japanese, only the Navajo could speak their language. Second, even Navajos who were not code talkers could not decipher this "wind talk." No one but the trained code talkers knew this secret language. One more thing made this language hard to decode: several different Navajo code words could be used for each English letter, and this confused the enemy.

_____

_____

G.   Mercury and Venus are closer to the sun than our planet, which is the third from the sun. Beyond Earth is the "red planet" called Mars. Next comes the Asteroid Belt. Here, thousands of rocks, from the size of your fist to ones that are nearly as large as our moon, circle the sun in an orbit between Mars and the giant planet Jupiter. Another giant, the ringed Saturn, is beyond Jupiter. Neptune and Uranus are the next two planets. At the outer edge of our solar system is the tiny planet Pluto. Together these nine planets, their moons, the asteroids, and an occasional comet make up our solar system.

_____

_____

H.   Yesterday, I overheard a man say, "It's sad. There's nowhere left to explore anymore." I say he is wrong. In my opinion, there are plenty of new and exciting places yet to discover. The biggest, of course, is outer space. There is an eternity of exploration waiting beyond this planet. Right here on Earth, we still have a place as dark and mysterious as outer space—the deep ocean. Only a tiny fraction of the oceans' bottoms have even been mapped. And only a handful of people have ever been into the world of the deep abysses that lay beneath the waves. In addition, one more place still unexplored is the human mind.

_____

_____

I.   During World War II, Australians fought alongside American troops in the South Pacific. British soldiers were there too. In Europe, Great Britain, Russia, and other smaller nations joined forces with the United States to defeat Hitler. In both Europe and the South Pacific, the United States had to work closely with its allies to win the war.

_____

_____

J.   Why is the Mayan writing so hard to translate? There are several reasons. First, the Mayans had no alphabet. Like the Egyptians, the Maya used a combination of logographs that represent ideas and glyphs that stand for sounds. These could be combined in many different ways to form words or sentences. Like in English, some of the symbols could have more than one meaning and are therefore easy to confuse. Unlike English, Mayan hieroglyphs were read not only from right to left, but also from left to right, top to bottom, or bottom to top. No wonder the Mayan language is still not completely understood.

_____

_____

Exercise 9-4   Finding the Implied Main Idea

First, read each paragraph. Second, choose from the sentences that follow the one that best states the main idea. Write the number of that sentence on the line provided. A sample has been provided for you.

Sample Paragraph

Drink lots of orange juice every day if you don't want to catch a cold. Be sure to dress warmly when you go out on a cold day. Also remember to wash your hands often if you want to stay healthy. You should also eat well and get lots of sleep if you don't want to catch a cold.

Sample Choices __4__

1. It is important to stay healthy.   [This answer is too broad.]

2. You should dress warmly when   [This is a specific detail.]
   it is cold.

3. Be sure to take good care of   [Again, this answer is too broad.]
   yourself.

4. There are several ways to   [This statement is the main idea.]
   prevent a cold.

Paragraph A

First, put a large pot of water on the stove. Then, add a dash of salt and a tablespoon of olive oil so the spaghetti will not stick. When the water is at a rolling boil, add the dry spaghetti. Stir it thoroughly with a wooden spoon so the spaghetti does not stick together. Next, turn down the heat to medium and cook. After 8 to 10 minutes, check to see if the spaghetti is ready. When a strand is the same color all the way through, drain off the water. Finally, add sauce and serve.

A. _____

1. There are many different ways to cook spaghetti.

2. You must watch spaghetti carefully so it does not overcook.

3. Follow these steps to properly cook spaghetti.

4. Spaghetti takes a lot of time and effort to cook.

Paragraph B

The cheetah, that long and lean big cat of southern Africa, is much faster than its cousins the lion and the tiger. A cheetah's speed is not the only way this cat is different. The cheetah does not growl or roar. Instead, it makes a hissing sound or a chirping bird sound. A cheetah's body is even built differently from that of other big cats. Unlike most cats, a cheetah's claws do not retract. They need them out at all times for traction while running. The cheetah's head is small for less wind resistance and its legs are very long for speed.

B. _____

1. The cheetah is faster than lions and tigers.

2. The cheetah is built for speed.

3. Cheetahs are very different from other big cats.

4. Cheetahs are unusual animals.

Paragraph C

Ride a bike to work tomorrow or, better yet, walk. You'll not only save gasoline and prevent pollution but improve your health as well. If you must drive, buy a car that gets good gas mileage and keep it tuned up not only to save on fuel bills but also to lessen the amount of pollutants your car puts into the air. Another way you can personally help the environment is to buy food in its natural state whenever possible. A fresh apple not only has more vitamins and fiber than applesauce but less calories. You also don't have the waste of a jar and lid that will end up in the dump. In fact, if you are concerned about the environment, be aware of everything you buy. Try to choose items with as little packaging as possible. Of course, everyone knows how important it is to recycle everything that you can.

C. _____

1. You should be careful when choosing your food and car.

2. Helping the environment is very important.

3. You should care about the environment.

4. There are things you can personally do to improve the environment.

Paragraph D

I saw my first coyote in Arizona. He was just where I expected him to be: running around the vast emptiness of the desert. Since then, I have seen coyotes sneaking down the back alleys of Phoenix, a city of over a million people, and lounging by the edge of a Florida swamp. A few years ago, I caught a glimpse of one checking out the hen house on a farm in Iowa, and last summer I heard them yipping at the moon near the beach in Oregon. Though I have never been to New York City, a friend tells me the wily coyote has also taken up residence there.

D. _____

1. I like to find out about coyotes.

2. In my experience, coyotes are to be found in many parts of the United States.

3. Coyotes travel over great distances.

4. Coyotes are found everywhere in the world.

Paragraph E

First, take a shoelace in each hand, then cross one lace over the next, making an X. Next, put the tip of the front lace through the opening at the bottom; go from the back of the X. Then pull the laces tight. Take that same lace and fold it in half to make a loop. Next, pinch the loop between your finger and thumb. With the other hand, run the second lace in a circle (going around the back) around the loop. Keep holding the loop pinched between finger and thumb. The second lace should go over your finger. When the second lace completes the circle in the back of the loop, pinch that lace into a small loop. Slowly, pull your index finger away while pushing the small loop through the space there. Grab both loops and pull tightly. Your shoe is now tied.

E. _____

1. There are several ways to use laces.

2. Pull your laces through each other.

3. Follow these steps to tie your shoe.

4. It takes two hands to tie a shoe.

Making Study Maps and Outlines

Making an outline or study map is a good way to check to see if you have correctly understood the facts and organization of a paragraph or reading. Learning this skill takes some role modeling and practice. Read the paragraph below, then look at the sample map and outline for this paragraph.

If you are interested in science, there are many different fields of study you might want to pursue. If you like rocks and minerals, you might consider geology. If plants or animals are of interest to you, you might want to study botany or zoology. Chemistry is another kind of science that might interest you if you like experimenting with chemicals. Astronomy might be the field for you if you like the stars and planets.

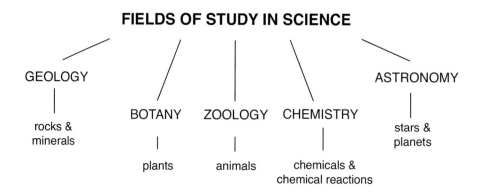

FIELDS OF STUDY IN SCIENCE

Fields of Study in Science

    I.   Geology

          A.   rocks

          B.   minerals

    II.   Botany

          A.   plants

    III. Zoology

          A.   animals

    IV. Chemistry

          A.   chemicals

          B.   chemical reactions

    V.   Astronomy

          A.   stars

          B.   planets

Steps to Making a Study Map or Outline

- Read carefully, noting clues to organization.
- Identify main idea—stated or inferred.
- Identify supporting details—major and minor.
- Organize your material into a map or outline.

For Your Information

TIPS FOR MAKING A STUDY MAP OR OUTLINE

- Abbreviate when possible.
- Use only key words or phrases.
- Use symbols, if they make sense to you.

Exercise 9-5 Sample Outline

Below is a sample outline for the following paragraph. Several facts have been left out. Complete the outline.

    If you cut potatoes into long strips and deep-fry them, you have French fries. Slit a potato on the top and put it in the oven for an hour, and you will have a baked potato. Slice up several potatoes, boil them in water until soft, drain, add butter, milk, salt, and pepper, and you have mashed potatoes.

If you have leftover mashed potatoes, you can mix them with milk and eggs and fry them to make potato pancakes. You can even eat a potato raw if the skin is no longer green. Obviously, the potato is very versatile.

The Potato—A Versatile Food

I.   French fries

II. _____

III. Mashed potatoes

IV. _____

V.   Raw potatoes

This was a simplified outline that did not list details. You can make your study map or outline as simple or complex as you need. If you are studying for a test and know the teacher expects you to remember details, you will want to include these in your map or outline. If the teacher does not care about details, it is not necessary to include them unless you want to for your own knowledge.

For Your Information

CHOOSING A TITLE FOR YOUR OUTLINE OR MAP

First, find the main idea of the paragraph or reading, then simplify that to a phrase. Then use that phrase to create your title.

Exercise 9-6 Making a Study Map or Outline

Read and study each paragraph, then first write the number of the stated main idea on the line provided. On your own paper, make a study map or outline. Paraphrase the topic sentence you have chosen for the title of your map or outline.

_____ 1.   [1]Thousands of feet below the sea's surface, where pressure is so great even a steel-hulled submarine would be crushed, live countless deep-sea animals. [2]In scalding hot springs and solidly frozen permafrost, there are bacteria. [3]Scientists have even discovered viruses that can survive the freezing vacuum of space. [4]Obviously, life can survive in very harsh conditions.

_____ 2.   [1]Is there life out there? [2]Most scientists believe that Earth is not the only place where life exists. [3]Evidence that life probably existed at one time on Mars seems to be growing. [4]There is also more and more evidence that there may be life on one or more of the moons of Jupiter. [5]Of course, there are the countless solar systems besides our own scattered throughout the universe where life may also exist.

_____ 3.   [1]During their journey of exploration from the Mississippi River to the Pacific Ocean, Lewis and Clark were some of the first white men to discover the amazing wildlife of the American West. [2]On the prairies, they saw thundering herds of bison as well as pronghorn, prairie dogs, coyotes, and the inquisitive raven. [3]Further west as they climbed into the mountains, they found an abundance of game animal: elk, mule deer, and bighorn sheep. [4]Of course, there were the predators as well. [5]Grizzly and black bears, mountain lions, wolverines, badgers, and gray wolves were common. [6]On the Pacific Coast, Lewis and Clark were awed by the rivers filled with trout and the beaches lined with seals and sea lions.

_____ 4.   [1]Would you find a desert in Alaska? [2]Most people would probably say no, but in fact there is a large desert in Alaska. [3]The word desert usually brings to mind a picture of the great white dunes of the Sahara in North Africa or perhaps the desolate emptiness of California's Death Valley or even the cactus-studded deserts of Arizona. [4]Though all deserts are places of little or no rain, not all deserts are hot. [5]Besides Alaska, there are deserts in other very cold places such as in South America and China. [6]In fact, deserts can be found in many different parts of the world.

_____ 5.   [1]Many people are terrified of taking a test, even when they know the material. [2]Why? [3]Test anxiety! [4]There is no reason, however, to allow this unnatural fear to ruin your grades. [5]Just follow this advice. [6]First, be prepared for the test. [7]Study for 20 or 30 minutes a day for a week rather than trying to cram the night before the test. [8]You want to be confident you know the material to be tested. [9]Also, be sure to go to bed on time or even a little earlier the night before, so that you are rested. [10]Next, be sure to arrive at your class 5 or 10 minutes early, so you are not rushed and have time to organize yourself and your material. [11]Lay out what you are going to need on your desk. [12]Several minutes before the test begins, close your eyes, take a few deep breaths, and let them out slowly. [13]Think of something quiet and pleasant like waves going in and out at the beach or wind blowing softly through the trees. [14]Do not think about the test. [15]Your mind works more efficiently when you are calm. [16]Finally, once the test arrives, preview it, then do the questions you know the answers to first. [17]This technique might help you find the answers to the difficult questions.

Exercise 9-7 **Outlining/Mapping Paragraphs with Implied Main Ideas**

After each paragraph is a choice of four possible titles for the paragraph (a paraphrasing of the main idea). Choose the best title and write its number on the line provided. Then on your own paper, make a map/outline.

A.   Words like canoe and moccasin were borrowed by the colonists from Native Americans. Rodeo, tomato, and countless other words were taken from the Spanish language. A few words came from the French fur traders, and even some from the slaves who had been brought to the New World from West Africa. Look at your dictionary, and you will find English words have also come to us from Greek, Hindi, Turkish, Norse, and a dozen other languages.

   A. _____

      1. English Words

      2. The History of English

      3. Where English Words Have Come From

      4. The English Language

B.   Get a good night's sleep and have a good breakfast before you come to school if you want to help improve your grades. Sit toward the front and center of the room in every class, so you can see clearly and can pay attention more easily. Always come to class prepared with your homework done and questions to ask the teacher. Another way to become a better student is to look for help when you need it. Check to see if your school has tutors, or find another student who is doing well and ask her or him for help. Study a little bit every day, so you only have to review the day before the test. Most important, always learn from your mistakes. Check your returned homework and tests and correct your errors.

   B. _____

      1. Be Prepared for School

      2. Ways to Become a Better Student

      3. Study Techniques

      4. Good Students

C.   Physicists study the magnetic fields of Mars to see if magnetic bacteria could survive there. Biochemists search for organic matter inside ALH 84001 and other space rocks. Microbiologists peer through their lenses looking for the tiny signs of living matter from soil samples collected on Mars and the moon. Exobiologists, most of all, are searching for confirmation that life exists, or did exist at one time, beyond the earth.

C. _____

    1. Studying Mars

    2. Kinds of Scientists

    3. The Study of Life

    4. Scientists Looking for Proof of Life on Mars

Reading 9 is another fact-based essay filled with new vocabulary and concepts. After you have read the reading once, read it again carefully, noting the organization of both the paragraphs and the reading as a whole. Note how the main ideas are supported.

The Mystery of the Moving Continents

READING 9

THE MYSTERY

1   Take a look at the map below, and you will see a mystery that puzzled scientists for hundreds of years. Can you see how neatly the shape of the west coast of Africa fits into the shape of the east coast of South America? They match so closely they almost look like two pieces of a jigsaw puzzle. In 1858, a geographer named Antonio Snider-Pellegrini drew a map showing exactly how closely the continents fit together.

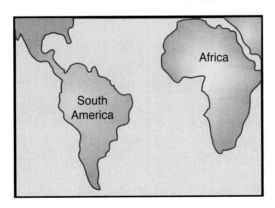

2   In 1915, the German geologist Alfred Wagener tried to explain this mysterious jigsaw puzzle with a theory he called **continental drift**. Wagener hypothesized that over 200 million years ago all the continents were part of one gigantic **landmass**. He called this **supercontinent** Pangaea (păn' jē' ə). Pangaea means "all-earth" in Greek. He believed that

Pangaea had somehow split apart, and the new smaller continents, which were large plates of the earth's crust, floated apart from each other atop the liquid mantle. Few scientists of his day supported Wagener's theory of continental drift. It seemed impossible that such huge chunks of the earth could move such great distances.

3   It was not until the 1960s that scientists from many different fields of study began to support the idea of continental drift. **Paleontologists** studying ancient plant and animal life discovered similar fossils in South America, Africa, and India. Their only explanation was that these plants and animals had been at one time in the same place on an ancient super-continent. The discovery of tropical-plant fossils in the now frozen Antarctica also suggested that this far southern continent was once near the equator. Geologists studying the sequence of rock layers found similar evidence. Rock layers along the east coast of South America were almost identical to those along the west coast of Africa. Glacial striations, deep scratches in the rocks left by huge ice sheets moving across the land, also seemed to match from one continent to the other.

SOLVING THE MYSTERY

4   Fossil and geological evidence as well as the near perfect fit of Africa and South America supported Wagener's theory. Still, scientists could not explain how the continents moved. The secret to the mystery of the moving continents, scientists finally discovered, lies below the sea. Exploration of the deep ocean has given geophysicists a better understanding of **geodynamics,** the power and motion of the earth.

5   In the 1960s, a new theory that explained continental drift was proposed. It was called **plate tectonics.** According to plate tectonics, the earth's rocky outer crust is not a solid shell. The crust is broken up into "plates" that are in fact like the pieces of a global three-dimensional jigsaw puzzle.

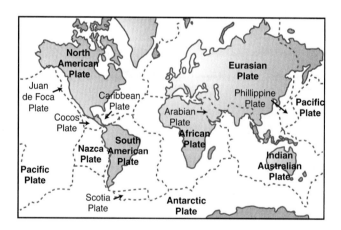

6   Over very long periods of time, these rocky plates can move across the planet. They can also grow or shrink as they run into each other. These plates of Earth's crust can be anywhere from 50 to 250 miles thick. Crust is always being created and destroyed. The average life of **oceanic crust** is about 55 million years, but the average life of **continental crust,** which is more stable, is 2.3 billion years.

THE MOVING CONTINENTS

7   New crust is constantly being made at the Mid-Oceanic Ridge, a ring of submarine volcanic mountains that circles the globe. Here magma wells up from deep in the earth, adding inch by inch new crust to these submarine mountain ranges.

8   Along the ridges, the seafloor is spreading. As it expands, the older crust is pushed farther and farther away. For example, Hawaii, which lies to the west of the Mid-Oceanic Ridge, is moving about 3 inches per year toward Japan and 3 inches a year away from the western shore of South America.

9   So, in fact, the continents are not drifting like a leaf on a pond. Rather, the continental plates, which are nothing more than enormous flat blocks of the earth's crust, are being moved as if they were on a gigantic conveyor belt. Newly created crust pushes older crust farther and farther away from its source. Eventually, old crust is destroyed.

WHEN PLATES COLLIDE

10   Interesting things happen when plates meet. If a thinner oceanic plate runs into a thicker continental plate, the oceanic plate is forced down into the earth. The crust from the oceanic plate is changed back into magma. Where two oceanic plates collide, magma from the mantle is squeezed up between the plates and volcanoes form. Perhaps most dramatic is what happens when two continental plates run up against each other. Look at a world map and see the result of the Indian/Australian Plate pressing into the Eurasian Plate. There you will find the Himalayas. These are the largest mountains in the world and are still growing several inches per year. In some places, as along the California coast, two plates are sliding along each other. In this situation, you will find an area of frequent **seismic**—volcanic and earthquake—activity.

11   Today, most scientists agree that 200 million years ago there was indeed a single landmass that they have named Pangaea. During the Jurassic Period, the time of the dinosaurs, Pangaea broke into two smaller supercontinents, which have been named Laurasia and Gondwanaland. These were separated by the Tethys Sea. Eventually, Laurasia separated into the lands of the northern hemisphere and Gondwanaland into what is mostly the southern hemisphere. The Mediterranean is all that remains of the Tethys Sea.

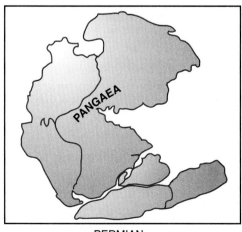

PERMIAN
225 million years ago

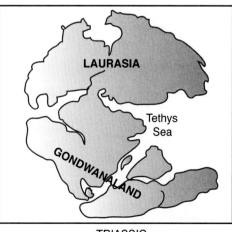

TRIASSIC
200 million years ago

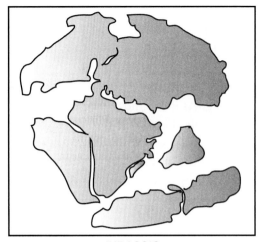

JURASSIC
135 million years ago

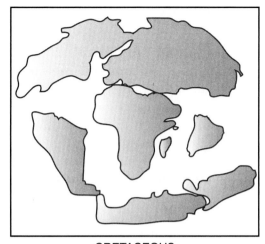

CRETACEOUS
65 million years ago

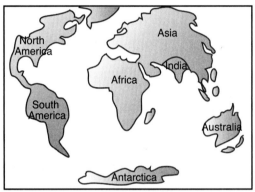

PRESENT DAY

THE FUTURE

12   And this restless earth is not finished changing yet. The Himalayans will continue to grow. The Atlantic Ocean will continue to widen while the Pacific narrows. The Mediterranean Sea will eventually disappear completely. As it has for millions of years, this planet will continue to reshape itself.

Exercise 9-8 **Finding the Correct Pronunciation**

_____ 1. seismic
   a. sēs´ mək
   b. sīz´ mək

_____ 2. tectonics
   a. tĕk tŏn´ ĭks
   b. tĕk tō´ nĭks

_____ 3. paleontologist
   a. pā´ lē ŏn tŏl´ ə jĭst
   b. päl ē´ ŏn tōl ə jĭst

Exercise 9-9 New Vocabulary

Use context clues to choose the correct word from the Answer Box to complete each sentence below.

> ANSWER BOX
>
> landmass   continental drift   oceanic plate
> ice sheets   seafloor   continental plate
> paleontologists   plate tectonics   glacial striations
> magma   seismic   dramatic

1. At one time, all the land on Earth was one gigantic

   _____. This supercontinent was called Pangaea.

2. In the 1960s, the theory of _____, which replaced Wagener's theory of continental drift, finally explained how the continents separated.

3. An _____ is much thinner and younger than most continental plates.

4. Scientists were amazed to find so many new species of animals living on the _____ of the deep ocean.

5. Ancient fields of ice moving across Pangaea left deep

   _____. These deep scratches can still be seen in Africa and South America today.

6. _____ studying ancient life forms noticed the similarity between the fossils in Africa and South America.

7. Two continental plates colliding can produce

   _____ results such as mountain building.

8. When a volcano erupts, _____ from deep in the earth flows out onto the surface of the planet.

9. Two plates sliding along each other such as those in California cause

   _____ activity such as earthquakes and volcanic eruptions.

10. During times of global cooling vast _____ moved out from the polar regions to cover massive areas of land and sea.

Exercise 9-10   Using Word Parts to Find Meaning

Use word parts and clues from the reading to match the word with its definition.

_____ 1. geologist

_____ 2. geographer

_____ 3. geodynamics

_____ 4. oceanic

_____ 5. submarine

_____ 6. subterranean

_____ 7. Pangaea

_____ 8. paleontologist

_____ 9. Mediterranean

_____10. Eurasian

a. relating to the power and movement of the earth

b. Middle Earth

c. beneath the ocean

d. person who studies the rocks and layers of the earth

e. person who studies ancient life

f. beneath the earth's surface

g. area where Asia and Europe overlap

h. relating to the seas

i. "all earth"

j. person who studies and maps the earth

Exercise 9-11   Finding the Right Meaning

Choose the right definition for each italicized word in the partial or complete sentences below. Write the number of that definition on the line provided.

_____ 1. Over very long periods of time, a continental *plate* can move across the planet.

> **plate** (plāt) *n.* 1. A sheet of hammered, rolled, or cast metal. 2. A shallow dish from which food is eaten. 3. A light sensitive sheet of glass or metal used in printing. 4. *Geol.* One of a large section of earth into which the earth's crust is divided. 5. Service or food for one at a meal.

_____ 2. . . . scientists from many different *fields* of study began to support the idea of continental drift.

> **field** (fēld) *n.* 1. A broad, level, open expanse of land. 2. A background area as on a flag. 3. *Sports* An area where a sporting event is played. 4. Profession, employment, or business. 5. *Comp. Sci.* A defined area of a storage medium. —*v.* 1. *Sports* To retrieve a ball. 2. To give an unrehearsed answer to a question.

_____ 3. . . . the earth's rocky outer *crust* is not a solid shell.

> **crust** (krŭst) *n.* 1. The hard outer surface of bread. 2. A stale piece of bread. 3. A pastry shell, such as a pie. 4. A hard covering or surface. 5. *Geol.* The exterior layer of the earth.

_____ 4. . . . the earth's rocky outer crust is not a solid *shell*.

> **shell** (shĕl) *n.* 1. The hard outer covering of some animals. 2. An outer covering on an egg, fruit, or nut. 3. A hard protective covering. 4. A thin layer of pastry. 5. A projectile or piece of ammunition such as used in a gun.

_____ 5. The discovery of tropical-*plant* fossils in Antarctica. . . .

> **plant** (plănt) *n.* 1. An organism such as a tree or shrub. 2. A factory. —*v.* 1. To place in the ground to grow. 2. To implant in the mind. 3. To place for the purpose of spying.

Exercise 9-12 Finding the Facts

Complete the following in sentences.

1. Who suggested the theory of continental drift? _____

   _____

2. Where did scientists finally find the secret to continental drift?

   _____

   _____

3. When did Antonio Snider-Pellegrini first notice the match between

   South America and Africa? _____

   _____

4. Describe how volcanoes are formed. _____

   _____

   _____

5. List three facts or discoveries that support the theory of continental drift.

   a. _____

   b. _____

   c. _____

6. Why are the Himalayan Mountains still growing? _____

   _____

7. What was the name of the first supercontinent? _____

   _____

8. What caused the glacial striations? _____

   _____

9. In the distant future, will the west coast of Africa be closer to or farther from South America than it is today? _____

   _____

10. Which lasts longer, in most cases, continental or oceanic crust?

   _____

   _____

Exercise 9-13 **Graphic Check**

The graphic below illustrates the sequence of development of the earth's landmasses. Fill in the missing information.

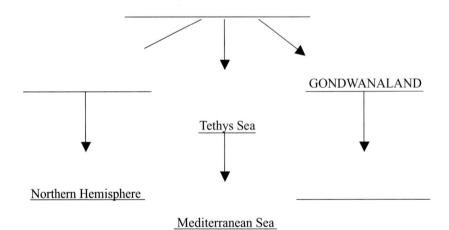

GONDWANALAND

Tethys Sea

Northern Hemisphere

Mediterranean Sea

Exercise 9-14 Main Idea

On the line provided, write the number of the stated main idea for each paragraph below. Then, on your own paper, make a study map or outline of the paragraph.

_____ A.   [1]Interesting things happen when tectonic plates meet. [2]If a thinner oceanic plate runs into a thicker continental plate, the oceanic plate is forced down into the earth. [3]The crust from the oceanic plate is converted back into magma. [4]Where two oceanic plates collide, magma from the mantle is squeezed up between the plates and volcanoes form. [5]Perhaps most dramatic is when two continental plates run up against each other. [6]Look at a world map and see the result of the Indian/Australian Plate pressing into the Eurasian Plate. [7]There you will find the Himalayas—the largest mountains in the world, still growing several inches per year. [8]In some places, as along the California coast, two plates are sliding along each other. [9]In this situation, you will find an area of frequent seismic—volcanic and earthquake—activity.

_____ B.   [1]It was not until the 1960s that scientists from many different fields of study began to support the idea of continental drift. [2]Paleontologists studying ancient plant and animal life discovered similar fossils in South America, Africa, and India. [3]Their only explanation was that these plants and animals had been at one time in the same place on an ancient supercontinent. [4]The discovery of tropical-plant fossils in the now frozen Antarctica also suggested that this far southern continent was once near the equator. [5]Geologists studying the sequence of rock layers found similar evidence. [6]Rock layers along the east coast of South America were almost identical to those along the west coast of Africa. [7]Glacial striations, deep scratches in the rocks left by huge ice sheets moving across the land, also seemed to match from one continent to the other.

Going Beyond

Research

Check the Internet or local library for any or all of these key words.

The Ring of Fire	vulcanism	seismology
Pompeii	Mid-Atlantic Ridge	Pangaea

Recommended

For an in-depth, in-motion look at continental drift/plate tectonics, visit the USGS online edition of *This Dynamic Earth: The Story of Plate Tectonics* by W. Jacquelyne Kious and Robert I. Tilling at: pubs.usgs.gov/publications/text/dynamic.html.

Study Strategy

Organizing Information

Challenge both your map and organizational skills by using the places in the Answer Box to correctly complete the outline provided. *Hint*: Try making a study map of the information before you try to outline. If this is too difficult to do by yourself, work with a partner or group.

ANSWER BOX

Japan	North America	Australia	Mexico	South America
Egypt	Great Britain	Oceania	Algeria	New Zealand
China	Antarctica	France	Europe	United States
Asia	Argentina	Vietnam	Sudan	Italy
Peru	Thailand	Brazil	Africa	Greece

The World

I. _____   V. _____

II. _____   A. _____

   A . _____   B. _____

   B . _____   C. _____

III. _____   VI. _____

   A . _____   A. _____

   B . _____   B. _____

IV. _____   C. _____

   A . _____   D. _____

   B . _____   VII. _____

   C . _____   A. _____

                                                         B. _____

                                                         C. _____

                                                         D. _____

CHAPTER 9 REVIEW

- Topic and Main Idea

The main idea is the statement the author wants to make about the topic.

- Where to Look for the Main Idea

The main idea can be found in a variety of places:
  - in the first sentence of the paragraph
  - near the beginning of the paragraph with:
    - hook
    - introduction
    - definition
  - in the middle of the paragraph
  - near the end of the paragraph
  - at both the beginning and end of paragraph

When the main idea is not stated, the reader must infer the main idea from the supporting details.

- Using Transition Clues

Transition clues are words that help the reader see changes in the writing, particularly supporting details. There are several kinds of transition clues:
  - addition
  - time
  - cause and effect
  - comparison
  - contrast

- A Strategy for Finding the Main Idea

Watch for transition clues as you read. Use these clues to identify the supporting details. Consider what all the supporting details have in common (your main idea). Note if there is a sentence that states this (a stated main idea), remembering that some main ideas are inferred.

To double-check that you have found the main idea, make sure that the supporting details do indeed support that statement.

- Making Study Maps and Outlines

Making a study map or outline of a paragraph will help you check your understanding of a paragraph's organization and make remembering the paragraph easier.

Using Graphic Aids

What Are Graphic Aids?

A picture is worth a thousand words! That is an old saying that is very true. **Graphic aids**—maps, graphs, charts and tables, timelines, photographs, illustrations, cartoons, and others—are picture representations of ideas.

Reasons to Use Graphic Aids

We use the term graphic aids because they **aid** (help) the reader. A quick preview of the graphics before you read will give you an idea what the reading is about. They are also good supports for comprehension. Graphics show in picture form the same facts or ideas that the text is trying to communicate. They can also give the reader missing background information. When you study for a test, looking over the graphics in a chapter is a good way to review your information. You can also create your own graphic aids to help you organize, study, and remember the information you read.

Using Graphic Aids

To the reader, graphic aids are also a storehouse of information. To find that information, however, you must first know how to understand the graphics. Here are a few simple steps to follow:

1. First, familiarize yourself with the graphic. Ask yourself:

   What is the title?

   What is the purpose of the graphic?

   How is the graphic organized?

   Is there a key (also called **legend**) to any symbols?

   Do you understand the vocabulary being used?

   What connection does the graphic have to the reading?

2. Next, scan for key words or concepts to find the facts you need.

3. Last, check to be sure the information in the graphic makes sense based on what you have read in the text.

Reading Graphic Aids

Different kinds of graphics give different information in different ways. Even the same kind of graphic aids, such as maps, can have very different forms. As with text, you must be an active reader to comprehend the information in graphic aids. Following is a discussion of a few of the different kinds of graphic aids along with some exercises that will let you practice using graphics to find facts.

Maps

There are many different types of maps. Road maps show you how to get from place to place. Other maps give you the names of countries, states, or other places. School textbooks often have maps that specify information about the people, animals, resources, or other aspects of a particular area. As different as they are, most maps have several things in common.

1. North should be toward the top of the map. If it is not, there should be an arrow somewhere on the map pointing toward north.

2. If the map uses symbols, there should be a key or legend on the map to decode those symbols. To use the legend, identify the meaning of the symbols, then use that interpretation to find information from the map. The legend may also include a **map scale** that helps you measure distances on the map. Find the map scale on the map below. Could you use the map scale to judge the distance between the bank and the school? You might need a ruler or straight edge to help you. You might also need to do a little math.

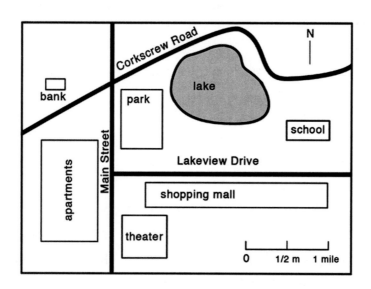

Reading Maps

Here are two examples of maps you might find in a textbook. Map A has no legend. You must draw the information from the map itself. Map B has a legend. You must familiarize yourself with the symbols in that legend in order to answer the questions in the exercises.

A. Map Without a Legend

POPULATION OF THE WORLD BY CONTINENTS

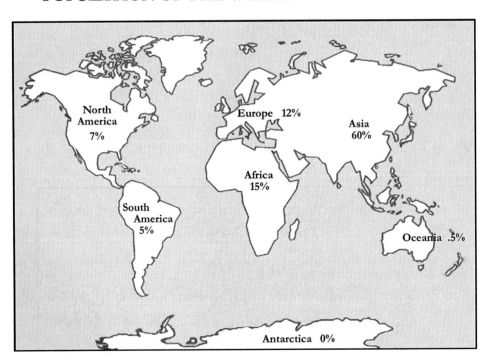

Exercise 10-1 Maps Without a Legend

1. Which continent has the largest population?

   _____

2. Which continent has no permanent population?

   _____

3. Which inhabited continent has less than 1 percent of the world's population? _____

4. Which has a larger population—North or South America?

   _____

5. Which has a smaller population—Africa or Europe?

   _____

B. Map with a Legend

Natural Resources of Western States

Exercise 10-2 **Maps with a Legend**

1. In which two Western states is timber not one of their natural

   resources? _____   _____

2. Which state has the most kinds of natural resources?

   _____

3. What state has only timber as a resource?

   _____

4. Which two states have gold as their only natural resource?

   _____   _____

5. What do the states of Washington, Oregon, and Idaho have in

   common? _____

Graphs

There are three major kinds of graphs: circle, bar, and line. Each has a different purpose. See if you can find the facts in these graphs.

Circle Graph

A circle graph is also called a **pie chart**. Circle graphs are used to show how a whole is divided into parts.

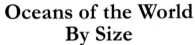

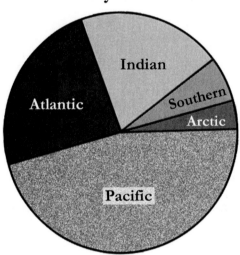

Oceans of the World By Size

Exercise 10-3

Use the circle graph to answer the following questions.

1. Which of the world's five oceans is the largest?

   _____

2. What ocean is the smallest?

   _____

3. Is the Southern Ocean larger or smaller than the Indian Ocean?

   _____

4. True or False: The Pacific Ocean is almost as large as all the other

   oceans combined. _____

5. True or False: The Atlantic Ocean is about half the size of the Pacific.

   _____

Bar Graph

A bar graph lets the reader compare facts in a general way. You do not get specific information, but can easily *see the big picture*.

When using a bar graph, be sure to check to see how the graph is organized and what facts are being shown. Bar graphs may run **horizontally** (side to side) or **vertically** (up and down).

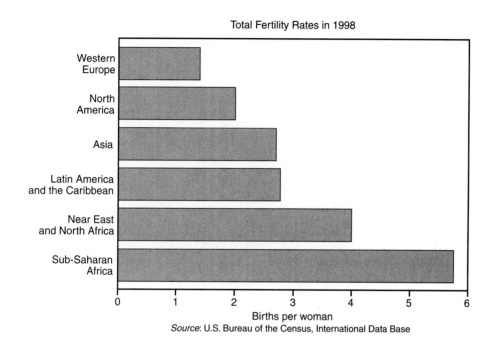

Total Fertility Rates in 1998

Births per woman
Source: U.S. Bureau of the Census, International Data Base

Exercise 10-4

Use the bar graph to answer the following questions.

1. In what region of the world do women have the most children?

_____

2. What two regions of the world have about the same fertility (birth/woman) rate?

_____   _____

3. How many children does the average woman in North America have?

_____

4. How many children does the average woman in Sub-Saharan Africa have? _____

5. How many children does the average woman in Egypt have?

_____

Line Graph

A line graph also lets the reader make comparisons but with specific information. Be sure to check the information on both axes (ăk´sēz´). An **axis** is either the vertical or horizontal line of the graph.

Line graphs are useful when you want to show how one thing changes in comparison to something else. For example, using a line graph is an excellent way to show in a visual form how the world's population grows year after year.

Take a look at the following line graph. Notice that the horizontal axis shows each **decade** (ten-year period). The vertical axis shows the population. Did you note that the numbers on the vertical axis (1, 2, 3, 4 . . .) represent the world population in billions? Noting these details is very important to finding the correct information.

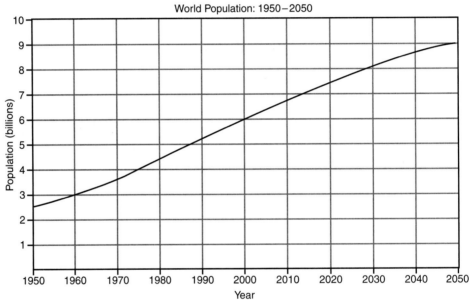

World Population: 1950–2050

Source: U.S. Bureau of the Census, International Data Base

Exercise 10-5

Use the line graph to answer the following questions.

1. In what year did the world population first reach 3 billion?

_____

2. What was the world's population in the year 2000?

_____

3. In what year will the world population reach 9 billion if this projection is correct? _____

4. About what was the world's population in 1970?

_____

5. If this projection is correct, will the world population have increased more between 1960 and 2000 or between 2000 and 2040?

_____

Charts and Tables

Charts and tables are used to give large amounts of information in an organized way. Again, it is very important to remember to study the organization of the chart or table so you understand the information being provided.

World Vital Events per Time Unit: 2003 (Figures may not add to totals due to rounding)			
Time Unit	Births	Death	Natural Increase
Year	128,758,963	55,508,568	73,250,395
Month	10,729,914	4,625,714	6,104,200
Day	352,764	152,078	200,686
Hour	14,699	6,337	8,362
Minute	245	106	139
Second	4.1	1.8	2.3

Source: U.S. Bureau of the Census, International Data Base

Exercise 10-6

Use the chart to answer the following questions.

1. How many babies are born every second in the world?

_____

2. How many people die every second?

_____

3. What is the natural increase to the world population every year?

_____

4. True or False: The world birth rate is more than twice the world death rate. _____

5. How much does the world's population increase every hour?

_____

Time Line

A time line is used to present events in chronological sequence.

World Population Time Line

2049   World population will be 9 billion.*
2028   World population will be 8 billion.*
2013   World population will be 7 billion*

1999   World population is 6 billion.
1987   World population is 5 billion.
1974   World population is 4 billion.
1960   World population is 3 billion.
1927   World population is 2 billion.
1804   World population is 1 billion.
1650   World population is 500 million.
BCE ---
8000   World population is 5 million.

*Based on current trends projected by the U.S. Bureau of Census, 2003.

Exercise 10-7

Use the time line to answer the following questions.

1. What was the world population in 1804?

   _____

2. If the projection is right, what will the world population be in 2049?

   _____

3. How long did it take the world population to increase from 1 billion to 2 billion? _____

4. How long did it take the world population to double from 2 billion to 4 billion? _____

5. From what source was the projection of future population numbers (trends) taken? _____

Other Graphic Aids

Illustrations, photographs, cartoons, and other graphic aids give you valuable information if you will take the time to read them carefully.

Illustration

CROSS-SECTION OF THE EARTH

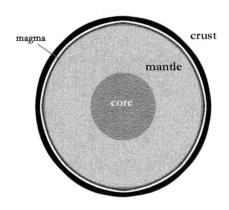

Exercise 10-8   Using Illustrations

Use the illustration to answer the following questions.

1. What is the center of the earth called?

   _____

2. On what part of the earth would you find mountains and cities?

   _____

3. Between what two parts of the earth do you find a thin, semiliquid layer of magma?

   _____   _____

4. Which is the thickest part of the earth?

   _____

5. Which is thicker, the core or the crust?

   _____

   If you take courses in the sciences or other content courses, you will find textbook assignments very similar to Reading 10. The material is dense with new vocabulary and concepts. The reading may seem boring and difficult to read. Yet to succeed as a student, you must be able to successfully complete the assignment.

Secrets to Success

READER'S EXPECTATIONS

Not all reading is fun or easy. If you know this is true, you can set your goals realistically. You should expect a boring or difficult reading to take more time and energy than a more interesting reading. If you know this and accept it, you will be more likely to succeed.

READING 10

The Mysterious Human Brain

1   Why do you cry when you are sad? When you touch something hot, why does your hand jerk back? How do you find your way home from school or work every day? What gives you the ability to write letters on a page or to read the words in this book? The answer to all those questions is: your brain.

WHAT IS YOUR BRAIN?

2   Stored inside the thick, **protective**, bony covering called the **skull** is a soft, wrinkled, somewhat moist collection of **neurons** (nerve cells) and other **cells** that together look something like a huge, pinkish head of cauliflower. The average human brain weighs only 3 pounds but contains more than 10 billion (that's 10,000,000,000) nerve cells plus 50 billion other cells.

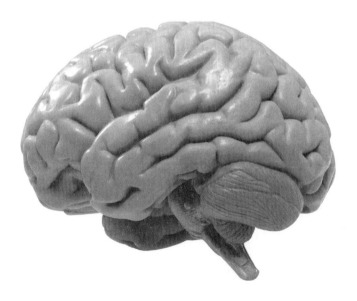

3   The outer surface of the brain is folded in on itself, over and over, somewhat like a crumpled newspaper. This folding allows more nerve cells to fit into a smaller area. If the brain was flattened out it would be about the size of an opened newspaper. There are lots of blood vessels in the brain. The **arteries** carry in a constant supply of oxygen-rich blood while the **veins** carry away carbon dioxide and other toxins.

WHAT DOES YOUR BRAIN DO?

4   The human brain allows you to think and dream, but it also does much more. The brain is the "mastermind" of the body. Without your brain, your heart would not beat, you could not breathe, your food would never digest. Without your brain, you could not see, hear, taste, smell, or feel anything. Without your brain, you could not walk or talk or move in any way. It is your brain that allows you to laugh and cry, to love and hate, to remember the past and imagine your future. Your complex, unique, mysterious brain gives you life.

HOW THE BRAIN WORKS

5   The neurons in the brain work something like a gigantic system of electrical lines. Messages are carried along the neurons (which are long and slender, similar to wires) by **electrical impulses**. These messages can travel over 200 miles per hour.

6   A neuron, like all cells in your body, has a **nucleus** inside a **cell body**. The cell body of a neuron is surrounded by tiny projections call **dendrites**. These are the signal receivers that pick up incoming messages from other neurons.

7   Extending out from the cell body is a long projection called the **axon** that carries the messages on toward other neurons. Axons range in size from a fraction of an inch to several feet in length. The axon is covered by a **myelin sheath**, which provides insulation. At the end of the axon are the **axon terminals**. It is here that the electrical messages are passed on to other neurons.

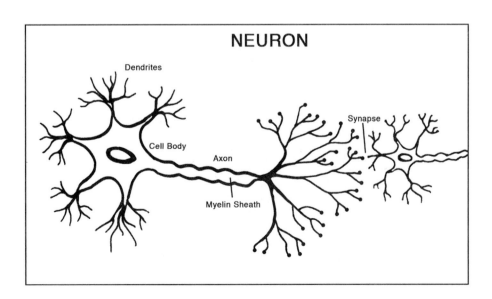

NEURON

8   Unlike electrical wires, the nerve cells do not touch each other. They are separated by tiny gaps called **synapses**. The electrical message is carried across the gap by chemicals called **neurotransmitters**. Research has found that many **neurological** diseases and even some mental illnesses such as depression can be traced to problems with these neurotransmitters.

THE ANATOMY OF YOUR BRAIN

9   Your brain is actually made up of several different "brains"—the brain stem, the cerebellum, and the forebrain. Each has a very different function. The **brain stem**, which is just above the **spinal cord**, is responsible for the basic functions of life like breathing, heart rate, and blood pressure. The word cerebellum in Latin means "little brain." The cerebellum is at the lower back of the head, below the forebrain. The cerebellum, which is divided into two halves, or **hemispheres**, is responsible for balance and movement. The largest part of the brain is the **forebrain**.

10   The forebrain actually consists of the **cerebrum** (also called the **cerebral cortex**) and the **diencephalon**, which is made up of the **thalamus** and the **hypothalamus**. Like the cerebellum, the cerebrum is divided into hemispheres. The two hemispheres of the cerebrum are connected by a thick, white band of nerve fibers called the **corpus callosum**.

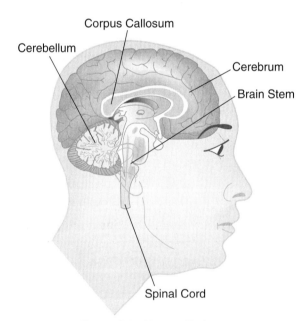

Parts of the Human Brain

11   The **cerebrum** has many important functions. Language, thought, memory, perception, and creativity—all come from the cerebrum. The cerebrum also allows us to move voluntarily and to control our emotions. Interestingly, it is the right hemisphere of your brain that is responsible for the left side of your body, and the left hemisphere that is responsible for your right side. An injury on the right side of the cerebrum could leave the left side of the body unable to move. Deep inside the cerebrum are the tiny thalamus and hypothalamus, the two parts of the diencephalon.

12   The thalamus is the "switching station" of the brain. Sensory messages from all over the body come to the thalamus. These messages are then sent to the correct part of the cerebral cortex. The cerebral cortex also sends messages back to this "switching station" to be passed on to other parts of the brain or spinal cord.

13   The hypothalamus, which is as small as a pea, is found at the base of the brain. Though tiny, it is very important too. The hypothalamus is your body's **thermostat**. It controls body temperature. It also controls hunger and thirst and your emotions.

14   **Neurologists**, who study the human brain, have discovered that particular functions like speech, vision, hearing, and others are located in particular areas of the cerebrum. Vision is at the very back of the cerebrum. Hearing is in the center, and speech is at the very front.

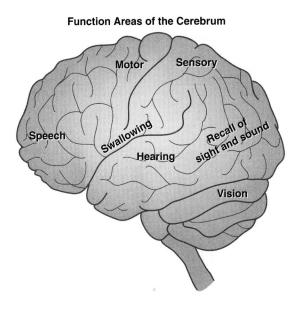

Function Areas of the Cerebrum

15   Your brain is something like a computer that is never switched off, even when you are sleeping. Your brain can process large amounts of information quickly and act based on that input. However, your brain is also very different from a computer. A computer cannot dream or feel emotions. There is one more thing that your amazing, mysterious human brain can do that no computer can: be conscious of itself. Your brain tells you that you exist. As far as scientists know, a human is the only animal that knows it lives.

Exercise 10-9 Noting Root Words

Underline the root word in the following words.

1. protective

2. pinkish

3. feelings

4. digestive

5. electrical

6. breathing

7. illness

8. hearing

9. snakelike

Challenge 10-9

Write out the root word in these words. There may be spelling changes.

1. mysterious _____

2. nervous _____

3. spinal _____

4. depression _____

Mastery 10-9

Break the following words into root(s) or root word and affixes.

1. neurotransmitter _____

Exercise 10-10 Word Families

Use word parts and your dictionary to match the words in this word family to their correct definition.

_____ 1. neuron

_____ 2. neurologist

_____ 3. neurological

_____ 4. neuritis

_____ 5. neurotransmitter

a. an inflammation of a nerve

b. a nerve cell

c. a doctor who deals with nerves and nerve problems

d. having to do with nerves and the brain (an adjective)

e. chemical that carries messages between nerves

Exercise 10-11 Using Your Dictionary

Use the dictionary entry below to answer these questions.

> **brain** (brān) *n.* 1. The portion of the vertebrate nervous system enclosed by the skull. 2. Often **brains**. Intellectual power; intelligence. 3. A highly intelligent person. —*v. Slang* 1. To hit in the head. —*idioms.* 1. **To beat one's brains out.** *Informal.* To try energetically. 2. **To pick someone's brain.** To explore another's ideas through questioning. [< OE *brægen*] —**braininess,** *n.* —**brainless,** *adj.* —**brainy,** *adj.*

1. How many syllables does the word brain have?

   _____

2. Does the first a in brain sound like the a in the word and or the a in

   the word age? _____

3. What is another noun form of brain?

   _____

4. The word brain can be used as what two parts of speech?

   _____   _____

5. Which definition of brain would you not use in an English paper?

   _____

6. Look at the sentence below. Which of the definitions is correct in this

   context? _____

   "Your son is such a brain. I bet he has straight A's in school."

7. Which definition is correct for the following sentence?

   _____

   "Hey, Joe. Did you hear the guy down at the gas station got brained
   by a robber last night?"

8. Which definition is correct for this sentence?

   _____

   The man was horrified to hear that his cancer had spread to his
   brain.

9. The word brain has two adjective forms. Which would you use for a

   person who is very foolish?

   _____

10. From what language did the word brain originate?

   _____

Exercise 10-12 Organizing the Facts

Below is a useful graphic aid: an outline. Use the reading to find the information needed to complete the outline.

Parts of the Human Brain

I. _____

   A. cerebrum or _____

   B. diencephalon

      1. _____

      2. hypothalamus

II. _____ or "little brain"

III. Brain Stem

Exercise 10-13 Finding Facts

Use the information from the reading to match the body function with the part of the brain that controls it.

_____ 1. breathing

_____ 2. balance

_____ 3. heart rate

_____ 4. reading

_____ 5. thirst

_____ 6. blood pressure

_____ 7. speech

_____ 8. memory

_____ 9. connecting the hemispheres

_____10. switching station

a. cerebrum

b. cerebellum

c. brain stem

d. hypothalamus

e. thalamus

f. corpus callosum

Exercise 10-14 Using Graphics

Use the graphics in the reading to answer these questions.

1. What part of the brain is at the back of the head, directly below the cerebrum? _____

2. What is the name of the covering of the axon?

   _____

3. True or False: If the lower back part of a person's cerebrum were badly injured, he or she would probably go blind. _____

4. What is the largest part of the brain?

   _____

5. In the axon, is the electrical impulse traveling toward or away from the cell body? _____

6. If a person has a stroke that damages the front of the cerebral cortex, is he more likely to lose the ability to move, hear, or speak?

   _____

7. What part of the brain is directly above the spinal cord?

   _____

8. Where would you find the nucleus of a neuron?

   _____

Exercise 10-15 Writing About What You've Read

Based on what you have read, write a short paragraph explaining why your hand jerks away if you touch something hot. Use your own paper.

Study Strategy

Using Graphics to Improve Comprehension

Exercise 10-16 Using the Clues

Use the information provided in the paragraph below, plus any additional maps in the Appendix you might need to support your background knowledge, to answer the following questions.

Discovering the Nile

More than 4,000 miles in length, the Nile River is the longest in the world. From its very first beginnings as a trickling spring high in the mountains of equatorial Africa to its mouth at the Mediterranean Sea far to the north, the river winds through jungles, swamps, and deserts across half the continent. Its waters are the lifeblood of millions of people of different races, cultures, and religions.

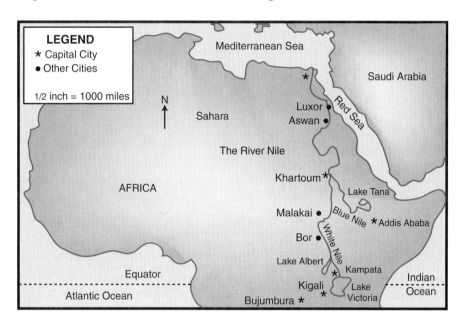

For millennia, explorers searched for the beginnings of this mighty river. In this exercise, you too can use your knowledge of maps, plus the information provided, and other resources as needed, to discover more about the Nile. Don't forget the map of Africa in the Appendix.

1. In what country does the Nile finally end its journey at the Mediterranean Sea? _____

2. If the Nile flows from near the equator to the Mediterranean Sea, what direction is it flowing? _____

3. The Nile is actually formed by two rivers: the Blue Nile and the White Nile. Near what city do the two rivers meet?

   _____

4. The beginnings of the Blue Nile were known to Europeans centuries before the source of the White Nile was finally discovered. In 1603, Father Pedro Paez, a Portuguese priest, was the first European to see the Ethiopian lake where the Blue Nile begins. What is the name of that lake? _____

5. In 66 CE, the Roman emperor Nero sent an expedition from Cairo up the Nile in search of its source. The Romans were stopped by a natural barrier called the Sudd. In the Sudd, the Nile widens out into the world's largest swamp. The Roman explorers could find no way through this reed-clogged waterway. The Sudd extends from just south of Malakal to about 100 miles north of Bor. Approximately how many miles of this swamp would the Romans have had to cross to reach the other side: 10, 100, 500, or 1,000 miles? _____

6. Near the equator in the countries that are now Uganda and the Congo is a range of ice-capped mountains much taller than the European Alps. Around 150 CE, Ptolemy, a geographer from Alexandria, Egypt, believed the waters of the Nile came down from these rugged peaks he called the Mountains of the Moon then passed through two lakes. Just north of Kampala there is a lake that is, indeed, part of the Nile. What is the name of that lake? _____

7. In part, it was Ptolemy's theory that sent British explorers searching deep into the heart of Africa. In 1858, Richard F. Burton and John Speke hunted in vain for the Nile's mysterious source. John Speke along with Augustus Grant set off again in 1860. Grant fell ill, but Speke continued on past Lake Albert farther south and east until he discovered a larger lake that he was certain was the source of the Nile. What is the name of that lake? _____

8. Another British explorer, Dr. David Livingstone, returned that same decade to try to find the exact source of the river. When he disappeared, Henry M. Stanley was hired to find the missing man. In 1871, when the two finally met, Stanley uttered that famous line: "Dr. Livingstone, I presume." Despite his years of wandering in the African bush, Livingstone was unsuccessful in finding the river's source. Why? He was looking in Tanzania. Was he looking too far north, too far south, or too far west? _____

9. In 1937, the German explorer Burkhart Waldecker traced the very beginning of the Nile to a small bubbling spring near the town of Bujumbura. A pyramid now marks the site. In what country is the true source of the Nile River? _____

10. Today, the Nile is much changed. In the 1960s and 70s, the Aswan High Dam was constructed for the purpose of supplying hydroelectric power and conserving water for dry years. Thousands of people and several ancient temples had to be relocated as Lake Nasser drowned much of the ancient region known as Nubia. Lake Nasser is just south of the city of Aswan. In what country is the Aswan High Dam?

_____

Going Beyond

Research

One day, a shockingly horrible accident happened to a young man named **Phineas Gage**. Go to the Internet or your local library and research this man's incredible story. On your own paper, write a short description of what happened to Phineas Gage and why it was so remarkable.

Recommended

If you would like to learn about the dangers and terrible hardships the British explorers experienced on their search for the source of the Nile, watch the movie *Mountains of the Moon* (1990).

Just for Fun

A Reading Riddle

According to *The American Heritage Dictionary,* a riddle is a "puzzling question or statement requiring thought to answer or understand." See if you can use your thinking skills to solve this riddle.

What Am I?

It is always dark in my world, but I can see light.
There is no sound in here, yet I hear everything.
The things I smell are not from here, but out there.
I am without color, but people call me gray.
While I am running, I do not move.
I taste everything, but I eat nothing.
My body sleeps, but I do not rest.
I live in a world surrounded by fluid
And am attached to my body by a stem.
My list of best friends includes electricity and oxygen.
Open your mind.
What am I?

© 2002 Monique Ilharreguy

What is being described in this riddle? _____

CHAPTER 10 REVIEW

- **What Are Graphic Aids?**

  There are many kinds of graphic aids—maps, graphs, charts, tables, illustrations, timelines, photographs, and more. Graphic aids are designed to help the reader by providing a visual presentation of the information.

- **Reasons to Use Graphic Aids**

  A preview of graphic aids will tell you what the reading is about. They offer support for comprehension because they give facts in picture form and can supply missing background information. You can create graphics to help organize, study, and remember information. A review of graphics is a good way to study for a test.

- **Using Graphic Aids**

  To use graphic aids effectively, first familiarize yourself with the graphic; note important information, then compare it to what you have read.

- **Reading Graphic Aids**

  Different types of graphics have different purposes.

  Maps give information about places and often the relationship of people and things with specific places.

  - Circle graphs (pie charts) show the relationship of parts to the whole.

  - Bar graphs compare information in a general way.

  - Line graphs compare information in a more specific, detailed way.

  - Charts and tables can provide large quantities of information easily.

  - Illustrations and photographs can explain concepts through pictures.

Putting All the Puzzle Pieces Together

In the first ten chapters of this text, you learned and practiced all the strategies and skills to become a successful reader. By now, you should know how to find both the pronunciation and meaning of a new word, phrasal, or idiom. You should also know how to use the context and graphics of the reading, your own background knowledge, and other resources such as your dictionary, the library, or the Internet to comprehend what you have read. In addition, you should be able to create concept maps or outlines if necessary to help you improve comprehension or study the material.

Up to this point in the text, you have read paragraphs and readings of short or medium length. But some outside readings, particularly in college-level courses, can be long, complex, and difficult. Don't worry! There is a strategy that can help you conquer even the most challenging reading . . . if you take the time and effort to follow it.

A 5-STEP READING STRATEGY FOR LONG OR DIFFICULT READINGS

1. Preview before you read.
2. Read the first time without stopping.
3. Do the work.
4. Read again for full comprehension.
5. Check your comprehension.

Step 1: Preview Before You Read

Many poor readers make the same mistake. They look at the first word on the page and just start reading. The general of an army would never send his troops into battle before his scouts or spies brought information about the enemy's strength and location. A basketball coach who wants his team to win has someone go to several of the opponent's games to watch how that team plays. Why? Both the general and the coach need information to win the war or the game.

You need information when you read. Information is power. When you **preview**, you are collecting information that gives you the power to improve your comprehension.

Previewing only takes a few seconds. But remember that previewing is more than just looking at the reading material. You must also be:

■ thinking about what you see

■ asking yourself questions

■ evaluating (judging) the vocabulary and the subject matter

When you are done previewing, you should have a good idea what the reading is about, how hard the material will be for you, and how much work and time it will take to understand what you will be reading.

How to Preview

1. Read the title and ask yourself questions about it.

   ■ Does the title give you a clue to what the reading is about?

   ■ Are you already familiar with this subject?

2. Read the first and last paragraph.

   ■ Often the **central idea** (main idea of the reading) is introduced and/or summarized in these paragraphs.

3. Look for bold-faced words.

   ■ As in this text, many authors boldface words that are new or important.

   ■ You don't have to learn these words during the preview. Just having seen a new word may help improve comprehension when you read the material.

4. Look over the graphic aids if there are any.

   ■ Remember: A picture is worth a thousand words.

5. Try to see how the reading is organized.

   ■ Are there headings? Subheadings?

Preview Practice

In less than a minute, preview the following reading, "What's Happening to the American Family?" Read only the first and last paragraph, headings, and bold-faced words, and glance at the graphic aids. Do not read the entire essay.

What's Happening to the American Family?

THE TRADITIONAL FAMILY

The year is 1950. Dad goes off to work each morning. Mom's job is homemaker. After school, the children rush home for milk and cookies. By the U.S. Census Bureau's definition, this is the **traditional** family: a father that works, a mother who is a homemaker, and their children. Times have changed, however, and so has the American family. In 2002, only 7 percent of all American households fit this pattern.

WHAT HAPPENED TO THE TRADITIONAL FAMILY?

So what did happen to this so-called traditional family? Lots. First is **economics**. Raising a family in the twenty-first century is expensive. Women, who previously would have stayed at home, now want or need to work. Second, divorce rates are around 50 percent. Third, many young Americans have decided to **postpone** marriage or to not marry at all. In 1970, 89 percent of American women had been married at least once by the time they reached 30. In 2002, only 60 percent of the women this age had decided to marry. In 2003, more than one-quarter of all American households were classified as "single-person."

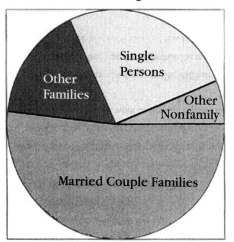

U.S. Households 2003

WHAT IS A FAMILY?

Is the concept of family disappearing? The answer to that question depends on how you define family. According to the U.S. Census Bureau, a family household is one "composed of two or more individuals who are related by birth, marriage, or adoption." In 2000, 69 percent of American households were still **classified** as "family." It is the makeup of the family that has changed so much in the last 50 years. Today, instead of only the traditional two parents with children, there are a variety of family types.

TODAY'S FAMILY

Perhaps the biggest change is that many children are now living in **single-parent** homes. The caregiver is usually the mother, though more and more fathers are demanding **custody** of their children. Some children of divorced parents belong to two families, if their parents share custody. **Merged** families are also common today. A merged family is one in which parents with children from previous relationships combine their families.

Stepbrothers, stepsisters, and half-**siblings** are more common. Many grandparents are also now raising their grandchildren. Because of economic conditions, many adult children still live with their parents. A large number of elderly parents live with their middle-aged children too. All these nontraditional combinations fit the Census Bureau's definition of family.

Is that definition of family, however, broad enough to include all of today's families? Even the U.S. Census Bureau is not sure. Today's attitudes and behaviors have changed greatly from the 1950s. Many couples who have not married (and may never marry) consider themselves family. Interestingly, if one of these couples has a child they will be reclassified by the Census Bureau as a "family household." Today, gay and lesbian couples also marry, even if that union is not recognized by the government. They may even have or adopt a child. These couples, on the other hand, are not reclassified as family even when they are raising a child. Because of the **complexity** of this issue, the Census Bureau is struggling to find new ways to define a household other than by family/nonfamily.

FAMILY IN THE PAST

Though people talk about the traditional family, historically the concept of family has always been changing. In the ancient world, many families were **matriarchal**; the mother was the head of the household. In some early Native American cultures, children were raised by their mother's brother rather than by their own father.

The typical American family itself has changed greatly from pre-1900 to the so-called traditional family of the 1950s. Before the **Industrial Revolution**, most people were farmers. Farm life was difficult and demanded large families. The **extended family**, which included grandparents, parents, brothers, sisters, aunts, and uncles, was the basis of many early American homes. Everyone was needed to help and support each other. Today, particularly for economic reasons, smaller families are the trend.

FAMILY IN THE FUTURE

Times change. So do families. Like people and the world in which they live, the concept of family will continue to evolve to meet the needs of the future.

Exercise 11-2 Preview Check

Answer the following questions about your preview.

1. What is the title of this reading? _____

2. Did you have a good idea what the story might be about by reading the title? Why or why not? _____

3. List two things you learned by reading the first and last paragraphs.

   _____

   _____

4. Did you recognize most of the bold-faced words? _____

   If not, do you think the vocabulary in this reading will be hard for

   you? _____

5. Does this reading look like it will be easy or hard for you?

   _____

6. List two things you learned from the graphic aid.

   _____

   _____

7. This reading is organized into sections. Each is listed with a bold-

   faced heading. How many sections are there? _____

   _____

   What is the name of each section? _____

   _____

   _____

8. Now that you have previewed the reading, write what you think this

   reading is about. _____

   _____

Remember that reading for comprehension is like putting together a jigsaw puzzle. You have to have a plan. Previewing a reading is like putting the **borders** (edges) of the puzzle together first. Previewing gets you started and gives you clues to what you are about to read.

Step 2: Read the First Time Without Stopping

Another common error many readers make is to stop at every word that they do not understand, so they can look it up in the dictionary. Don't make that mistake! Every time you stop, you break the flow of ideas that are forming in your mind.

Do this instead. Have a pencil or pen as you read. When you find a word you don't know or are unsure of, <u>underline</u> it. If something in the reading doesn't make sense, quickly write a question mark (?) over it or in the margin nearby.

Many times if you keep reading, you will find the definition to an unknown word in the next few sentences. Continuing to read might also give you comprehension clues.

Secrets to Success

BE AN ACTIVE READER!

Remember, you are a reading detective. As you read this first time, look for basic facts, clues, and any information that might help you solve the mystery. Continually question yourself.

Exercise 11-3 First Reading

Go back and do a first reading of "What's Happening to the American Family?" and remember—do not stop. Keep reading! <u>Underline words you don't know</u> and put question marks (?) beside the things you don't understand.

Step 3: Do the Work

In reading as in life, success takes hard work. You must do the work of the reading detective to find meaning. After the first reading:

- Look for clues to meaning—word, vocabulary, grammar, etc.
- Look up unfamiliar words in your dictionary, if necessary.
- Reread sentences or paragraphs that are confusing.
- Review the graphic aids; they may help explain the more difficult ideas.
- Look for clues to organization.
- Use aids such as your dictionary, the Internet, or a reference librarian to find background information you might be missing.

1. List any words in "What's Happening to the American Family?" that you did not understand, and do your best to define them.

_____

_____

_____

_____

_____

_____

_____

_____

2. Use an encyclopedia or check the Internet to find out information about the **Industrial Revolution.** On the lines below, write a brief description of the that era. _____

_____

_____

_____

Before taking on your second reading, do these following exercises to check your vocabulary.

Exercise 11-4 Decoding Check

Choose the correct pronunciation of these new words.

_____ 1. economics
   a. (ēk´ ōn ŏm´ ĭks)
   b. (ĕk´ ə nŏm´ ĭks)

_____ 2. postpone
   a. (pōst pōn´)
   b. (pŏst´ pōn)

_____ 3. merge
   a. (mĕrg)
   b. (mûrj)

Exercise 11-5 Vocabulary Check

_____ 1. traditional

_____ 2. family

_____ 3. economic

_____ 4. postpone

_____ 5. custody

_____ 6. merged

_____ 7. reclassified

_____ 8. complexity

_____ 9. matriarchal

_____10. extended family

a. having to do with money and spending money

b. a unit of people related by birth, marriage, or adoption

c. having the right to supervise, being in charge of

d. customary, done the way of previous generations

e. put together, combined

f. a group that includes parents, grandparents, siblings

g. to put off until later

h. something that is complicated or has many parts

i. to change to new group or category

j. having to do with a mother

Step 4: Read Again for Full Comprehension

Students are usually very busy and would rather not take the time and effort to read something again. If full comprehension is important, however, then it is equally important to make time to do a second reading. If your time is extremely limited, at least scan over the reading again, checking for places where your comprehension may be weak, and reread those sections. As you do your second reading, find as many _pieces of the puzzle_ as you can. Hopefully, if you have done the necessary work, the pieces will fit together to give you the whole picture.

For Your Information

MISSING INFORMATION

Sometimes, a few pieces of the puzzle are missing even after you have read something twice. Don't worry! Comprehension is not always 100 percent. Do the best you can, and remember that the more you read and work at being a reading detective, the better you will become at seeing the clues that will help you solve the mysteries of reading.

Step 5: Check Your Comprehension

There are many ways to check your comprehension.

- Retell what you have read. You can do this in your head, write it down, or tell a friend.
- Complete textbook or homework exercises.
- Draw your own graphic aids, such as a concept map or outline, to organize information.

For Your Information

CHECKING YOUR COMPREHENSION

Checking your comprehension helps you clarify what you have read. It also helps you remember the information. If you can talk or write about the story easily, you probably have most of the pieces put together.

Now do the following exercises to check your comprehension of the story.

Exercise 11-6 Comprehension Check

1. Define the traditional family. _____

   _____

2. In 2002, what percent of American households were classified as traditional families? _____

3. List three reasons the traditional family is changing.

   1. _____

   2. _____

   3. _____

4. What kind of family was common in the United States in the 1800s?

   _____

5. What would you call a family that was made up of a husband with his two sons from an earlier marriage and his wife with a daughter also from a previous marriage?

   _____

6. In 2003, were there more people living in Single-Person Households or in Family Households that did not include married couples?

   _____

7. The traditional American family is patriarchal. The father is the head of the household. Who was the head of the household in a matriarchal family?

   _____

8. What government agency is in charge of counting the number of people in different households in the United States?

   _____

Exercise 11-7 Sequencing

In the Answer Box, there are four different kinds of family from early to modern times. Put them in chronological order based on when they were most common, starting with the oldest.

ANSWER BOX

traditional family	matriarchal family
extended farm family	single-parent family

1. _____

2. _____

3. _____

4. _____

Exercise 11-8 Retelling

Now that you have done all the work, you should have a good under-standing and memory of the reading. On your own paper, retell in your own words what this story was about. Remember, you don't have to tell all the details but try to tell all the important parts. You may want to do a quick outline or map to help organize your thoughts before you begin.

Using Your Strategy

Now you are ready to try your new strategy on a longer, more difficult reading. In Reading 11, you will be taken through the strategy one step at a time. In future readings, you will have to follow the strategy on your own. That is why it is important to practice the steps now.

Step 1: Previewing

1. Preview the title of your reading

Navajo Code Talk:
The Mystery the Japanese Army Never Solved

Exercise 11-9

Write three questions that this title brings to your mind.

1. _____

2. _____

3. _____

2. Preview the first and last paragraphs

War in the South Pacific

The year was 1942. The world was at war. In Europe and Africa, British and Americans troops and their **allies** were fighting against the **invading** German soldiers known as the Nazis. Halfway around the world in the Pacific, there was a very different kind of war being fought against the Japanese.

* * * * *

Until recently, only a few people knew about the brave deeds of the Navajo code talkers. The code talkers had been classified as "top secret" be-cause of the importance of the job they were doing during the war. Finally, in 1992 at the Pentagon in Washington, DC, the Navajo code talkers were honored for their "worth, intelligence, bravery, **sacrifice**, and patience, dur-ing a very critical period in our history."

Exercise 11-10   Inferring Facts

*After reading only the first and last paragraph of this story, decide whether the statements that follow are true (T), false (F), or unclear (UC) based on what you can **infer** (make an educated guess about) from the preview.*

—— 1. Nazis were German.

—— 2. The United States and Germany fought together against Japan.

—— 3. War was also being fought halfway around the world from Europe.

—— 4. Great Britain and the United States were enemies.

—— 5. The world was at war in 1940.

—— 6. The Navajo code talkers were very famous in 1942.

—— 7. The Navajo code talkers helped the Japanese.

—— 8. The Navajo code talkers did something very important during World War II.

For Your Information

DIFFERING ANSWERS

When previewing, how much you comprehend often depends on your background knowledge about the subject you are reading. Answers that are inferred may differ from one person to another, depending how much each person knows about the subject. So don't worry if your answers are different from someone else's. As long as you can prove your answer from the text, you are correct.

3. Preview the entire reading

Do not actually read the story! Try to take less than a minute or two to complete your preview. Don't forget to check the following things:

- bold-faced words
- graphic aids
- organization:
  - major heading (often bold-faced)
  - minor headings

You should also see if you notice any dates or notice a sequence of events, if possible. Does the reading seem to follow in chronological order? Or do the events appear out of time sequence?

Navajo Code Talk: The Mystery the Japanese Army Never Solved

WAR IN THE SOUTH PACIFIC

1   The year was 1942. The world was at war. In Europe and Africa, British and Americans troops and their **allies** were fighting against the **invading** German soldiers known as the Nazis. Halfway around the world in the Pacific, there was a very different kind of war being fought against the Japanese.

2   In 1941, the Japanese Air Force had attacked the United States Navy at Pearl Harbor in Hawaii. The Japanese planes destroyed much of the U.S. **naval** fleet in the attack. Almost immediately after, the United States declared war against Japan.

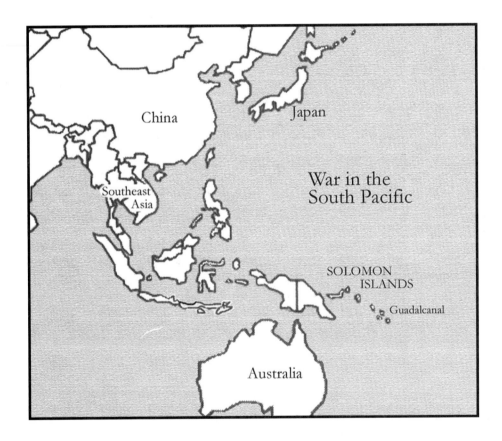

3   By 1942, Japan had already taken control of much of China and **Southeast Asia** (the countries now known as Vietnam, Thailand, Burma, and others). The Japanese Army and Navy had also moved south almost to Australia. They had taken control of many of the thousands of islands in the **South Pacific**. Today, this area is called **Oceania** because it is mostly ocean.

4   Among the many islands of the South Pacific was one of great importance to the United States—**Guadalcanal**. Guadalcanal is the largest of a group of islands just north of Australia that are called the **Solomon Islands**.

5   Both Japan and the United States knew that Guadalcanal was important because the U.S. military supply ships had to pass by the island on their way to and from **Australia**. Australia was an ally of the United States during World War II. The American and Australian commanders knew that the Japanese had begun building an airbase on Guadalcanal. They also knew this military base had to be destroyed.

THE ATTACK ON GUADALCANAL

6   The day was August 7, 1942. There were boatloads of U.S. Marines just beyond the beach at Guadalcanal. They were waiting for orders to land. At last, a Marine **communication specialist** received a message over his wireless radio. "AL-TAH-JE-JAY!"

7   Aboard a Japanese warship, an enemy communication specialist also heard the coded command. The Japanese, however, could not understand this American code, so they did not know the attack on Guadalcanal had begun.

FINDING AN UNBREAKABLE CODE

8   In any war, it is essential that the military can communicate without the enemy knowing what is being said. To do this, expert linguists create codes. Unfortunately, there are also other experts known as **code breakers**. It is very difficult to make a code that cannot be broken. The American military knew they had to have a code that could not be decoded if they were going to win the war. But how?

9   A man named Philip Johnston, who was a **veteran** of World War I, had an idea to use the Navajo language as a code. As a child, he had lived on the Navajo reservation in northern Arizona. The **Navajo** are a tribe of Native Americans who live in the Four Corners area of Arizona, New Mexico, Utah, and Colorado.

10   The Navajo language is unwritten and very complex. At the time of World War II, fewer than 30 people other than Navajos could speak the language. None of these people were Japanese. Johnston also remembered that Choctaw Indians had been used in World War I to **encode** and send messages, so he was sure that his idea made sense.

NAVAJO CODE TALKERS

11   In early 1942, Johnston convinced the American military leaders of the value of using the Navajo language to create a code. In May 1942, the first 29 Navajo Marines came to Camp Pendleton in California. They developed the Navajo code. By the end of the war, around 400 Navajo men had been trained and served as **code talkers** in the war in the South Pacific. It took both skill and courage to be a Navajo code talker.

12   Navajo code talkers served as Marines. Their primary job was to send and receive messages about the enemy by telephone or radio. They also went into battle. The Japanese were very frustrated because they could

not decode the Navajo code. Japanese leaders knew that the only way to break the code was to capture a Navajo code talker alive. Fortunately, none were ever captured.

NAVAJO CODE TALK

13   One Navajo soldier was captured by the Japanese, but he was not a code talker. The Japanese were very upset when even their prisoner could not understand the Navajo code. The reason was that some of the Navajo words actually stood for English letters, not Navajo words. These letters were then put together to spell out English words. Instead of letters, other Navajo words meant a particular object or idea, usually a military term.

14   For example, let's say a code talker wanted to send the word fire. He could say, "TSA-E-DONIN-EE YEH-HES DAH-NES-TAS AH-NAH."

15   Here's how it worked.

TSA-E-DONIN-EE means FLY, which stands for the letter F.

YEH-HES means ITCH, which stands for the letter I.

DAH-NES-TAS means RAM, which stands for the letter R.

AH-NAH means EYE, which stands for the letter E.

To make the code even more difficult, there were three different Navajo words that could be used for each letter of the English alphabet.

16   There was also a dictionary of 450 Navajo words that meant specific military terms. These Navajo words were often taken from nature. The words were usually **similar** (nearly the same) in some way to the object or idea described. For example, a battleship was called LO-TSO, which meant "whale." A DAH-HE-TIH-HI, which means "hummingbird" in Navajo, meant "fighter plane." A bomb was called A-YE-SHI, which means "egg." A tank resembling a giant turtle was called CHAY-DA-GAHI.

HONORING THE NAVAJO CODE TALKERS

17   Until recently, only a few people knew about the brave deeds of the Navajo code talkers. The code talkers had been classified as "top secret" because of the importance of the job they were doing during the war. Finally, in 1992 at the Pentagon in Washington, DC, the Navajo code talkers were honored for their "worth, intelligence, bravery, **sacrifice**, and patience, during a very critical period in our history."

Exercise 11-11 Preview Check

*There are six bold-faced **headings**. List them below.*

1. _____

2. _____

3. _____

4. _____

5. _____

6. _____

Exercise 11-12   Preview Check

Now that you have previewed the bold-faced vocabulary and the maps, look over the list of subjects listed below and put a check mark next to any that you think might appear in this story.

—— Navajo language   —— New York City   —— code breakers

—— Atlantic Ocean   —— Pacific Ocean   —— India

—— Guadalcanal   —— Italians   —— islands

Step 2: Read without Stopping

Now it is time to actually read the story. Remember not to stop as you read. Have your pencil and pen handy to <u>underline</u> unknown or confusing words or to put a question mark (?) by ideas you do not understand.

Step 3: Do the Work

Exercise 11-13   New Words to Define

Define any new words you do not know.

_____

_____

_____

_____

_____

_____

Exercise 11-14   Checking Your Background Knowledge

This reading was filled with geographical references. To comprehend fully, you need knowledge about the places that were referred to in the reading. Look at the maps in the Appendix and study the map in Reading 11 to find the following places. Place a check beside each when you have located it.

—— Europe   —— The South Pacific   —— The American Southwest

—— Germany   —— Australia   —— California

—— Great Britain   —— Guadalcanal   —— Southeast Asia

—— Japan   —— China   —— Solomon Islands

Step 4: Reading for Comprehension

Read the story again slowly and carefully. Take all the time you need. When you are finished reading, pause for a moment and try to remember the important facts. If there are parts that you cannot remember or are still confused about, go back and read that section again.

Step 5: Check Your Comprehension

You have now previewed and done two readings. Are you ready to check your vocabulary and comprehension? If you feel unsure of the facts, make some notes before you try these exercises. Go back to the text whenever you need to.

Exercise 11-15   Decoding

Choose which of the two word pronunciations are correct. Write the letter of the correct pronunciation on the line. Number 1 has been done for you.

__b__ 1. ally
   a. (ăl′ ē)
   b. (ăl′ ī)

____ 2. code
   a. (kōd)
   b. (kŏd)

____ 3. sacrifice
   a. (să′ krī ə fiz′)
   b. (săk′ rə fīs′)

____ 4. Navajo
   a. (năv′ ə hō′)
   b. (nā′ və jō′)

____ 5. Nazi
   a. (năt′ sē)
   b. (nā zī′)

Exercise 11-16   Vocabulary Check

Use the words in the Answer Box below to complete the following incomplete sentences. Use each word only once.

	ANSWER BOX			
military	decode	similar	Vietnam	Guadalcanal
code	Navajo	classified	allies	Oceania
Nazis	nature	opposite	encode	the Four Corners

1. _____ is one of the Solomon Islands.

2. During World War II, Navajo soldiers spoke a top secret

   _____ that the Japanese could not understand.

3. Australians and Americans are _____ in many ways. They are very much the same.

4. During World War II, the Germans were also called the

   _____.

5. The code talkers were _____ as "top secret" because the U.S. Marines did not want anyone to know what they were doing.

6. The U.S. _____ includes the army, navy, air force, and marines.

7. Australia, Great Britain, and the United States were

   _____ during World War II. They often fought side by side.

8. The area of the world including Australia and the islands of the South Pacific are now known as _____.

9. The Japanese could never _____ the mysterious Navajo messages.

10. Many of the words used in Navajo code talk were taken from

   _____. They were words for animals or plants.

Exercise 11-17

Answer the following questions about the reading.

1. What is a code? _____

   _____

2. Who was/were the:

   Navajo code talkers? _____

   _____

   code breakers? _____

   _____

   Philip Johnson? _____

   _____

3. Where were the Navajo code talkers first used in battle during World
   War II? _____

   _____

4. When were the Navajo code talkers first recruited and trained?

   _____

   _____

5. Why was the Navajo language perfect for using as a code?

   _____

   _____

   _____

6. How did the Navajo code work? _____

   _____

   _____

   _____

Exercise 11-18 Map Check

*Identify the location of each place listed by writing its number on the line
at the correct location.*

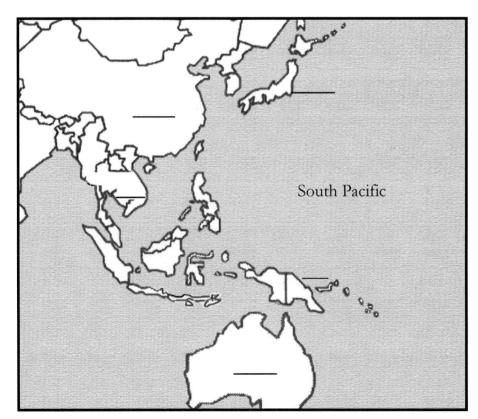

1. China
2. Japan
3. Australia
4. Southeast Asia
5. Solomon Islands

Exercise 11-19   Finding Facts from a Map

Look at the map in this reading more closely; then decide whether the sentences below are true (T) or false (F).

_____ 1. The Solomon Islands are south of Australia.

_____ 2. Vietnam is Japan's closest neighbor.

_____ 3. Japan's eastern shore is the Pacific Ocean.

_____ 4. Australia is larger in size than Japan.

_____ 5. Southeast Asia is southwest of Japan.

Exercise 11-20   Completing a Time Line

The beginning of this reading is very difficult because it is not in chronological order. Your job as the reader is to make sense of the sequence of events. Reread this first portion of the reading; then use this information to fill in any of the missing information in the time line that follows.

WAR IN THE SOUTH PACIFIC

The year was 1942. The world was at war. In Europe and Africa, British and Americans troops and their allies were fighting against the invading German soldiers known as the Nazis. Halfway around the world in the Pacific, there was a very different kind of war being fought against the Japanese.

In 1941, the Japanese Air Force had attacked the United States Navy at Pearl Harbor in Hawaii. The Japanese planes destroyed much of the U.S. **naval** fleet in the attack. Almost immediately after, the United States declared war against Japan.

By 1942, Japan had already taken control of much of China and **Southeast Asia** (the countries now known as Vietnam, Thailand, Burma, and others). The Japanese Army and Navy had also headed south almost to Australia. They took control of many of the thousands of islands in the **South Pacific**. Today, this area is called **Oceania** because it is mostly ocean.

Among the many islands of the South Pacific was one of great importance to the United States—**Guadalcanal**. Guadalcanal is the largest of a group of islands just north of Australia that are called the **Solomon Islands**.

Both Japan and the United States knew that Guadalcanal was important because the U.S. military supply ships had to pass by the island on their way to and from **Australia**. Australia was also an ally of the United States during World War II. The American and Australian commanders knew that the Japanese had begun building an airbase on Guadalcanal. They also knew this military base had to be destroyed.

THE ATTACK ON GUADALCANAL

The day was August 7, 1942. There were boatloads of U.S. Marines just beyond the beach at Guadalcanal. They were waiting for orders to land. At last a Marine **communication specialist** received a message over his wireless radio. "AL-TAH-JE-JAY!"

Aboard a Japanese warship, another communication specialist also heard the coded command. The Japanese, however, could not understand this American code, so they did not know the attack on Guadalcanal had begun.

Time Line

1941

- **Japanese** attacked and destroyed the **U.S.** Navy at Pearl Harbor.
- _____ declared war on **Japan**.

1942

- **World** was at war. (Note: From the reading, you do not know for how long the war had already been in progress.)

In **Europe/Africa**:

_____ and **Americans** fight **Nazi Germany**.

In **South Pacific**:

Japanese had taken control of _____, Southeast Asia, and threatened to take over the South Pacific (**Oceania**).

Americans and _____ want to protect

Guadalcanal because of its importance to the United States and threat to Australia.

August 7:

U.S. forces attack **Japanese** forces on _____.

Exercise 11-21 **Sequence of Events**

Put the events in the Answer Box in the correct chronological order on the lines that follow. Number 1 has been done for you.

ANSWER BOX

Navajo code created.

War in the South Pacific ends.

United States attacks Guadalcanal.

Code talkers honored in Washington.

Code talkers trained in California.

United States enters war against Japan.

1. United States enters war against Japan.

2. _____

3. _____

4. _____

5. _____

6. _____

Exercise 11-22 **Making a Concept Map or Outline**

On your own paper, make a study outline or map of Reading 11.

Exercise 11-23 **Writing About What You Know**

On your own paper, write a paragraph or two explaining why the Navajo code talkers were so important in World War II.

Going Beyond

Research

For additional information, check the Internet or your local library for any of these key words.

Navajo code talkers	secret codes	World War II
Navajo culture	decoding	South Pacific Theater

Recommended

You might also want to rent the movie *Windtalkers* (2002), which tells the story of two Navajo code talkers during World War II.

Study Strategy

Self-Check

Self-check is a study strategy you might also want to learn if you would like to become a better student. A self-check helps you learn about your own learning. When you know your own strengths and weaknesses, you have the power to improve.

Exercise 11-24 Self-Check

Try the self-check for this chapter. Remember to answer honestly. This information is for you. It can help you grow as a learner.

1. Was the reading difficult for me? _____ If it was difficult, why? Was the vocabulary too hard? The reading too long? _____

2. Did I do each strategy to the best of my ability? _____ If not, what could I have done better? _____ _____

3. Put a check next to any of the strategies you think you need to improve.
   - ■ ____ Preview before you read
   - ■ ____ Read the first time without stopping—underline and question
   - ■ ____ Do the work
   - ■ ____ Read again for full comprehension
   - ■ ____ Check your comprehension

4. What could I have done better to improve my comprehension? _____ _____

Just for Fun

Navajo Code Words

Exercise 11-25

Try matching the military words used during World War II with its Navajo code word. You may want to do this with a partner or in a group.

English Word	Navajo Code Word
____ 1. commanding general	a. Toh-yil-kah (much water)
____ 2. America	b. Tal-kah-silago (sea soldier)
____ 3. submarine	c. Yas-nil-tes (crusted snow)
____ 4. river	d. Besh-lo (iron fish)
____ 5. combat	e. Chido-tso (big auto)
____ 6. December	f. Ne-he-ma (our mother)
____ 7. navy	g. Bih-ke-he (war chief)
____ 8. truck	h. To-altseh-hogan (temporary place)
____ 9. camp	i. Da-ah-hi-jih-ganh (fighting)
____ 10. machine gun	j. A-knah-as-donih (rapid fire gun)

Challenge 11-25

____ 1. enlarge	a. Ni-ma-si (potatoes)
____ 2. artillery	b. Nih-tsa-goh-al-neh (make big)
____ 3. creek	c. Be-al-doh-tso-lani (many big guns)
____ 4. dive bomber	d. Toh-nil-tsanh (very little water)
____ 5. grenades	e. Gini (chicken hawk)

Mastery 11-25

____ 1. amphibious	a. Ah-deel-tahi (blow up)
____ 2. radar	b. Na-hos-ah-gih (thereabout)
____ 3. pontoon	c. Chal (frog)
____ 4. vicinity	d. Esat-tsanh (listen)
____ 5. demolition	e. Tkosh-jah-da-na-elt (floating barrel)

CHAPTER 11 REVIEW

Use This Five-Step Strategy for Long or Difficult Readings

Step 1: Preview Before You Read

- Read the title and ask yourself questions about it.
- Read the first and last paragraph.
- Look at the bold-faced words.
- Look at the graphic aids.
- See how the reading is organized.

Step 2: Read the First Time Without Stopping

- Underline any words you do not know.
- Put question marks over or beside things you do not understand.

Step 3: Do the work

- Look for clues to meaning—words, vocabulary, grammar, etc.
- Look up unfamiliar words.
- Reread sentences or paragraphs that are confusing.
- Review the graphic aids; they may help explain the more difficult ideas.
- Use aids such as your dictionary, the Internet, or a reference librarian to find background information you might be missing.

Step 4: Read Again for Full Comprehension

- Use all your strategies and knowledge to put together the pieces of the puzzle to find comprehension.

Step 5: Check Your Comprehension

- Retell what you have read. You can do this in your head, write it down, or tell a friend.
- Complete textbook or homework exercises.
- Draw your own graphic aids.
- Use a concept map or outline to organize information.

CHAPTER 12

Mystery Solved!

Wrapping Up the Case

Do you remember in "The Mystery of the Missing Necklace" (Chapter 1) that Detective Lee's job was not done, even after she discovered who had stolen the necklace? She still had to carefully think through the entire crime and then write up a report of the case. As a reader, you are not completely finished even after the final reading. You need to take a moment to think about the entire reading and consider the central idea (the main idea of the reading). If the reading is for a class, you might also have to prepare an outline or study map or write a **summary** about the reading. To do either, you must have correctly identified the central idea and seen how the author supported that point.

Central Idea

Essays, chapters, or even entire books are groups of paragraphs organized around one idea. This is the central idea that organizes all the main ideas, major supporting details, and minor supporting details. You might want to think of the central idea as the **working title** of the reading because a well-chosen title should give you a good idea about what you are reading.

How to Find the Central Idea in an Essay: Review

Do you remember the first step of the 5-step reading strategy you learned in Chapter 11? Preview! The **review**, the last thing when you are ready to find the central idea or write a summary, is nearly the same as the preview except there is one more step. To review:

Step 1: Reread and think about the title.

Step 2: Reread the first and last paragraphs.

Step 3: Reread the bold-faced words and headings.

Step 4: Take another quick look at the graphics.

Step 5: Think about the organization of the reading.

Step 6: Put all the pieces together to find meaning.

Step 1: Reread and Think About the Title

Most authors think long and hard before choosing a title. The title is important because it must either be a hook to interest the reader in the reading or in some way let the reader know what the reading is about, or both. A good title should give the reader a strong clue about the central idea of the reading.

Step 2: Reread the First and Last Paragraphs

Like paragraphs, many readings have introductions. These should do just that, introduce the central idea. The first paragraph might also give necessary background information, or explain important vocabulary or concepts. The last paragraph may serve as a conclusion. A good conclusion will restate the central idea and the major supporting details of the reading. Some final paragraphs draw some conclusion about the central idea.

Step 3: Reread the Bold-Faced Words and Headings

Words and headings are bold-faced for emphasis. They are the words and concepts that are critical to understanding what the writer is trying to say.

Step 4: Take Another Quick Look at the Graphics

Often, reading the titles of graphics will provide clues to the main ideas covered in the reading. The graphics themselves are usually explanations of those ideas.

Step 5: Think About the Organization of the Reading

If you are lucky, the reading will have subheadings (most are even bold-faced). These often represent the major supporting details of the central idea. If there are no subheadings in the reading, you will have to skim over each paragraph looking for the topic sentences. In a well-written essay, each paragraph, except the introduction and conclusion, should support the central point.

Step 6: Put All the Pieces Together to Find Meaning

Based on all the clues and information you have gathered, decide what you think the writer is trying to say.

Exercise 12-1 Reviewing a Reading

Below is the reading "What's Happening to the American Family?" for you to reread. When you are done, you will review the reading step-by-step.

What's Happening to the American Family?

THE TRADITIONAL FAMILY

The year is 1950. Dad goes off to work each morning. Mom's job is homemaker. After school, the children rush home for milk and cookies. By the U.S. Census Bureau's definition, this is the traditional family: a father that works, a mother who is a homemaker, and their children. Times have changed, however, and so has the American family. In 2002, only 7 percent of all American households fit this pattern.

WHAT HAPPENED TO THE TRADITIONAL FAMILY?

So what did happen to this so-called traditional family? Lots. First is economics. Raising a family in the twenty-first century is expensive. Women, who previously would have stayed at home, now want or need to work. Second, divorce rates are around 50 percent. Third, many young Americans have decided to postpone marriage or to not marry at all. In 1970, 89 percent of American women had been married at least once by the time they reached 30. In 2002, only 60 percent of the women this age had decided to marry. In 2003, more than one-quarter of all American households were classified as a "Single Person."

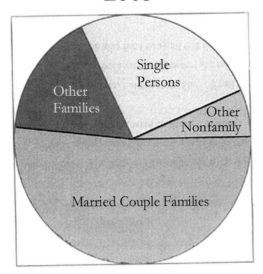

U.S. Households
2003

WHAT IS A FAMILY?

Is the concept of family disappearing? The answer to that question depends on how you define family. According to the U.S. Census Bureau, a family household is one "composed of two or more individuals who are related by birth, marriage, or adoption." In 2000, 69 percent of

American households were still classified as "family." It is the makeup of the family that has changed so much in the last 50 years. Today, instead of only the traditional two parents with children, there are a variety of family types.

TODAY'S FAMILY

Perhaps the biggest change is that many children are now living in single-parent homes. The caregiver is usually the mother, though more and more fathers are demanding custody of their children. Some children of divorced parents belong to two families, if their parents share custody. Merged families are also common today. A merged family is one in which parents with children from previous relationships combine their families.

Stepbrothers, stepsisters, and half-siblings are more common. Many grandparents are also now raising their grandchildren. Because of economic conditions, many adult children still live with their parents. A large number of elderly parents live with their middle-aged children too. All these nontraditional combinations fit the Census Bureau's definition of family.

Is that definition of family broad enough, however, to include all of today's families? Even the U.S. Census Bureau is not sure. Today's attitudes and behaviors have changed greatly from the 1950s. Many couples who have not married (and may never marry) consider themselves family. Interestingly, if one of these couples has a child they will be reclassified as a "family household." Today, gay and lesbian couples also marry, even if their union is not recognized by the government. They may even have or adopt a child. These couples, on the other hand, are not reclassified as family, even when they are raising a child. Because of the complexity of this issue, the Census Bureau is struggling to find new ways to define a household other than by family/nonfamily.

FAMILY IN THE PAST

Though people talk about the traditional family, historically the concept of family has always been changing. In the ancient world, many families were matriarchal; the mother was the head of the household. In some early Native American cultures, children were raised by their mother's brother rather than by their own father.

The typical American family itself has changed greatly from pre-1900 to the so-called traditional family of the 1950s. Before the Industrial Revolution, most people were farmers. Farm life was difficult and demanded large families. The extended family, which included grandparents, parents, brothers, sisters, aunts, and uncles, was the basis of many early American families. Everyone was needed to help and support each other. Today, particularly for economic reasons, smaller families are the trend.

FAMILY IN THE FUTURE

Times change. So do families. Like people and the world in which they live, the concept of family will continue to evolve to meet the needs of the future.

Review

Step 1: Reread and Think About the Title

Consider this title: "What's Happening to the American Family?" A central idea is almost never a question, but it is often the answer to an introductory question.

In your own words, write a sentence that answers the title's question based on the information in this reading.

_____

_____

_____

Step 2: Reread the First and Last Paragraphs

■ Look at the first paragraph:

> The year is 1950. Dad goes off to work each morning. Mom's job is homemaker. After school, the children rush home for milk and cookies. By the U.S. Census Bureau's definition, this is the traditional family: a father that works, a mother who is a homemaker, and their children. Times have changed, however, and so has the American family. In 2002, only 7 percent of all American households fit this pattern.

There is a lot of background information in this paragraph; however, one sentence states the main idea of the paragraph. Write it on the lines provided.

_____

_____

■ Now look at the last paragraph in this reading.

> Times change. So do families. Like people and the world in which they live, the concept of family will continue to evolve to meet the needs of the future.

Do you see any similarities in this paragraph to the sentence you chose as the main idea in the first paragraph? To the title? *In your own words*, write the main idea for this last paragraph. _____

_____

_____

In this essay, the first and last paragraphs are saying the same thing in slightly different ways: *Families, or at least concepts about what a family is, change with time.* A skilled reading detective would deduce that this is the central idea of this essay.

Does this sentence actually answer the question in the title—"What's Happening to the American Family?" Yes, it does. You have found the central point of the reading.

Step 3: Reread the Bold-Faced Words and Headings

There are no bold-faced vocabulary words in this reading. Only the sub-headings have been bold-faced.

List the subheadings in this reading.

_____

_____

_____

_____

_____

What do these subheadings have in common? _____

_____

Step 4: Take Another Look at the Graphics

The only graphic with this essay is a chart that shows how different the makeup of the American family was in 2002 compared with the traditional family of the 1950s. Does this information seem to support the title and information about the central idea you discovered in the first and last paragraphs and subheadings?

Step 5: Think About the Organization

Here are brief summaries of the information in each of the 6 sections.

First section states central idea that families are changing over time.

Second section has an inferred main idea that families today have changed since the 1950s for several reasons.

Third section includes this topic sentence: "It is the makeup of family that has changed so much in the last 50 years."

Fourth section offers the explanation for this change. "Today's attitudes and behaviors have changed greatly from the 1950s."

Fifth section supports the central idea with the main idea that "historically the concept of family has always been changing."

Sixth section repeats the central idea that families are and always have been changing.

What do all of these have in common? Write your answer in a complete sentence. _____

_____

Your review is complete. In your mind, you should now have a good idea of the central idea of the reading. Be careful! Don't be too **broad** in your statement. The central idea should cover only what is discussed in the essay. Don't be too **narrow** either. You need a statement that covers everything in the essay.

Here are three choices for a possible central idea for "What's Happening to the American Family?" Put an X on the line next to the sentence that best states the central idea of this essay. Think carefully.

_____ 1. The traditional family is disappearing in the United States.

_____ 2. Like families of the past, the American family continues to change over time.

_____ 3. The extended family was important in the past.

Exercise 12-2   Finding the Central Idea of an Essay

If you have completed this text to this point, you have read 11 essays. One by one, take a moment to review each chapter reading. When you are done with the review, choose the answer that best states the central idea for each. Write the letter of your choice on the line provided. Skip the question if you have not read the essay.

1. _____ "Solving the Mystery of Using Your Textbook"

   a. It is important to know how to use a textbook.

   b. If you understand the purpose and organization of this text, you will know how to use it more effectively.

   c. A textbook can be very complicated.

2. _____ "The Rosetta Stone: The Key to Egyptian Hieroglyphs"

   a. For centuries, Egyptian hieroglyphs were a mystery to linguists.

   b. With the discovery of the Rosetta Stone and its meaning, linguists were finally able to decipher the mysterious Egyptian hieroglyphs.

   c. The Rosetta Stone was discovered near the Nile by French soldiers.

3. _____ "Mayan Hieroglyphs: The Unsolved Mystery"

   a. The Maya wrote in hieroglyphs.

   b. Linguists and epigraphers are studying Mayan hieroglyphs.

   c. The Maya used a complex form of hieroglyphs that researchers are still trying to completely decipher.

4. _____ "Where in the World Did English Come From?"

    a. English is a close relative of Dutch.

    b. English evolved from the common Indo-European language.

    c. The origin of the English language is complex, and even today the language continues to evolve.

5. _____ "Did the Anasazi Really Vanish?"

    a. The Anasazi civilization did not vanish; the people were forced to leave their homeland for a variety of reasons.

    b. There are many reasons civilizations like the Anasazi disappear.

    c. The Anasazi were forced to leave their homeland because they had become overpopulated and resources became scarce.

6. _____ "Is There Life on Mars?"

    a. Scientists continue to search for life, or at least the possibility of life, on Mars.

    b. Some scientists believe ALH 84001 is proof of life on Mars.

    c. Mars is an inhospitable place, probably too cold to support life.

7. _____ "Into the Abyss"

    a. The tubeworms of the abyss are unique animals.

    b. The deep sea is filled with an amazing variety of life that is only beginning to be explored.

    c. There have been many explorations into the abyss.

8. _____ "Who Killed the King?: The Mysterious Disappearance of Dinosaurs"

    a. Sixty-five million years ago, all but one of the dinosaurs became extinct.

    b. The tyrannosaurus rex was the biggest of the dinosaurs.

    c. Scientists now believe that the impact of a gigantic meteorite is what caused the extinction of the dinosaurs.

9. _____ "The Mystery of the Moving Continents"

    a. Scientists' explanation of how the continents move has changed over time.

    b. At one time, there was a gigantic supercontinent called Pangaea.

    c. Geologists are studying continental drift.

10. _____ "The Mysterious Human Brain"

    a. The human brain has three major parts.

    b. The complex human brain is responsible for most aspects of our lives, for our consciousness, and for our self-awareness.

    c. Without our brains, humans could not live.

11. _____ "Navajo Code Talk: The Mystery the Japanese Army Never Solved"

    a. The code talkers were Navajo Indians.

   b. The unbreakable Navajo code and the brave men who used it helped the United States defeat the Japanese in World War II.

   c. People from many countries, including the Navajos, fought in World War II.

Writing a Summary

A summary is a shortened version of the original reading. A **rule-of-thumb** (accepted rule) is that a summary should be no more than one-quarter to one-fifth the length of the original reading. For example, the summary of a five-page reading would probably not be longer than a page. You should also remember to use your own words.

Caution

PLAGIARISM

Plagiarism is stealing. It is using someone else's words as your own without giving that person credit. At many schools and colleges, a student who plagiarizes may be expelled, so remember it is very important to write a summary in your own words. If you must use the author's words, put quotes around that portion.

There are several steps to writing a summary for a paragraph or reading.

1. Find the central idea of the reading.

2. Find the major supporting details that support that central idea.

3. Use the central idea plus the major supporting details to write the summary. You might want to make an outline or concept map to help you organize your thinking before writing.

4. Read your completed summary carefully to be certain that you have not left out any important facts or included details that are not of importance.

Secrets to Success

CHECK THOSE SUBHEADINGS IN THE READING

Don't forget that the subheadings of a reading are often major supporting details of the central point. You can rewrite these in sentence form to use in your summary. If there are no subheadings, then you can paraphrase the topic sentences of paragraphs instead. Remember that introductory and conclusion paragraphs are usually some restatement of the central idea.

Sample Summary

Here is a sample of what a summary of Reading 11, "What's Happening to the American Family?" might look like.

> Times have changed, and so has the American family. In the past, American farm families were large and were extended to include many relatives. A mother, father, and their children made up the traditional American family of the 1950s and 1960s. Since then, hard economic times, a high divorce rate, and young people postponing marriage have changed the definition of family. Today, there are many new kinds of families—single-parent families, merged families, families with gay parents, and more. In the future, families will probably change again to meet the needs of the time.

Secrets to Success

CHRONOLOGICAL SEQUENCE

Did you notice that the summary did not follow the same sequence as the reading? To make the summary easier to understand and remember, it is often a good idea to put events in chronological order if possible.

Exercise 12-3 Summarizing a Reading

Choose one (or more) of the chapter readings and summarize it on your own paper. You may want to make an outline(s) or study map(s) before you begin writing to help you organize all the information.

The following reading is very long and filled with information—names, dates, places. Remember to use the five-step strategy:

- Do a quick preview.
- Read through once.
- Don't keep stopping to look up new words.
- Do all the work necessary to prepare for your second reading.
- When you are done, you can check your comprehension.

Later you will have the chance to review the reading, find the central idea, and write a summary.

What Really Happened to Amelia Earhart?

THE YOUNG AVIATOR

1   In 1937, the name Amelia Earhart was a household word. She was known not only in the United States but worldwide. Why? She was famous around the world because she was trying to do something no other woman had ever done. She was trying to fly her airplane all the way around the earth.

2   Even as a child Amelia was bold and adventuresome. While other little girls played with dolls, Amelia climbed trees, fished, played baseball, and explored the fields and woods around her birthplace—Atchison, Kansas. Many of the neighbors disapproved of Amelia being a **tomboy**. Amelia's mother, though, encouraged her daughter to try new things. She understood Amelia because Mrs. Earhart liked adventure too. When she was younger, Amy Earhart had been the first woman to climb to the top of Pikes Peak in Colorado.

3   Young Amelia moved a lot as she grew up. Her father had a problem with drinking and had a hard time keeping a job. Fortunately, Amelia's grandparents were wealthy. They made sure that she and her sister Muriel went to the best private schools and later to college.

4   In 1914, **World War I** began in Europe. Amelia was still a schoolgirl. It was not until she visited her sister in **Canada** that Amelia saw the true horror of that war. "There for the first time," Amelia remembered, "I realized what the World War meant. Instead of new uniforms and brass bands, I saw only the results of four years' desperate struggle; men without arms and legs, men who were paralyzed, and men who were blind." Amelia quit school and trained as a **nurse's aide**. She worked at a military hospital until the war ended.

5   Afterward, Amelia went to Columbia University to study **pre-med**. A year after her parents and sister moved to Los Angeles, Amelia moved to California to join them. She planned to continue her studies and become a medical researcher.

6   Then something happened. At an **air show** in Long Beach, Amelia took her first airplane ride. The **biplane** had an **open cockpit** so she could feel the wind in her hair and the sun on her face. "As soon as we left the ground," Amelia remembered later, "I knew I had to fly."

7   Amelia quit school again to work. She needed money to pay for her flying lessons. Amelia's family did not see her often once she started flying. Amelia worked all week then spent every weekend at the airport. She even got extra work to help earn the money she needed. For a while, she drove a truck for a sand-and-gravel company. In 1922, Amelia Earhart

finally earned her pilot's license. She was one of only a dozen women in the world who were licensed to fly.

8   As a birthday present, Amelia's mother and sister helped her buy a **secondhand** plane. Amelia **nicknamed** the bright yellow biplane the Kinner Canary. She practiced and practiced. She had several minor accidents, but that did not frighten her. She was fearless. In October 1922, she soared to an altitude of nearly three miles high. This was a record for a woman pilot. This was the first of Amelia Earhart's many record-breaking flights.

9   Unfortunately, owning an airplane is very expensive. Amelia had tried to find work in aviation, but had no luck. Finally, she had to sell her plane. She used the money to buy a brightly colored car that she nicknamed "The Yellow Peril."

10   Her mother wanted to move to Boston, so Amelia drove Amy from California to Massachusetts. Cross-country travel by automobile was very uncommon in the 1920s. There were no **superhighways** in those days. People were especially surprised to see two women making such a long journey.

11   Amelia stayed in Boston and found a job as a novice **social worker**. She spent her time and money on flying and trying to interest other people in flying, especially women. A newspaper in Boston called her one of the best women pilots in the United States. Unfortunately, without her own plane Amelia had to watch others set flying records.

12   In 1927, a man named Charles Lindbergh became the first person to fly a plane solo across the **Atlantic Ocean**. People around the world were excited about Lindbergh's amazing accomplishment. A woman in London, England, who loved flying decided it was time a woman crossed the Atlantic by plane too. She bought a seaplane and named it the *Friendship*. She thought this name would show the **goodwill** between the United States and England. Now all she needed was a woman of adventure. A short time later, Amelia Earhart got a phone call that would change her life.

AMELIA EARHART—RECORD-SETTER

13   On June 7, 1928, the seaplane *Friendship* lifted off from **Newfoundland** in eastern Canada and headed across the wide Atlantic Ocean. Aboard was 30-year-old Amelia Earhart. Amelia was really just a passenger. There was a pilot and mechanic on the plane. Still, the trip was very dangerous. Three women had already died trying to cross the Atlantic.

14   Twenty hours and four minutes later, the plane touched down in Wales, which is part of Great Britain. Amelia had become the first woman to fly over the Atlantic Ocean. Papers around the world ran her picture. People nicknamed her "Lady Lindy." Some people even said she looked like Charles Lindbergh. She was tall and thin with the same short hair. Amelia also wore trousers and **flying gear** similar to Lindbergh's.

15   For the next 4 years, Amelia Earhart traveled, giving speeches and at-
tending air shows. She also continued breaking records, often her own.
She was the first woman to fly solo across the United States. She set several speed records. She even flew an **autogyro**, an aircraft that is part hel-
icopter and part plane, to a record-setting altitude of 18,451 feet. There
was one record, however, she still wanted to break. She wanted to be the
first woman to fly solo across the Atlantic Ocean.

16   No one, man or woman, had flown from the United States to Europe
alone since Charles Lindbergh's **transatlantic** crossing. Amelia surprised
the world when she announced she not only planned to make the flight
but to do it in an airplane with wheels rather than **pontoons**. If she went
down in the ocean, she would sink without these floats.

17   On May 20, 1932, the fifth anniversary of Lindbergh's famous flight,
Amelia Earhart took off from Newfoundland alone. All she took with
her was a thermos of water and a can of tomato soup. Since she did not
drink coffee or tea, she took **smelling salts**. These would wake her up
quickly if she started to fall asleep.

18   The trip went badly from the beginning. First, her **altimeter** failed.
Without it, Amelia had no way of knowing her altitude above the sea unless she could see the water. Next, flames started shooting out of her exhaust. Then she ran into a storm. When she tried to fly above the storm,
heavy ice formed on the plane's wings. Amelia knew she had to descend. ■

The clouds were so low and thick when she did come down, Amelia's plane almost crashed into the waves.

19   As bad as things were, Amelia knew she must not fail. She would die. So hour after hour, with fire shooting out the back of her plane, the young woman piloted the trembling plane. At last she found land. After flying for 15 hours and 18 minutes, Amelia Earhart landed her plane in a cow pasture in northern Ireland.

20   Her historic flight set several records. She was the first woman to fly solo across the Atlantic, and the first woman to have made the transatlantic crossing twice. This was also the longest nonstop flight by a woman. And she had made the trip from the United States to Europe in the shortest time ever recorded. Amelia Earhart was welcomed back to New York with a **ticker-tape** parade.

21   From 1932 to 1935, the brave, young **aviatrix** continued to set records. One was the first nonstop solo flight from Hawaii to California. Ten other pilots had already died trying. There seemed nothing Amelia Earhart would not try. In 1935, Amelia announced she was going to attempt to **circumnavigate** the world. Others had flown all the way around the world, but no one had ever flown the entire distance around the equator. The total distance would be more than 27,000 miles.

THE LAST FLIGHT

22   Amelia was not making this journey alone. She hired Fred Noonan as her **navigator**. Fred knew a lot about the islands of the South Pacific. That was important because the journey over the broad Pacific Ocean would be the hardest and most dangerous part of their long flight.

23   On May 21, 1937, Amelia's plane took off from **Oakland, California**. She headed southeast, stopping in **Florida** and **Puerto Rico**. She then flew south, following the eastern edge of South America before heading out across the Atlantic toward Africa. From Africa she flew across the **Middle East** and **India** and then down across Southeast Asia to Australia. She finally stopped for a short rest on the island of **New Guinea** in the South Pacific on June 27. She and Fred Noonan had already traveled 22,000 miles.

24   People who saw Amelia in New Guinea said she looked very tired and ill. Supposedly she was suffering from an illness called **dysentery**. Three days later, however, she was ready to fly the next leg of her journey. Her destination was **Howland Island**, a tiny speck of land more than two thousand miles to the east in the middle of the wide Pacific Ocean. A U.S. Coast Guard cutter called the *Ithaca* was waiting offshore. The ship was to help with radio navigation, so Amelia and Fred could find the tiny island more easily.

25   On July 2, 1937, Amelia Earhart and Fred Noonan took off from New Guinea, heading east toward home. The *Ithaca* received several garbled radio messages but could not get a fix on the plane's location. The last message received said, "Gas running low." Her plane was never seen again.

AMELIA EARHART'S JOURNEY

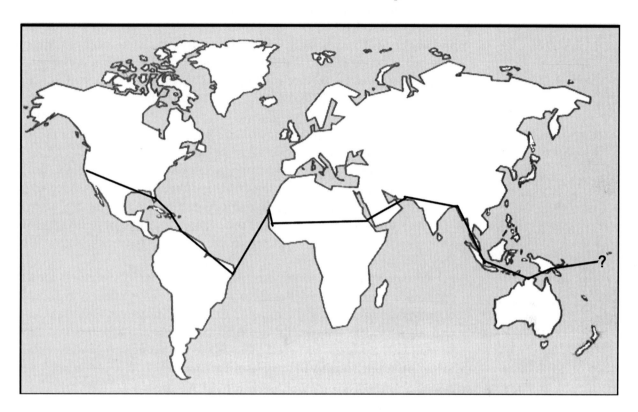

26   For weeks, nine naval ships and 66 aircraft searched the South Pacific for the famous aviator and her navigator. There was hope that the empty fuel tanks on the plane would float. On July 18, the search was ended. Amelia Earhart and Fred Noonan were declared "lost at sea."

WHAT REALLY HAPPENED TO AMELIA EARHART?

27   The United States government still insists that Amelia Earhart's plane ran out of fuel and crashed at sea, but there are many people who believe other theories. Some people even think the government knows the truth but does not want people to know it.

28   One theory is that Amelia Earhart and Fred Noonan were actually on a spy mission for the United States. In 1937, four years before the United States went to war with Japan, the leaders in Washington were already beginning to worry about the Japanese military. U.S. generals suspected that the Japanese were building a large naval base on a small island called Truk.

29   In the days before spy **satellites**, there was no way to see what other countries were doing. Some people believe that Amelia took a **detour** in her flight to fly over **Truk Island**. This would have been very dangerous, but the United States badly needed the information that only she could gather. Because of this extra distance and bad weather in the area, Amelia may have run low on fuel and been forced to head back to find land. If she did, she would have landed in Japanese territory. Other people refuse

to believe that Amelia and Fred were spying but do believe that they crash-landed on Japanese-held islands and were taken prisoner.

30   One researcher says he has **eyewitness** stories about a woman pilot and her navigator who had been captured after crashing near a tiny island that belonged to Japan. The two were supposedly held prisoner on the Japanese-controlled island of **Saipan**. The eyewitnesses said that the woman finally died of dysentery. The day after her death, the man was executed. Some veterans of World War II even swear they saw Amelia's plane in an airplane hangar in Saipan. The hangar was destroyed in a U.S. bombing raid, so the story can never be proven.

31   Amelia Earhart was well aware of the dangers of this flight, as she wrote in this letter to her husband some time during the last **leg** of her trip. Despite the dangers, she had good reasons for making the attempt. "Please know I am quite aware of the hazards. . . . I want to do it because I want to do it. Women must try to do things as men have tried. When they fail, their failure must be a challenge to others."

32   What did happen to Amelia Earhart? Did her plane crash into the sea? Or did she die in a Japanese prison camp? That mystery will probably never be solved. What happened to Amelia, however, is not as important as what she did during her lifetime. With her life and her death, Amelia Earhart inspired future **generations** of women to challenge themselves and their roles in the world.

Exercise 12-4 Finding the Facts

Scan the text to find the facts you need to match the following people, places, or dates (1–12) with the reason they are important (a–l).

_____ 1. 1928

_____ 2. Fred Noonan

_____ 3. New Guinea

_____ 4. *Friendship*

_____ 5. Truk Island

_____ 6. July 2, 1937

_____ 7. Kansas

_____ 8. 1897

_____ 9. 1922

a. last place Amelia seen alive

b. seaplane that Amelia rode in first transcontinental flight

c. possible Japanese naval base

d. U.S. naval ship waiting for Amelia at Howland Island

e. the day Amelia Earhart disappeared

f. Amelia's solo transatlantic flight

g. Amelia earns her flying license

h. Japanese controlled island where Amelia may have been a prisoner

i. Amelia Earhart's birthplace

_____10. *Ithaca*

j. Amelia's navigator on the circumnavigation of world

_____11. Howland Island

k. the place Amelia never reached

_____12. Saipan

l. the year of Amelia Earhart's birth

Exercise 12-5 Compound Words

Write the letter of the definition on the right that best matches the meaning of the italicized compound word in each sentence on the left.

_____ 1. Amelia owned a *secondhand* airplane because it would have been too expensive to buy a new one.

_____ 2. At least one *eyewitness* swears to have seen Amelia's plane in a hangar on a Japanese-held island.

_____ 3. The cutter *Ithaca* was waiting *offshore* to help Amelia find Howland Island.

_____ 4. Amelia Earhart *nicknamed* both her first plane and her first car.

_____ 5. There was a lot of *goodwill* between France and the United States after Lindbergh's first flight.

_____ 6. Amelia quit school to work as a *nurse's aide* so she could help wounded World War I soldiers.

_____ 7. As a child, Amelia was such a *tomboy* her mother allowed her to wear pants instead of a dress.

_____ 8. Amelia's *cross-country* drive took her from California to Massachusetts.

_____ 9. For several years of her life, Amelia and her sister were members of her grandparents' *household*.

_____10. News of Amelia Earhart's goal to fly around the globe spread *worldwide*.

a. to give a funny or cute name to something

b. an old-fashioned word for an active girl

c. used, not new

d. all over the planet

e. a job helping in a hospital

f. from one border to the other

g. a feeling of friendship between people(s)

h. in the water, just off the coastline

i. the people living in a home

j. a person who sees something, like a crime

Exercise 12-6 Using Word Parts to Find Meaning

Use a word from the Answer Box below to complete the following sentences. In each sentence, <u>underline</u> the clue word(s) that gave you the correct meaning.

ANSWER BOX

uniform	mechanic	dysentery	solo	historic
exhaust	equator	thermos	altimeter	transatlantic

1. When the _____ stopped working, the pilot had no way to judge if his plane was high enough to clear the 12,000-foot-high mountain.

2. If the _____ pipe on your car is clogged, dangerous gases from your engine cannot get out and may back up into your car.

3. A _____ is good to have if you want to keep your soup hot or your juice cold.

4. Today, many people have made the _____ flight across the Atlantic Ocean from New York to Paris.

5. Just before her disappearance, Amelia was suffering from _____, an illness that affects your intestines.

6. Amelia Earhart's attempt to circumnavigate the globe at the equator was a _____ event because no man or woman in history had ever attempted this dangerous mission.

7. Like Lindbergh, Amelia Earhart flew _____ across the Atlantic Ocean. She was all alone in the plane.

8. A good _____ can often fix any kind of machine, whether it is an airplane or a car.

9. Many schools now have students wear a _____ because there seem to be fewer problems when everyone wears one type of clothing.

10. The _____ is an imaginary line that cuts the

    earth into equal parts—north and south.

Exercise 12-7 Choosing the Right Definition

Find the correct definition of each italicized word as it is used in the sentence. If more than one part of speech is listed, list both the part of speech and the number. Example: ___v. 3___

____ 1. "Instead of new *uniforms* . . . I saw only the results of four years' desperate struggle."

> **uniform** (yo͞o nə fôrm) *adj.* 1. Always the same. 2. Being the same as another.—*n.* 1. A distinctive outfit worn by a particular group.

____ 2. "This was a *record* for a woman pilot."

> **record** (rĭ kôrd') *v.* 1. To set down for preservations, as in writing. 2. To register or indicate. 3. To register sound or images in permanent form such as on a record or tape. —*n.* (rĕk' ərd) 1. A written account of events. 2. An unsurpassed measurement, such as a *world record* in weightlifting.

____ 3. "Charles Lindbergh became the first person to fly a plane *solo* across the Atlantic Ocean."

> **solo** (sō' lō) *n., pl.,* **-los** 1. *Mus.* A composition for an individual voice. 2. A performance or accomplishment done by a single individual. *adj.* 1. Alone.

____ 4. The Ithaca received several garbled radio messages but could not get a *fix* on the plane's location.

> **fix** (fix) *v.* 1. To place securely. 2. To correct or make right. 3. To spay or castrate an animal. *n.* 1. The act of adjusting or repairing. 2. A solution, such as a *quick fix*. 3. The position, as of a ship or airplane, based on observation or equipment.

_____ 5. If Amelia had not disappeared, the next *leg* of her journey from Howland Island would have ended with a stopover in Hawaii.

> **leg** (lĕg) *n.* 1. A limb used for locomotion or support. 2. A part resembling a leg in shape or use, *a table leg.* 3. The part of a pair of trousers that covers the leg. 4. A stage or part of a journey.

Exercise 12-8   Checking the Details

Four of the five words or phrases grouped below have something in common to Amelia Earhart. Using your knowledge of this reading, find and <u>underline</u> the word that does not go with the group, then explain why it is different.

1. bold, wary, adventuresome, determined, courageous

   _____

2. nurse's aide, truck driver, medical researcher, pilot, social worker

   _____

3. North America, South America, Europe, Asia, Oceania

   _____

4. Newfoundland to Wales, Newfoundland to Ireland, South America to Africa, Hawaii to California, California to Massachusetts

   _____

5. First transatlantic flight, first woman to solo transcontinental United States, first nonstop solo from Hawaii to California, first attempt to circumnavigate the earth at equator, first woman to fly across Atlantic _____

Exercise 12-9   Sequence of Events

Follow Amelia Earhart's flight on the map, then put the places from the box on page 299 in the lines below in order from the beginning of her trip to the end.

1. _____

2. _____

3. _____

4. _____

5. _____

6. _____

7. _____

8. _____

```
┌─────────────────────────────────────────┐
│  PLACES ON EARHART'S JOURNEY              │
│                                           │
│  Florida          Australia               │
│  New Guinea       South America           │
│  India            Southeast Asia          │
│  Africa           California              │
└─────────────────────────────────────────┘
```

Exercise 12-10 Graphics Check

Use information from the graphics in the reading or maps in the Appendix to decide if the following sentences are true (T) or false (F).

_____ 1. New York is closer to Massachusetts than it is to Kansas.

_____ 2. When the Earharts drove from California to Massachusetts, they drove east.

_____ 3. When Amelia flew from Hawaii to California, she headed east.

_____ 4. Pikes Peak, Colorado, is located in the state next to Kansas.

_____ 5. Amelia was going to school in Pennsylvania the year she went to see her sister in Canada. To visit Muriel, Amelia had to travel north.

_____ 6. On her transworld flight, Amelia arrived in the Middle East before she visited Africa.

_____ 7. During her transworld flight, Amelia only flew south of the equator.

_____ 8. In Amelia Earhart's flight, Hawaii would have been west of Howland Island.

_____ 9. Amelia's flight across the United States was shorter than her flight across India.

_____10. Puerto Rico is south of Miami, Florida.

Exercise 12-11 Finding the Main Idea in Paragraphs

Read each of the paragraphs below and find the main idea. The topic sentence may be stated in the paragraph. If it is, you may copy it onto the line provided. If the main idea is implied, write the topic sentence yourself.

A.   The trip went badly from the beginning. First her altimeter failed. Without it, Amelia had no way of knowing her altitude above the sea unless she could see the water. Next, flames started shooting out of her exhaust. Then she ran into a storm. When she tried to fly above the storm, heavy ice formed on the plane's wings. Amelia knew she had to descend. The clouds were so thick when she did come down, Amelia's plane almost crashed into the waves.

A. main idea: _____

_____

B.   Amelia quit school again to work. She needed money to pay for her flying lessons. Amelia's family did not see her often once she started flying. Amelia worked all week then spent every weekend at the airport. She even got extra work to help earn the money she needed. For a while she drove a truck for a sand-and-gravel company. In 1922, Amelia Earhart finally earned her pilot's license.

B. main idea: _____

_____

C.   [Amelia Earhart's] historic flight set several records. She was the first woman to fly solo across the Atlantic Ocean, and the first woman to have made the transatlantic crossing twice. This was also the longest nonstop flight by a woman. And she made the trip from the United States to Europe in the shortest time ever recorded.

C. main idea: _____

_____

D.   On May 21, 1937, Amelia's plane took off from Oakland, California. She headed southeast, stopping in Florida and Puerto Rico. She then flew south, following the eastern edge of South America before heading out across the Atlantic toward Africa. From Africa she flew across the Middle East and India and then down across Southeast Asia to Australia. She finally stopped for a short rest on the island of New Guinea in the South Pacific on June 27. She and Fred Noonan had already traveled 22,000 miles.

D. main idea: _____

_____

Exercise 12-12 Central Idea of the Essay

Which of the following is the best statement of the central idea of this essay? Write the letter of that statement on the line.

1. ____

   a. After a historic flight nearly three-quarters of the way around the world, Amelia Earhart was lost at sea.

   b. Amelia Earhart was an adventurous woman whose determination and courage in life and flying caught the attention of the world and inspired women to challenge themselves.

c. Brave women and men like Amelia Earhart and Charles Lindbergh were the pioneers of flying.

Exercise 12-13 Writing About What You've Read

*A **role model** is someone who sets an example for others. A role model is someone to look up to. A role model is someone you might want to "model" your life after. Amelia Earhart was a role model for many women. She showed women that if they had goals and the determination and courage to work for those goals they could succeed at anything. Many of today's women astronauts say that Amelia Earhart inspired them to fly.*

Think about someone in your life who has been a role model for you, someone you want to be like. On your own paper, write about that person. Tell what it is about that person that you admire.

Going Beyond

Research

Though Amelia Earhart vanished more than 50 years ago, her disappearance is still a much-debated mystery. Some people are convinced that there has been a conspiracy to hide the government's knowledge; others say that is absolute nonsense. To learn more about this, check out the key word "Amelia Earhart" on the Internet or at your local library or read the books *The Search for Amelia Earhart* (1996) by Fred Goerner and *Amelia Earhart's Shoes: Is the Mystery Solved?* (2001) by King, Jacobson, Burns, and Spading.

Recommended

If you'd like to experience firsthand the incredible adventures of another early flier, read the book *Wind, Sand, and Stars* (1940) by Antoine de Saint-Exupéry.

Enhancing Your Thinking

Analogies

One way to increase vocabulary, improve your comprehension, and enhance your critical thinking skills is by studying the relationship between words. You can do this by working with analogies. An **analogy** is a comparison of four words or phrases. For example:

hand is to arm as foot is to leg

This can also be written as:

hand : arm :: foot : leg

Do you see the relationship between these two pairs of words? Your hand is a part of your arm in the same way that your foot is a part of your leg. There are many kinds of relationships. This relationship is a *part to a whole* relationship. Here are a few more examples.

1. **Antonym** (opposite meaning words) Analogy

   big : small :: tall : short

2. **Synonym** (similar meaning words) Analogy

   female : woman :: male : man

3. **Cause-and-Effect** Analogy   trip : fall :: cut : bleed

4. **Noun/Verb** Analogy   snake : hisses :: cat : meows

5. **Other Analogies** There are many, many other relationships words can have to each other. Here's one: before : after :: pretest : post test. Do you see the relationship?

Exercise 12-14 Analogies

Try to complete these simple analogies. Choose your answers from the Answer Box.

ANSWER BOX				
game	cow	disappear	car	whether
drink	hard	cowardly	sad	crow

1. dog : bark :: rooster : _____

2. win : lose :: happy : _____

3. feather : soft :: rock : _____

4. run : race :: play : _____

5. arrive : depart :: appear : _____

6. sail : ship :: drive : _____

7. plane : plain :: weather : _____

8. candy : eat :: cola : _____

9. strong : weak :: brave : _____

10. rooster : hen :: bull : _____

Challenge 12-14

Try these analogies on your own.

1. solar : sun :: lunar : _____

2. cub : bear :: kitten : _____

3. drought : dry :: monsoon : _____

4. bride : groom :: salt : _____

5. loan : lone :: pear : _____

6. biologist : life :: geologist : _____

7. herbivore : grass :: carnivore : _____

8. starvation : food :: thirst : _____

9. solve : problem :: answer : _____

10. stars : telescope :: bacteria : _____

Mastery 12-14

Find the answers to these analogies in your background knowledge. Be sure you can explain the relationship before you choose your answer.

1. early Anasazi : petroglyphs :: ancient Egyptians : _____

2. 100 : century :: 1,000 : _____

3. Hawaii : state :: Australia : _____

4. Maya : South America :: Anasazi : _____

5. Martian : Mars :: Terran : _____

6. pieces : puzzle :: clues : _____

- Wrapping Up the Case

  The last thing you do is find the central idea of the reading.

  You may also have to write a summary.

- Central Idea

  The central idea is the main idea of the reading. **How to find the central idea:**

  Step 1 Reread and think about the title.

  Step 2 Reread the first and last paragraphs.

  Step 3 Reread the bold-faced words and headings.

  Step 4 Take another quick look at the graphics.

  Step 5 Think about the organization of the reading.

  Step 6 Put all the pieces together to find meaning.

- Writing a Summary

  1. Find the central idea of the reading.

  2. Find the major supporting details that support that central idea.

  3. Use the central idea plus the major supporting details to write the summary.

  4. Read your completed summary carefully to be certain that you have not left out any important facts or included details that are not of importance.

Additional Readings

D. B. Cooper: The Amazing Disappearing Skyjacker

1   On February 24, 1971, a daring skyjacker strapped the $200,000 he had **extorted** from the airline around his waist and jumped from the back of a Boeing 727 jetliner into the darkness over the wilds of the Pacific Northwest. For weeks, a manhunt led by the FBI searched the cold, wet forests of Washington and Oregon for this man known by the **media** as D. B. Cooper. He was never found.

2   This story began at the Portland International Airport on the day before Thanksgiving. In the days before tightened airport security, there was no need for identification papers, no scanning of baggage or checks for explosives. On that afternoon, a middle-aged nondescript man calling himself Dan Cooper bought a one-way ticket to the Seattle-Tacoma International Airport with cash, then walked onto the plane carrying a black attaché case with what may, or may not, have been a bomb. He went to the back of the plane and sat by himself in row 18.

3   Shortly after Northwest Orient Airlines Flight 305 took off at 4:35 that afternoon, the man calmly handed the flight attendant a note informing her that he had a bomb. His demands were $200,000 in unmarked $20 bills and four parachutes. Thinking the passenger was giving her his phone number or asking for a date, Flo Schaffner put the note in her pocket while she finished her work. When she finally opened it a short time later, the alarmed flight attendant rushed to the cockpit to tell the captain. She was sent back to **verify** that the man in fact had a bomb. At her request, the man who was now wearing black wraparound sunglasses opened his case. Inside were a series of red cylinders, either sticks of dynamite or flares, connected with wire. The flight attendant rushed back to the cockpit. Captain William Scott immediately contacted authorities. He was told to circle SEA-TAC (Seattle-Tacoma) Airport until the FBI could collect the skyjacker's demands and position their people to capture the man while the plane was on the ground. The other 36 passengers on the plane were completely unaware of what was happening.

4   Before delivering the money, the FBI used a high-speed copy machine to electronically scan the **serial numbers** of the bills, so they would have a record of each and every bill. Cooper had been smart to ask for four parachutes. Not knowing if the extra three were for possible **hostages, the authorities** did not dare give him equipment that had been **rigged** to fail. The safety of the passengers and crew was the number-one priority.

5   At 5:45, the FBI notified the pilot that everything was ready. Once on the ground, the calm and cordial skyjacker released all the passengers and

all the crew except the pilot, co-pilot, and one flight attendant. The plane was in the air again at 7:44 with a full tank of gas and a destination of Mexico. The skyjacker had also given the pilot very specific instructions. The landing gear was to be kept down. The flaps were to be set at 15 degrees so that the plane could not exceed 170 mph. The pilot was also told not to fly over a 10,000-foot altitude.

6   The skyjacker had done his research. The Boeing 727 was the only commercial airline with a stairway that opened at the back of the plane. After asking the flight attendant how to open the back **hatch** (cargo doors were not locked in those days), he told her to return to the cockpit and stay there. During her last glance at the man, she saw him tying something, probably the bags of money, to his waist.

7   At 8:00 p.m., a red light on the pilot's dash came on, showing that a door was opened somewhere on the plane. At 8:11, the pilot felt a slight "pressure bump." Even though the pilots tailing five miles behind in Air Force 106's did not see anyone parachute from the back of the plane, authorities assumed that this was the time the skyjacker had made his escape. An intensive manhunt immediately began in this wilderness area near the Lewis River in southwest Washington. The search was difficult because of heavy rains.

8   In the beginning, the FBI believed the suspect was Daniel B. Cooper, **a.k.a.** D. B. Cooper. Even though this man was soon found and cleared of the crime, television and radio had already begun using that name for the skyjacker and continued to do so. The **misnomer** continues to this day.

9   As the days turned into weeks and no trace of the mystery man could be found, the FBI became convinced that the skyjacker had not survived the jump. Even for an experienced skydiver, the chances of survival under the conditions that night were very small. Dressed only in a suit and overcoat with a heavy bag of cash strapped around his waist, this slightly built, middle-aged man had jumped from a plane going almost 200 mph into the complete darkness of an early winter rainstorm. Authorities estimated that temperature, including the wind-chill factor, was at 70 degrees below zero.

10 If he did live through the sky dive, his chances for survival were still slim. The forest below was dense with evergreen trees. There were also dozens of lakes and a river where a man tangled in a chute would quickly drown in icy waters. Even if he did land safely, the forest was snow-filled and dark, and the man had no survival gear.

11 On February 10, 1980, a boy digging a fire pit on the shore of a river in Northwest Vancouver, Washington, found a bag with $5,800 worth of $20 bills. The serial numbers matched those from the skyjacking. Another mystery! How did the money get there? Had the skyjacker left a small bit of the money to throw the authorities off the track? Was this proof that the man they were seeking had survived his **harrowing** jump into the night?

12 One man, however, has no doubts about the fugitive's whereabouts. According to Ralph Himmelsbach, an FBI agent who continued the search for the notorious D. B. Cooper until his retirement in 1980, the skyjacker was "an outcast who died with his money in the wilderness of the Pacific Northwest." End of story.

13 Jo Weber, a widow in Florida, disagrees. She says that her husband, Duane Weber, told her on his deathbed that he was Dan Cooper. She had

no idea what he meant until she discovered a book about the infamous D. B. Cooper several years later.

14   Then the puzzle pieces started to fall into place. Not only was the name Dan Cooper the same, but he also fit the physical description given by the FBI. Like Cooper, her husband was a chain smoker of Raleigh filter-tip cigarettes and a heavy bourbon drinker (other traits identified by the authorities from the man's behavior on the plane). Another **red flag** was that her husband had a bad knee that he said he had received "jumping out of a plane." She told authorities that once, while visiting the Pacific Northwest, her husband showed her a logging road near the Columbia River and said, "That's where D. B. Cooper walked out of the woods." At the time, she thought he was joking. The FBI has not taken Mrs. Weber's theory seriously, but she continues to investigate.

15   So what did happen to D. B. Cooper and all that money? Did he die in the fall? Was he drowned, his body long vanished beneath the waves? Or will his remains be found one day in the wilderness still dangling from a parachute caught high in a tree? Or did he survive and walk out of that dark, cold forest to spend the rest of his life living happily ever after in warm, sunny Florida? Most likely, the disappearance of D. B. Cooper will remain one of the greatest mysteries of the twentieth century.

Exercises

I. Noting Compound Words

There are more than 20 compound words in this reading, including some hyphenated and some spaced compound words. Find at least 10 of those compound words.

1. _____   6. _____
2. _____   7. _____
3. _____   8. _____
4. _____   9. _____
5. _____   10. _____

II. Finding the Correct Meaning

Write the part of speech and the number of the correct definition of each italicized word as used in the sentences below. Example: n. 3

_____ 1. Before giving the skyjacker the money, the FBI electronically *scanned* all of the $20 bills.

> **scan** (skăn) *v.* 1. To examine closely. 2. To look over quickly.
> 3. *Elect.* To move a beam of light over a surface to reproduce an image. 4. *Comp. Sci.* To search for data systematically.

_____ 2. Before September 2001, the D. B. Cooper case was one of the only successful skyjackings of a *commercial* American jetliner.

> **commercial** (kə mûr′ sh əl) *adj.* 1. Having profit as a chief gain. 2. Supported by advertising. —*n.* 1. An advertisement on television or radio.

_____ 3. The FBI was afraid to *rig* the parachutes to fail in case they were used by hostages instead of the skyjacker.

> **rig** (rĭg) *v.* **rigged, rigging** 1. To equip or fit, often a ship. 2. To do or make in a makeshift way. 3. To manipulate dishonestly for gain. —*n.* 1. The arrangement of masts and sails on a sailing vessel. 2. Gear used for a particular sport.

_____ 4. The authorities *estimate* that the wind-chill factor at that altitude was 70 degrees below zero.

> **estimate** (ĕs′ tə māt′) *v.* **-mated, -mating.** 1. To calculate the approximate amount. 2. To evaluate. —*n.* (ĕs′ tə mĭt) 1. A rough calculation. 2. An estimate of the cost of work to be done.

_____ 5. In the 1970s, the *hatch* to the cargo stairs was never kept locked.

> **hatch**[1] (hătch) *v.* 1. To emerge from an egg. 2. To devise a plan in secret.
> **hatch**[2] (hătch) *n.* 1. An opening, as in the deck of a ship or aircraft.
> **hatch**[3] (hătch) *v.* 1. To shade by drawing fine parallel or crossed lines.

III. Understanding New Vocabulary
Write the letter of the correct definition (a–j) on the line beside each word (1–10).

_____ 1. extort

_____ 2. media

_____ 3. verify

_____ 4. authorities

a. a wrong name

b. to check out the truth about something

c. very distressing, agonizing

d. to get something by use of a threat

_____ 5. misnomer

_____ 6. serial

_____ 7. harrowing

_____ 8. infamous

_____ 9. hostage

_____10. a.k.a.

e. numbered in order

f. also known as

g. the people in charge

h. a means of mass communication: TV, radio, newspapers

i. having a bad reputation

j. a person held against her or his will by force

IV. Using New Vocabulary

Choose a word from the list in Exercise III to complete the following sentences. Don't forget to watch for context clues.

1. Before television, radio was the people's favorite form of

   _____.

2. Jumping from a plane, even on a bright sunny day, would be a

   _____ experience for me. I'd be terrified.

3. Guinea pig is certainly a _____ for that cuddly

   little rodent. Don't trust its name. It is not from New Guinea, and it

   certainly is not a pig.

4. Charles Lutwidge Dodgson, _____ Lewis

   Carroll, is best known for his book *Alice in Wonderland*.

5. Blackbeard was an _____ pirate. His name was

   known and feared throughout the Caribbean.

6. Most products today are marked with _____

   numbers. That's so the product can be identified in case of a recall.

7. When it comes to interpreting the laws, the Supreme Court justices

   are the highest _____ in the United States.

8. A cashier should always _____ a person's iden-

   tity before approving a credit card purchase.

9. The school bully would _____ the young kids'
   lunch money every day by threatening to hurt them if they didn't
   give it to him.

10. The bank robber held the security guard _____
    until he had collected all the money.

V. Finding the Facts

*Use the information in the Reading to answer the following questions in
complete sentences.*

1. Who was the pilot of Flight 305? _____

   _____

2. What was the FBI's number-one priority when dealing with the skyjacker? _____

   _____

3. What was the original destination of Flight 305? _____

   _____

4. What did the flight attendant see in the skyjacker's attaché case?

   _____

   _____

5. Where did "Dan Cooper" buy his plane ticket?

   _____

   _____

6. Where did the skyjacker sit in the plane?

   _____

   _____

7. When was some of the stolen money finally found?

   _____

   _____

8. How did the skyjacker escape the plane? _____

   _____

9. Why did the flight attendant wait to read the note given to her by

the skyjacker? _____

_____

10. Why do you think the skyjacker asked for four parachutes instead of

one? _____

_____

VI. Sequencing
Put the events in the Answer Box into the correct chronological order.

ANSWER BOX

Flight 305 leaves SEA-TAC Airport.
A massive manhunt for "D. B. Cooper" begins.
Skyjacker gives flight attendant a note.
Jo Weber suspects that her late husband was D. B. Cooper.
Flight 305 leaves Portland.
The F.B.I.'s manhunt is called off.
The skyjacker parachutes from the plane.
A boy finds a bag of the extorted $20 bills.

1. _____
2. _____
3. _____
4. _____
5. _____
6. _____
7. _____
8. _____

VII. Finding the Main Idea
Write the number of the sentence in the paragraph that best states the main idea of the paragraph.

_____ 1.   [1]If he did live through the sky dive, his chances for survival were still slim. [2]The forest below was dense with evergreen trees. [3]There were dozens of lakes and a river where a man tangled in a chute would quickly drown in icy waters. [4]Even if he did land safely, the forest was snow-filled and dark, and the man had no survival gear.

VIII. Finding the Central Idea

Choose the letter of the sentence that best states the central idea of this reading.

_____ 1. a. "D. B. Cooper" was a notorious skyjacker.
   b. Despite all the information known about the skyjacking, the truth about what happened to the mysterious "D. B. Cooper" may never be known.
   c. The FBI, after years of investigation, are certain that the skyjacker known as "D. B. Cooper" is dead.
   d. The daring skyjacker Dan Cooper successfully stole over $200,000.

IX. Analogies

Using the information from the reading, choose a word or phrase from the Answer Box to complete the following analogies.

1. Arizona : Southwest :: Oregon : _____

2. identification : ID :: also known as : _____

3. time sequence : chronological :: number sequence : _____

ANSWER BOX			
SEA-TAC	serial	parachute	pilot
organized	a.k.a.	Mexico	Northwest
misnomer	Florida	D. B. Cooper	flight attendant

4. 4:35 p.m. : Portland :: 7:44 p.m. : _____

5. Himmelsbach : FBI agent : Schaffner : _____

6. extort : bomb :: skydive : _____

X. Writing About What You've Read

A skyjacking like the one done by the man calling himself Dan Cooper would be very difficult today. Explain why.

The Tuareg: Mysterious People of the Sahara

1   For centuries, the wealth of North Africa—gold, salt, and slaves—crossed the vast Sahara along ancient **caravan** routes. The undisputed masters of these caravan routes were the fierce and proud **Tuareg** (twä rĕg). These camel-riding nomads were also known as the Blue Men of the Sahara because of the dark-blue veils and turbans they always wore. Taxation of the caravan travel was not the Tuareg's only livelihood. This nomadic people also tended herds of camels, goats, and cattle and were known to **plunder** neighboring peoples on occasion. Though much has changed for this ancient people, the mysterious Tuareg still survive today.

HISTORY OF THE TUAREG

2   Some historians believe the ancestors of the Tuareg, who are an ethnic branch of a larger group of North Africans called the **Berbers**, came to North Africa nearly 4,000 years ago, long before the Arabic people arrived. The first recorded proof of the Berbers' existence in the Sahara was written in the fifth century BCE by a Greek historian named Herodotus.

3   In the middle 1600s, nomadic Arab tribes began to invade North Africa. The Tuareg resisted the Arab Conquest by migrating into the central and western portions of the Sahara Desert. From their mountain strongholds, **oasis** villages, and desert camps, the Blue Men of the Sahara dominated nearly 150,000 square miles of this arid land. Though the Tuareg eventually accepted the **Islamic** religion of the Arab conquerors, they fiercely resisted "Arabization." Many historians believe the Tuareg to be the purest surviving form of the pre-Islamic Berber culture and language.

4   Interestingly, the name Tuareg is an Arabic name that means "abandoned of God." Since the Tuareg people find this word insulting, they do not use it to refer to themselves. Instead they use one of several different names: Imashaghen (the noble and the free), Kel Tamashek (speakers of the Tamashek language), or Kel Taggelmoust (wearers of the blue veil).

THE TUAREG PEOPLE

5   In many ways, the Tuareg are like their Arab neighbors to the north and east. There are several puzzling differences, however, between this unique people and most other North Africans. For one thing, the Tuareg are Caucasian unlike most African tribes who are black. Their skin color, according to the *Encyclopedia Britannica*, "is the reddish yellow of southern Europeans." Though their eyes are usually brown, blue eyes are not uncommon. Another remarkable difference is the wearing of the veil. In Arab societies, the woman is usually veiled. In Tuareg tradition, the male wears the veil, not the woman. In fact, a man begins to wear the veil when he reaches **puberty**, and it is never removed, even with family or while sleeping. Another major difference is that this culture is **matrilineal** while in most Arabic cultures, power and property pass through the father's line.

6   Another slight difference the Tuareg have from their Arabic neighbors is in their practice of the Islamic religion. Though probably one of the earliest North African people to convert to Islam, the Tuareg are not strict followers of the Muslim faith. They do pray daily to Allah and are **devout** in their beliefs but often do not practice all the requirements of the faith. In fact, many of the pre-Islamic rituals are still practiced, and the cross, a symbol that may remain from their earlier Christian faith, is still used in their artwork today.

TUAREG SOCIETY

7   In the past, Tuareg tribes were typically made up of groups of 10 to 30 families. Interestingly, traditional Tuareg society in some ways is like **feudal** Europe during the Middle Ages. Tuareg society was **stratified** into three layers: nobles, **vassals**, and **serfs** (servants or slaves). Historically, the nobles or upper class were traders. The vassals were often farmers who had to pay **allegiance** to a local headman, who in turn reported to a noble. In the past, slaves, who were blacks rather than Tuareg, did much of the work. Today, the division of Tuareg society is still much the same. Even though slavery is now illegal, the descendants of these slaves are often still serfs, the lowest of the working class who do most of the heavy labor.

TUAREG WOMEN

8   The role of the woman in Tuareg society is quite remarkable. Unlike women in most Arabic societies, Tuareg women are independent, with a strong position in society. Tuareg women can own property and livestock in their own right. Because the Tuareg culture is matrilineal, power and land pass through the woman's family, not the man's.

9   Tuareg women have also always had a large responsibility for the success of the tribe. In traditional Tuareg culture, the men were traders and warriors; the women were responsible for the camps. They saw to the herds, food preparation, social matters, and the education of children.

Tuareg women were, and still are, the poets and musicians of the society. For centuries, the brave deeds of the men, love stories, and other memorable events have been recorded in verse and sung to the music of an imzad—a one-string violin. Perhaps most remarkable of all is that only the Tuareg women know how to write Tifinagh. This ancient script was brought to North Africa by the Phoenicians. Tifinagh is the only surviving written Berber language.

TUAREG ART AND CULTURE

10   The Tuareg's incredible poetry and music are not the only accomplishments of this unique culture. Even today, the Tuareg are known for their **exquisite** arts and crafts. Fine indigo cloth; gold, silver, and copper jewelry; carved wooden masks; leather and metal saddle decorations; and particularly the finely crafted swords for which Tuareg warriors are famous are all sought by art dealers around the world.

THE TUAREG TODAY

11   For more than a millennium, the Tuareg way of life remained the same . . . until the twentieth century. Actually, the first conflict between the emerging modern industrial world and this ancient nomad culture began in 1881 when the French decided to build a trans-Saharan railroad. The fiercely independent Tuareg resented this invasion. Despite the French Army's superior weapons, the Blue Men of the Sahara on their camels with nothing more than swords and determined courage **annihilated** the foreign troops. For 20 years, the French made no attempt to move into the Tuareg's territory. Eventually, however, warfare between the two began again. Unfortunately, even the Tuareg's bravery and skill in battle were not enough to defeat the motorized armies of Europe.

12   In the 1960s, the countries of North Africa began creating laws and policies that made the traditional life of the Tuareg nearly impossible. A revolt by the Tuareg in 1963 was quickly put down, and the Tuareg people

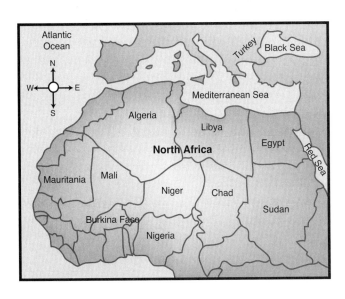

found themselves separated by political boundaries over which they had no say. The area that had once been the Tuareg homeland was now under the control of several different nations—Niger, Mali, Burkina Faso, Algeria, Libya, Mauritania, and Morocco. Since the 1970s, severe droughts and famine have forced many of this once-flourishing people into poverty and **degradation**. Many were forced to move to urban areas or to become farmers.

13   In the early 1990s, groups of Tuareg rebels began fighting for **autonomy**. Many on both sides have died. To escape the war, a great number of the Tuareg people fled to **refugee** camps in Mauritania or Libya. A cease-fire was finally signed between the Tuareg and the nations of Niger and Mali in the mid-1990s. Today, after more than a thousand years of nomadic life, the fierce and independent Tuareg are being forced to adapt to a sedentary lifestyle in the twenty-first century.

Exercises

I. Finding the Correct Pronunciation
Write the letter of the correct pronunciation on the line beside the word.

_____ 1. feudal
  a. fyo͞od′ əl
  b. fĕd′ ĕl

_____ 2. oasis
  a. ō ā′sēz
  b. ō ā′sĭs

_____ 3. annihilate
  a. ăn nīl′ lāt′
  b. ə nī′ ə lāt′

II. Finding the Correct Meaning
Use the context clues in each sentence to determine the correct meaning for each of the italicized words. Write the correct part of speech and number on the line provided. Example: _n. 3_

_____ 1. ". . . the ancestors of the Tuareg, who are an ethnic *branch* of a larger group of North Africans called the Berbers."

> **branch** (brănch) *n.* 1. One of the woody parts growing out from the trunk, limb or main stem of a tree or shrub. 2. A part or division of a larger whole. 3. A local unit or office, *the post office branch.* —*v.* 1. To put forth branches. 2. To develop divisions; diverge.

_____ 2. "Many historians believe the Tuareg to be the purest surviving form of the pre-Islamic Berber *culture* and language."

> **culture** (kŭl' chər) *n.* 1. The arts, beliefs, customs, institutions, and all other products of human work and thought at a particular time. 2. The qualities of mind and the tastes that result from appreciation of the arts and sciences. 3. The breeding of animals or growing of plants, especially to improve their development. 4. The growing of microorganisms for study. 5. Such a growth, of bacteria or tissue.

_____ 3. "This nomadic tribe also *tended* herds of camels, goats, and cattle . . ."

> **tend¹** (tĕnd) *v.* 1. To incline toward: *Stress tends to make her crazy.* 2. To be inclined: *She tends toward conservatism in money matters.*
> **tend²** (tĕnd) *v.* 1. To have the care of somebody or something; look after. 2. To apply one's attention; attend: *You should tend to your own business.*

III. Synonyms
Match the new vocabulary words with their synonyms.

_____ 1. wealth   a. layered

_____ 2. dominate   b. Muslim

_____ 3. Islamic   c. white

_____ 4. Caucasian   d. appearing

_____ 5. noble   e. escapee

_____ 6. convert   f. riches

_____ 7. stratified   g. destroy

_____ 8. annihilate   h. lord

_____ 9. emerging   i. rule

_____10. refugee   j. change

IV. Using New Vocabulary

Choose a word from the Answer Box to complete the following sentences using context clues.

ANSWER BOX			
caravans	undisputed	plunder	ethnic
oasis	devout	puberty	matrilineal
feudal	autonomy	exquisite	trans-Saharan

1. In many cultures, _____ is the time when a boy's responsibilities change to those of a man and a girl's to a woman's.

2. The Tuareg people are not the only ones who have fought for _____. Colonial Americans fought for their right to self-government and independence from England.

3. It would be almost impossible to build a _____ railroad because the drifting sands would continually bury the tracks in places.

4. Before motorized vehicles, camel _____ carried goods and people across the Sahara Desert.

5. A _____ society like that of the early Europeans and the Tuareg is one in which a poor working class serves the wealthy nobility.

6. The Tuareg are an unusual culture, particularly in the Arab world, because their society is _____. Power and property pass through the woman's family.

7. A desert _____ with its green palm trees and promise of clear, clean water was a welcome sight for travelers in the Sahara.

8. Tuareg blacksmiths are known worldwide for the _____ craftsmanship of their swords.

9. For more than a thousand years, the Tuareg were the _____ rulers of the Sahara. No one dared challenge their power.

10. There are many _____ differences between the Tuareg and their Arab neighbors. For one thing, in Tuareg society it is the man who wears the veil, not the woman.

V. Finding the Facts
Write the letter of the correct answer on the line provided.

_____ 1. Who first brought the Tifinagh form of writing to North Africa?
   a. Arabs
   b. Greeks
   c. Phoenicians
   d. French

_____ 2. Of what larger ethnic group of people are the Tuareg a part?
   a. Arabs
   b. Berbers
   c. Egyptians
   d. Phoenicians

_____ 3. To where did many of the Tuareg people escape during the fighting in the 1990s?
   a. Mali
   b. Egypt
   c. Niger
   d. Libya

_____ 4. When does a Tuareg man remove his veil?
   a. at night
   b. only when with his family
   c. never
   d. when there are no women present

_____ 5. Why were the Tuareg finally defeated by the French?
   a. The Tuareg were outsmarted by the French.
   b. The French soldiers were braver than the Tuareg warriors.
   c. The French were helped by the Arabs.
   d. The Tuareg on camels with only swords were no match for the French with their motorized vehicles, such as tanks and supply trucks.

_____ 6. How were important events recorded in the Tuareg culture?
   a. put to music and sang
   b. painted on pottery
   c. written in Tamashek
   d. kept in a journal by tribe historian

_____ 7. How large an area of the Sahara did the Tuareg once rule?
   a. 4,000 square miles
   b. 16,000 square miles
   c. 100,000 square miles
   d. 150,000 square miles

_____ 8. What language do only the Tuareg women know how to write?
   a. Berber
   b. Arabic
   c. Tifinagh
   d. Tamashek

_____ 9. What religion were the Tuareg before they were converted to the Muslim faith?
   a. Buddhist
   b. Christian
   c. Hindu
   d. Islamic

_____10. In which layer of Tuareg society would you find black Africans?
   a. traders
   b. vassals
   c. serfs
   d. nobles

VI. Noting Important Dates
Match the following dates with why they were important.

_____ 1. 1881

_____ 2. fifth century BCE

_____ 3. mid-1600s

_____ 4. 2000 BCE

_____ 5. 1960s

_____ 6. 1963

_____ 7. 1970

_____ 8. early 1990s

_____ 9. mid-1990s

_____10. twenty-first century

a. Nomadic Arabs began to invade North Africa.

b. Tuareg signed a cease-fire with Mali and Niger.

c. Severe droughts began in North Africa.

d. The ancestors of the Tuareg first arrived in North Africa.

e. The Tuareg people struggle to adapt to a new lifestyle.

f. The French tried to build a trans-Saharan railroad.

g. The Tuareg were noted by Greek historian Herodotus.

h. The Tuareg revolted.

i. The Tuareg began fighting for autonomy.

j. The countries of North Africa began making laws and policies that affected the Tuareg.

VII. Map Check

Use the map of Africa in the Appendix to answer the following questions. Write the letter of the correct answer on the line provided.

_____ 1. The Sahara Desert crosses the majority of which portion of Africa?
a. the North
b. the South
c. the East
d. the West

_____ 2. What large country is due east of Mali?
a. Burkina Faso
b. Mauritania
c. Nigeria
d. Niger

_____ 3. The Tuareg's original territory was divided between several countries. Which of the following is the smallest?
a. Burkina Faso
b. Mauritania
c. Algeria
d. Niger

_____ 4. When Tuareg refugees fled from Mali to Algeria, in what direction would they have traveled?
a. east
b. west or southwest
c. north
d. south

_____ 5. The Tuareg's ancestors originally came from Europe. Where is Europe in relationship to the Tuareg's present homeland?
a. north
b. south
c. east
d. west

VIII. Finding the Main Idea

Write the numbers of the sentence in each paragraph that best states the main idea of the paragraph. The main idea may be repeated.

_____ 1.   [1]There are several puzzling differences between the Tuareg and other African people. [2]First, the Tuareg are Caucasian while most Africans are black. [3]Another difference between the Tuareg and their Arab neighbors is that the Tuareg men wear a veil; in Arab culture women are veiled. [4]The fact that property and power is passed through the woman's family is another surprise. [5]Many African societies are not matrilineal.

____ 2.   [1]In Tuareg society, the women are independent with a strong position in society. [2]Traditionally, the women managed the camp while the men were traders and warriors. [3]Tuareg women are also well-known as accomplished musicians and poets. [4]Remarkably, it is the women only in this culture who are literate. [5]They alone know how to read and write the ancient script known as Tifinagh. [6]Obviously, Tuareg women play an important role in their society.

IX. Finding the Central Idea

Choose the letter of the sentence that best states the central idea of this reading.

____ 1. a. The Tuareg people are the purest surviving example of the pre-Islamic Berber culture.

b. A nomadic lifestyle like the Tuareg's is no longer possible in the modern world.

c. The Tuareg people are an ancient and unusual culture that after thousands of years is changing under pressure from the modern world.

d. The Tuareg were the rulers of the Sahara Desert.

X. Seeing Relationships

Based on what you have read, find the one word or phrase in each set that does not belong and cross it out. On the line, explain the relationship that connects the related words or phrases.

1. trucks   tanks   camels   cars   motorcycles

_____

2. Niger   Phoenicia   Mali   Libya   Algeria

_____

3. Imashaghen   Kel Tamashek   Tuareg   Arab   Kel Taggelmoust

_____

4. trader   sea captains   herders   plunderers   tax collectors

_____

5. property owners   camp managers   poets   warriors   musicians

_____

XI. Summarizing
On your own paper, write a summary of this reading.

Rainbows, Sundogs, and Other Meteorological Marvels

RAINBOWS

1   For **millennia**, rainbows have been a source of wonder and myths. European tales tell of the pot of gold at the rainbow's end. The Arawak Indians of South America consider a rainbow over the ocean to be a sign of good luck. Many cultures around the world see the rainbow as a bridge between heaven and Earth. Today, scientists know that a rainbow is nothing more than a combination of light rays and raindrops.

2   To understand how a rainbow is formed, you must understand two terms from physics—refraction and dispersion. **Refraction** is the bending of light. Put a pencil in a clear glass of water, and look at it carefully. Does the pencil seem to be bent? Your eye tells you that it is, even though your brain knows that it is not. But why does the pencil seem bent? The answer is refraction.

3   The next time you are at the swimming pool or in the lake, try running through the water. Is it easier to run on the ground (you are running through air) or through the water? Just like you, light can travel faster through air than it can through water. Glass slows down light rays even more. Air, water, and glass are all different kinds of **mediums**. When light travels from one medium to another, like from the air into the glass or from the glass into the water, it bends. This bending of light is called refraction.

4   Our eyes usually see light as white, but in fact a beam of light is made up of a series of colors—red, orange, yellow, green, blue, indigo,

and violet (the colors of the rainbow). If a beam of light hits a crystal or raindrop or other clear **prism**-like object, it is bent not only once but twice. Because different colors of light travel at different speeds, the second refraction breaks the white light into its many colors. This process is called **dispersion**. Together, refraction and dispersion create a rainbow.

5   The next time you see a rainbow, take note of two things. First, notice that the sun is always at your back (when you are facing the rainbow). Second, you will see that there is always a rain shower in the direction of the rainbow. This is because a rainbow is caused by the sunlight coming from behind you hitting the raindrops in front of you. The raindrops act like a prism, first refracting then dispersing the sunlight. The raindrops also act as a mirror to reflect the colors back toward you. The best time to see rainbows is in the summer when there are local rain showers at the same time the sun is shining. You can even see a rainbow during a full moon if the conditions are just right. This rare sight is called a **moonbow**.

HALOS

6   Rainbows and moonbows are not the only marvels of nature that this combination of refraction and dispersion can create. If you know where and when to look and are lucky, you might also see halos, sundogs, mirages, or even the incredible **green flash**.

7   Have you ever looked up on a cold, clear winter's night to see the moon circled in a halo? Sometimes the halo around the moon seems a ghostly white, and other times the moon seems to be circled by a rainbow of its own. Actually, the halo only appears to be around the moon. The moon itself is in outer space. The halo is formed by moonlight passing through ice crystals in a thin layer of clouds high above the earth. The ice crystals refract the moonlight. The most common halos are called 22-degree halos because the circle of color appears at a 22-degree angle from the viewer's eyes. Under certain circumstances, halos can also be seen during daylight.

8   On cold, sunny mornings or evenings just when the sun is rising or setting, you might be lucky enough to see a very special kind of 22-degree halo—**sundogs**. Prism-like ice crystals near the horizon refract the sun's light to either side. Like a pair of dogs guarding a temple gate, two bright sundogs sit one to the right and the other to the left of the sun, looking in some ways like a small, round rainbow. The side of each sundog closest to the sun is bright red, and often there is a long, white tail pointing away from the sun. Sometimes you can just make out the rest of the halo on which the sundogs sit, but often the two false suns flanking the real one is all that can be seen. Scientists call these fragments of a rainbow **parhelia**.

9   A rainbow itself is, in fact, a kind of a halo. Usually the horizon cuts off the view of the bottom half of the circle. If you were lucky enough to

see a rainbow while high above the earth in an airplane, you would see a full circle of color with the shadow of your plane at the very center.

MIRAGES

10   There is another remarkable phenomenon caused by refraction—**mirages**. Have you ever been driving down a sizzling hot road on a summer's day and seen what appears to be a pool of water in the road ahead of you? The water, however, always seems to disappear before you can get to it. This phenomenon is called a **highway mirage**. It is much like the **desert mirage** that travelers crossing Death Valley or the Great Sahara might experience—an inviting pool of water that is nothing more than sand. These are called simple mirages.

11   If you have ever tried to walk barefoot on a black-topped road in summer, you know how very hot the pavement can be. The air directly above the pavement is also very hot, much hotter even than the air only inches away. Hot air is much less **dense** than cold air. Just as light bends when it moves from air to water, so light bends as it moves from cooler air into hot air. In a mirage, the light that would normally travel directly to your eye from the roadway is bent away from your eye, while the light from the blue sky is refracted off the layer of hot air directly toward you. The water your brain thinks it sees on a hot roadway is actually an image of the blue sky.

12   Mirages, like highway and desert mirages, that appear below where the real object exists are called **inferior**. In this case, inferior means lower rather than of less value. Sometimes, the image created by the mirage appears above the real object. When an image appears above its true location it is called a **superior** mirage.

13   People have reported seeing mountains, buildings, ships, even armies floating in the sky. In rare cases, when layers of air temperature were just right, light has been refracted from places far below the horizon. In 1897, an exploration team in Alaska saw a "Silent City" floating over the ice.

Some scientists now think that the mirage was the image of the English town of Bristol. Remarkably, the light from the city had refracted from several different layers of the atmosphere and sent the **image**, the mirage, more than 2,500 miles away.

14 Mirages at sea are also very common. They are called **Fata Morgana**. When the water is colder than the air above, such as just after dawn, before dusk, or when a storm is building, light is more likely to refract. There have been many legends of phantom ships, the most famous being the Flying Dutchman. Scientists today believe that mirages are the source of these tall tales.

15 At sea is probably the best place to see the incredible green flash. If conditions are absolutely perfect—the horizon is far in the distance and the sky is completely clear of clouds—you might see this brief yet spectacular event. Just as the sun rises or sets, there may be a second or two when you can see a brilliant green flash from the upper edge of the sun. Even rarer is the **blue flash**, and most rare of all the **violet flash**. All are caused by the dispersion of sunlight by the atmosphere.

16 Today, green flashes, mirages, halos, sundogs, rainbows, and other atmospheric marvels can all be explained by science. They are nothing more than the results of refraction and dispersion. Still, knowing how they are created does not take away from the magic of these wonders of Mother Nature.

Exercises

I. Finding the Correct Pronunciation
Write the letter of the correct pronunciation on the line beside the word.

_____ 1. myth
    a. mĭth
    b. mīth

_____ 2. prism
    a. prĭsm
    b. prĭz´ əm

_____ 3. phantom
    a. phānt´ əm
    b. făn´ təm

_____ 4. mirage
    a. mī´ răg
    b. mĭ räzh´

II. Finding the Correct Meaning

Use the dictionary entries given below to choose the correct meaning for each italicized word as it is used in that context. If there is more than one choice, give both the part of speech and the number of the definition. Example: <u>n. 3</u>

_____ 1. Light refracts as it moves from one *medium* to another.

> **medium** (mē′ dē əm) *n., pl.* **media** or **mediums**. 1. A means or way to do, transport, or transfer something: *English is used as a medium of instruction.* 2. A substance or element: *Water is the medium of fish.* 3. A technique or material used by artists. 4. A person who claims to be able to speak with the spirit of the dead. 5. *pl.* **media**. A way of sending information to large numbers of people: *Television and newspapers are good advertising media.* —*adj.* 1. Halfway between extremes; intermediate: *of medium height.*

_____ 2. A city floating in the air is an example of a *superior* mirage.

> **superior** (soo pîr′ ē ər) *adj.* 1. High or higher in order, degree, or rank; *superior court or superior officer.* 2. Higher in quality. 3. Excellent. 4. Situated above or over. —*n.* 1. A person who is above another in rank. 2. The head of a religious community such as a monastery or convent: *Mother Superior.*

_____ 3. A *beam* of sunlight can be refracted by raindrops.

> **beam** (bēm) *n.* 1. A long, rigid piece of wood. 2. A stream of particles or rays, as of light, sound, or other radiation. 3. One of the main horizontal supports of a building or ship. —*v.* 1. To give off light; shine. 2. To smile broadly. 3. To emit or transmit signals.

III. Using New Vocabulary

Choose a word from the Answer Box to complete the following sentences using context clues.

ANSWER BOX			
millennium	refraction	dispersion	prism
horizon	conditions	atmospheric	fragments
sizzling	inferior	dense	myths

1. Glass is a more _____ medium than water.

2. If the _____ are perfect—a distant horizon and an absolutely clear day—you may see a green flash.

3. Rain and sunshine are the two _____ conditions that must be present for a rainbow to appear.

4. Both refraction and _____ are needed to make a rainbow.

5. When white light refracts through a _____ it disperses into the colors of the rainbow.

6. Sundogs are _____ of a rainbow. The other parts of the 22-degree halo on which they appear are usually not visible.

7. Scientists believe that mirages may be the source of many _____ and legends such as phantom ships and even UFOs.

8. A desert mirage is called _____ because the mirage is seen below the actual object.

9. The sun has actually moved below the _____ a few moments before we "see" the sun disappear. This effect is due to refraction.

10. A simple mirage is caused by the _____ of light off the layer of hot air just over the highway's surface.

IV. Finding the Facts

Write the letter of the best answer on the line provided.

_____ 1. Which is not one of the colors that make up white light?

    a. green

    b. orange

    c. brown

    d. violet

    e. indigo

_____ 2. In which medium listed below does light travel the fastest?

    a. air

    b. water

    c. glass

    d. clouds

    e. empty vacuum of space

_____ 3. What makes a pencil in a glass of water appear to be bent?

    a. refraction

    b. reflection

    c. dispersion

    d. mirage

    e. optical illusion

_____ 4. Who saw a floating city in Alaska?

    a. Arawat Indians

    b. seamen

    c. the English

    d. an exploration team

    e. a physicist

_____ 5. Why are most rainbows not a complete circle?

    a. They are not halos.

    b. You cannot see the part below the horizon.

    c. There are not enough raindrops.

    d. The sun is not bright enough to create a full circle.

    e. Only halos are complete circles.

_____ 6. Where would you be most likely to see a green flash?

    a. out on a boat on a fine, clear day

    b. near tall mountains

    c. in the rainforest

    d. on a hot summer highway

    e. in sand dunes

_____ 7. Which of the following is not necessary to make a rainbow?
  a. raindrops
  b. reflection
  c. refraction
  d. sun
  e. cool air

_____ 8. Which is not a 22-degree halo or part of a 22-degree halo?
  a. a mirage
  b. a ring around the moon
  c. a rainbow
  d. a moonbow
  e. a sundog

_____ 9. When would you probably not see a Fata Morgana?
  a. at sunrise in the Sahara
  b. before a storm from a Hawaiian beach
  c. just after sunrise from a sailboat
  d. just after sunset from a cruise ship
  e. at the end of sunny day aboard a ship in the Arctic Ocean

_____ 10. What do the Arawak believe a rainbow over water represents?
  a. a clear day to come
  b. a bridge to heaven
  c. good luck
  d. bad weather on the way
  e. a pot of gold waiting at the end

V. Sequencing
Put the events in the Answer Box into the correct chronological order.

> ANSWER BOX
>
> The water droplets disperse the white light into the colors of the rainbow.
> The observer sees a rainbow.
> The colored light is reflected back toward the observer.
> A beam of sunlight (white light) hits water drops.

1. _____

2. _____

3. _____

4. _____

VI. Finding the Main Idea
Write the number of the sentence in each paragraph that best states the main idea of the paragraph.

_____ 1.   [1]For millennia, rainbows have been a source of wonder and myths. [2]European tales tell of the pot of gold at the rainbow's end. [3]The Arawak Indians of South America consider a rainbow over the ocean to be a sign of good luck. [4]Many cultures around the world see the rainbow as a bridge between heaven and Earth. [5]Still others see it as a connection between the living and the dead.

_____ 2.   [1]A halo circles the moon on a crisp winter's night. [2]A dazzling rainbow arches across the sky. [3]Phantom ships sail overhead. [4]Shining pools of water shimmer in the desert but always disappear before the thirsty traveler can reach them. [5]A rare green flash at sunset delights seamen. [6]Sundogs guard the setting sun. [7]Moonbows arch above a waterfall on a full-moon evening. [8]Rainbows dance across the surface of a soap bubble! [9]The simple bending of light creates all these beautiful natural wonders.

VII. Finding an Implied Main Idea
Write the letter of the sentence below that best states the main idea of the paragraph.

_____ 1.   [1]The next time you see a rainbow stop for a moment. [2]Notice that the sun is at your back, and that you are facing the rainbow. [3]The sunlight coming from behind you strikes the raindrops, is refracted and dispersed into its color, then the light is reflected back to you. [4]The beautiful arch of color you are seeing is yours alone. [5]Even a person standing next to you sees a slightly different rainbow because the light is bouncing back to that person at a different angle.

a. Rainbows are made of light and rain.
b. The rainbow that you see is a unique result of refraction and dispersion.
c. Everyone sees a different rainbow.
d. Rainbows only happen when it is raining.

VIII. Finding the Central Idea
Choose the letter of the sentence that best states the central idea of this reading.

_____ 1. a. Rainbows and sundogs are atmospheric marvels.
b. Rainbows, moonbows, and sundogs are all 22-degree halos created by light bending through layers of air.
c. Refraction and dispersion can cause amazing natural phenomena.
d. Mother Nature can be incredible.

IX. Analogies

Using the information from the reading, choose a word or phrase from the Answer Box to complete the following analogies.

ANSWER BOX

air	phantom	refract	Fata Morgana
halos	rainbow	ice crystals	inferior
colors	Sahara	sundogs	blue flash

1. moon : moonbow :: sun : _____

2. whole : parts :: white light : _____

3. Flying Dutchmen : superior :: highway mirage : _____

4. sundogs : parhelia :: ocean mirages : _____

5. scarce : rare :: green flash : _____

6. highway mirage : hot road :: desert mirage : _____

7. twist : turn :: bend : _____

8. summer day : mirages :: winter night : _____

9. rainbow : raindrops :: halo : _____

10. legend : tall tale :: ghost : _____

X. Writing About What You've Read

On your own paper, explain how a mirage is created.

READING 4

The Power of Symbols

1   **Symbols** are everywhere around us. A red **octagonal** sign tells you to stop even if you cannot read the letters written there. A skull and crossbones on a bottle warns, "Poison!" without saying a word. In the midst of battle, a flag is held high to urge the soldiers onward. Gang members fight over graffiti spray-painted on "the wrong" wall. These symbols and thousands more are an **integral** part of our everyday life. But what is a symbol, and why do symbols have such an amazing power over us?

2   The *American Heritage Dictionary* defines a symbol as "something that represents something else by association, resemblance, or convention." A slightly different definition of symbol is "a **visible** sign of an **invisible** reality." In fact, both definitions are true. The symbol of the skull and crossbones on the bottle of poison is a visible picture that warns

of the invisible danger that lies within. The symbol, however, has no meaning or value to us if we cannot associate the sign to the invisible reality it symbolizes. Just as it is impossible to read Chinese if you do not know the characters of the Chinese language, so a symbol is meaningless if a person does not know its significance.

3   Symbols are a means of communication. As the old **axiom** says, "A picture is worth a thousand words." Symbols can warn us of danger, guide us in the right direction, help us find a common understanding for those "invisible" realities like friendship, gratitude, service, courage, love, and many more. From a road sign to a ring of gold given at a wedding, symbols are a powerful part of our lives.

4   Symbols are also found in literature. In one story, a tree may symbolize the connection of Earth and heaven. In another, a river might represent cleansing or baptism into a new life. The use of symbolism allows an author to examine those **intangible** realities that drive not only a good story but our lives.

5   Within a culture, the power of a symbol comes from its shared understanding and use by a group of people. The American flag is only a piece of cloth, but to millions of people in this world it is much more. For many Americans, the stars and stripes represent this country, our freedom, our courage, and many other values. To **desecrate** the American flag by allowing it to touch the ground or burning it in defiance is seen by many as an attack on these values, if not the country itself. The symbolism of this rectangle of cloth is so strong that an **etiquette** has been developed over the years for the "proper" use, handling, and respectful destruction of the American flag.

6   For the religions of the world, symbols are a **concrete** portrayal of a spiritual belief. Christians have the cross. A Star of David symbolizes Judaism. A mandala created with sand, the circular yin-yang, prayer flags, and other symbols have importance to Buddhists. Some say that the crescent moon and star that appear on many of the flags of Islamic countries are symbols of that faith, though others say that the Muslim religion has no symbol. Even older religions now gone had symbols such as the tree of life, the rising sun, and the Egyptian ankh.

7   Surprisingly, perhaps the most ancient symbol, one that is thousands of years old and found in almost every culture in the world, is now one of the most hated—the swastika. This symbol dates back at least 3,000 years. Coins and pottery from ancient Troy carry this unmistakable marking. The swastika has also been found in ancient Rome, in a 2,000-year-old Jewish temple, on Buddhist idols, Chinese coins, and Irish doorways.

8   Until its use by the Nazis during World War II, the symbolism of the swastika was always positive. It stood for life, the sun, strength, power, or good luck. The ancient Sanskrit word *svastika* from which the word *swastika* comes means "to be good." For centuries, Native Americans wore **amulets** of swastikas for good luck. In early nineteenth-century America, the symbol was said to represent interlocking "L's" for Love, Life, Light, and Luck. Swastikas were once common on pins, jewelry, cigarette cases, and were incorporated into buildings or walkways. Even today in Washington, DC, you can find several decorative swastikas built into the U.S. Capitol Building.

9   How then did a symbol with such positive energy become **perverted** into perhaps the most hated in the world? **Association!** Adolf Hitler used this ancient symbol to unite the Germans, then used the power of their anger and hatred to kill millions of people, particularly Jews and gypsies. Instead of love, life, light, and luck, under the Nazis' reign of terror, the once-loved symbol became associated with death, darkness, degradation, and despair.

10   Symbols do have amazing power. World War II ended more than 50 years ago, but the power of the swastika is still strong, especially for the Jewish people. For Jews and others, the mere sight of the symbol brings back memories of the horror of Hitler's **genocide** in much the same way the symbolism of the Confederate flag brings back memories of the horrors of slavery and **racism** for African Americans in the United States.

11   Many argue that people should forget the negative aspects of both these symbols. They believe the ancient, positive meanings of the swastika should be recognized again; that the Confederate flag should now be seen only as a symbol of Southern pride. However, the power of a symbol is strong and difficult to change. That is especially true when both these symbols are, in fact, still used today to spread hatred and fear. Neo-Nazi groups who still believe in Hitler's teachings have adopted the swastika as their symbol of recognition, and organizations and individuals who still preach racism use the Confederate flag with pride.

12   And that is another power of the symbol—to both unite and identify groups of people. Many Christians wear a cross on a chain around their neck to show the world which religious group they belong to. Sorority and fraternity members use the Greek letters of their organization, such as ΔΣΩ, on clothing or jewelry to identify themselves. The sudden appearance of the American flag on everything from T-shirts to bumper stickers after 9/11 is an example of the American people's need to show **solidarity** and to **reaffirm** their beliefs in the ideals of the United States. Gang symbols serve much the same purpose. A certain tattoo or particular colored shirt or hat tells those familiar with the symbolism which gang an individual belongs to.

13   Marketing experts, whose job it is to sell you their products, long ago recognized the appeal of symbols. **Logos** of professional sports teams are popular on clothing and other **merchandise** because people want to show publicly that they support their favorite team. Even name brands like Nike have symbols, so the person wearing the shoes or clothing can announce to the world that they belong to the in-style group.

14   Symbols are as ancient as the human race because they are a form of communication that can take us beyond both the written and spoken word. Symbols can cross the boundaries of time and countries. Symbols allow us to share the experience of being human. Look around. Notice the symbols of your world.

Exercises

I. Finding the Correct Pronunciation
Write the letter of the correct pronunciation on the line beside the word.

_____ 1. ankh
   a. ănk
   b. ăngk

_____ 2. axiom
   a. ăsk´ əm
   b. ăk´ sē əm

_____ 3. reign
   a. rēn
   b. rān

II. Finding the Correct Meaning

Use the dictionary entries given below to choose the correct meaning for each italicized word as it is used in that context. If there is more than one choice, give both the part of speech and the number of the definition. Example: <u>n. 3</u>

_____ 1. "... something that represents something else by association, re-semblance, or *convention*."

> **convention** (kən věn′ shən) *n.* 1. A formal meeting or assembly. 2. An international agreement. 3. General usage or custom. 4. An accepted or prescribed practice.

_____ 2. "The *power* of the symbol comes from its shared understanding and use. . . ."

> **power** (pou′ ər) *n.* 1. The ability or authority to act effectively. 2. A specific capacity or ability, *the power of concentration.* 3. Strength or force; might. 4. A person, group, or nation having control over another. 5. The energy by which a machine is operated. 6. Electricity. 7. *Phys.* The rate at which work is done. —*v.* 1. To supply with energy, especially mechanical.

_____ 3. "... symbols are *concrete* portrayals of spiritual beliefs."

> **concrete** (kŏn krēt′ or kŏn′ krēt′) *adj.* 1. Relating to an actual specific thing. 2. Existing in reality. 3. Formed by the joining of separate particles. —*n.* 1. A construction material made of sand, gravel, and mortar or cement. 2. A mass formed by the joining of particles.

_____ 4. "... both symbols are still used today to *spread* hatred and fear."

> **spread** (sprĕd) *v.* **spread, spreading.** 1. To open or be extended more fully. 2. To separate more widely, open out. 3. To distribute over a surface in a layer. 4. To distribute widely. —*n.* 1. The act or process of spreading. 2. An open area of land. 3. A cloth cover for a bed or table. 4. *Informal.* An abundant meal laid out on a table. 5. Two facing pages of a magazine or newspaper. 6. A difference, as between two totals.

III. Understanding New Vocabulary
Write the letter of the correct definition on the line beside each word.

_____ 1. genocide

_____ 2. solidarity

_____ 3. Neo-Nazis

_____ 4. etiquette

_____ 5. sorority

_____ 6. perverted

_____ 7. amulet

_____ 8. defiant

_____ 9. desecrate

_____10. integral

a. sisterhood, organization of women

b. resistant to authority

c. to violate the sacredness of something

d. the planned, systematic destruction of a people or race

e. practices of social conventions, manners

f. good luck charm, often worn around the neck

g. new Fascists

h. corrupted, twisted

i. essential (necessary) for completion or wholeness

j. unity of interest

IV. Using New Vocabulary
Choose a word from the list in Exercise III to complete the following sentences. Don't forget to watch for context clues.

1. Susan and Marie were as excited about joining the _____ Phi Kappa Delta as they were starting college.

2. A husband and wife must show _____ when disciplining their children. They should be united in their decision of what punishment to use.

3. Carson's _____ is a rabbit's foot he wears on a chain around his neck. He thinks it brings him good luck.

4. Doing homework assignments is an _____ part of being a successful student.

5. During World War II, Hitler's campaign of _____ killed millions of Jews and gypsies.

6. Today, _____ still preach hatred against people of color.

7. It is hard to imagine how a person can become so _____
that the only emotions they feel are anger and hatred.

8. According to tradition, allowing an American flag to touch the
ground will _____ this symbol of the country.

9. Blowing your nose at the dinner table is not considered good
_____.

10. My little brother was so _____ he ran away from
home rather than do the chores my parents gave him.

V. Symbolism
Match its meaning to each symbol.

_____ 1. ⬣   a. Christianity

_____ 2. ☠   b. love

_____ 3. ☺   c. STOP

_____ 4. ♥   e. Judaism

_____ 5. ☪   f. Have a nice day!

_____ 6. $ g. music

_____ 7. ✡   h. poison

_____ 8. †   i. money

_____ 9. ♪   j. Islam

VI. Finding the Facts
Use the information in the reading to answer the following questions.
Write the letter of the correct answer on the line provided.

_____ 1. Who uses Greek letters to identify themselves?
    a. fraternity members
    b. Greek Orthodox church members

c. Buddhists
d. sorority members
e. both a and d

_____ 2. Which is not a "power" of symbols?
a. can warn of danger
b. can communicate unseen "reality"
c. can be used to identify members of a group
d. is understood by everyone
e. can be used to sell merchandise

_____ 3. The ankh was a symbol used by what people?
a. gang members
b. Muslims
c. Native Americans
d. Egyptians
e. Irish

_____ 4. Why is the continued use of the Confederate flag still offensive to many people?
a. The flag symbolizes the South's defeat.
b. To some people, the flag still symbolizes what the Confederacy stood for—slavery and defiance of the United States.
c. Northerners are still angry with Southerners because the South started the war.
d. The flag represents Southern pride.
e. The flag symbolizes independence and freedom.

_____ 5. When did the symbol of the swastika become perverted from its original meaning?
a. during World War I
b. during World War II
c. during the Civil War
d. 2,000 years ago
e. 3,000 years ago

_____ 6. Where would you *not* likely find a swastika today?
a. on antique jewelry
b. on a Neo-Nazi uniform
c. at the U.S. Capitol
d. in a Buddhist temple
e. in a modern Jewish temple

_____ 7. For which of the major religions is the Star of David a symbol of the faith?
a. Islam
b. Christianity
c. Buddhism
d. Judaism
e. none of the above

_____ 8. Gang members wear certain color clothing for the same reason sorority girls wear a sweater or jacket embroidered with their Greek sorority letters. What is the reason for this behavior?
a. To show they are a member of a particular group.
b. Because they want to be different from everyone else.
c. To show they have the power or money to do whatever they want.
d. To make other people angry.
e. To dare other people to be like them.

_____ 9. The date 9/11 is now symbolic of many things. Which of the following would *not* be "communicated" by that date?
a. shock
b. anger
c. bravery
d. fear
e. hopefulness

_____ 10. Why might it be dangerous not to know the symbols of a particular culture or people?
a. You might not notice a warning signal, such as a railroad-crossing sign.
b. You might misunderstand what the person is trying to communicate.
c. You might accidentally insult a person by not paying the appropriate respect to their honored symbols.
d. You might not be able to travel because you could not interpret the meaning of road signs.
e. All of the above.

VII. Finding the Main Idea
Write the letter of the sentence that best states the main idea in each set of sentences below.

1. _____ a. Swastikas were once common on pins, jewelry, and cigarette cases.
b. This symbol used by the Nazis was once commonly used in buildings, such as Irish homes and even the Capitol Building in Washington, DC.
c. The interlocking L's were once believed to stand for Luck, Life, Light, and Love.
d. Before World War II, the swastika was a commonly used symbol that represented good luck.
e. Native Americans wore amulets with swastikas engraved them to ensure good hunting.

2. ____ a. The skull and crossbones warn us of dangerous poisons.
   b. A Star of David identifies someone of the Jewish faith.
   c. The red, white, and blue of the American flag inspires respect.
   d. A golden wedding band symbolizes eternal love.
   e. Symbols are a common and powerful presence in our lives.

VIII. Finding the Central Idea
Choose the letter of the sentence that best states the central idea of this reading.

____ 1. a. Symbols are as old as human beings.
   b. A symbol can only communicate meaning if a person noting it is familiar with that symbol.
   c. Symbols, a common part of our daily lives, have both positive and negative power.
   d. The meaning of symbols, like the swastika, can be perverted.

IX. Writing About What You've Read
Think of a symbol that is an important part of your life; explain why it is important to you.

Secrets of the Mummy Revealed

READING 5

1   Think **mummy**, and a picture probably comes to mind. In a shadowy Egyptian tomb, a linen-wrapped figure walks, arms outstretched. Fortunately, mummies only walk in Hollywood movies. In reality, a mummy is nothing more than a dead body that has been preserved.

2   Unlike a skeleton, a mummy still has some of its body's soft tissue, such as skin or muscle. Normally, when a person dies, bacteria and fungus begin to grow on the body. This causes the body to decay. However, if the bacteria and fungus cannot grow for some reason, much of the body can be preserved. This process is called **mummification**.

3   Mummification can happen naturally. **Freeze-drying** is one way. Just as the cold, dry air in a freezer can **dehydrate** a piece of chicken, frigid dry air in the cold regions of the world can preserve a body. For example, a person who dies in an **avalanche** in Alaska might be found perfectly preserved hundreds, even thousands, of years later. Extremely hot, dry air or intense, direct sunlight like that in the Sahara Desert will also mummify a body. Since bacteria and fungus cannot grow without oxygen, it is not surprising that mummies have

also been found in peat bogs. A **peat bog** is like a cold swamp. The peat moss on top of the bog grows so thickly that air cannot reach the layers below. Salt, mud, and chemicals can also naturally mummify a body.

EGYPTIAN MUMMIES

4   Most mummification has been done **artificially**, such as the mummification done by the ancient Egyptians. Believing the body needed to be preserved for the afterlife, Egyptians mastered the art of mummification thousands of years ago. For centuries, the Egyptians' process of **embalming** the body, the first step in mummification, was a secret known only to the priests. After years of research, however, scientists now believe they have unraveled the mystery of how Egyptians so successfully preserved their dead.

5   The first step Egyptians used in embalming was to make a cut on the left side of the body. The stomach, liver, intestines, and lungs were removed through the cut. The heart was left because it was thought to be the center of thought. The brain was next removed through the nose with a long hook. Afterward, the body was rinsed with wine (alcohol kills bacteria) then packed in salt. Four days later, the salt was removed and the dried body rubbed with oil to soften the skin. The body cavity was then stuffed with padding. Finally, the mummy was coated with **resin**, a waxy substance made from plants, then wrapped in linen.

6   Researchers think that more than 70 million Egyptians were mummified over a 3,000-year period. The Egyptians were not the only people practicing mummification, however, and certainly not the first. Mummies have now been discovered on every continent except Antarctica.

SOUTH AMERICAN MUMMIES

7   In South America, on the north coast of what is now Chile, lived a tribe of fishermen called the Chincochoros. They were embalming their dead as early as 5,000 BCE, almost 1,500 years before the Egyptians made their first mummy. These embalmers took the body completely apart, including the head. The parts were dehydrated with heat and chemicals then tied back together. The body cavity was then stuffed with feathers or grass. The arms and legs were strengthened with sticks. Afterward, the skin was stretched back over the body. The last step was to cover the mummy with a white ash and clay mixture and to paint it.

8   A thousand years later, another South American people, the Palomans, used salt (as the Egyptians would later use) to embalm their dead. These mummies were wrapped in matting made from reeds then buried under the floor of their homes. Their descendants, the Incas, were still embalming their dead more than 5,000 years later. Incan mummies were wrapped in leather or cloth then placed in baskets or large ceramic pots. They were buried with food, clothing, and personal belongings for their journey into the afterlife. When the Spaniards invaded South America in the 1500s, they outlawed the practice of mummification and burned all the mummies they could find. Only a few survived.

9   Several unexpected Incan mummies have been found on the high peaks of the Andes Mountains. Many of these were the remains of children who had been sacrificed to the Incan gods. Their bodies had been preserved naturally by the frigid, dry air at the high altitude.

NORTH AMERICAN MUMMIES

10   Mummification was also practiced in North America. Nearly 2,000 years ago, there was a tribe of Native Americans known as the Anasazi living in the American Southwest. Anasazi mummies have been found in caves and rock holes. These mummies were wrapped in fur or leather blankets, and many were wearing new sandals. Scientists are still **perplexed** by the Anasazi's embalming process. Since the region is hot and dry like Egypt, a process similar to early Egyptian embalming may have been used.

11   The Aleuts, who lived on the cold, wind-swept islands off the coast of Alaska, embalmed their dead in a very different way than others did. They would remove the internal organs and stuff the body cavity with grass. The body would then be laid in a very cold stream. The water would wash away all the body's fat. All that would be left was bone, muscle, and skin. The body was then air-dried, wrapped in waterproof leather, and put in a cave. Some mummies were hung from the ceiling. Others were put on shelves above the cave floor.

MUMMIES OF OCEANIA

12   Villagers in hot, humid Papua, New Guinea, found a different way to mummify. Their dead were smoked in a method similar to the way fish or meat is preserved. Once dehydrated by the smoke, the bodies were covered with clay and the mummies propped up on platforms to look down on their villages.

NATURAL MUMMIFICATION

13   Like the sacrificial mummies of the Andes, some of the best-preserved and oldest mummies have been naturally mummified. The "Ice Man" (see photo) found frozen in 1991 on a glacier in Germany is believed to be more than 5,000 years old. In Greenland, eight perfectly preserved bodies were found in an abandoned settlement. The icy winds and dry cold had freeze-dried these women and children so quickly that neither their bodies nor their clothing had decayed in more than 500 years. A **CAT scan** of the bodies even showed the food still in their stomachs.

14   In Europe's peat bogs, hundreds of mummies dating back to the time of the Roman Empire have been found. They were preserved by the oxygen-free bogs in which they had been buried. Like the mummies of China's cold Takla Makan Desert and those from the high Andes, these mummies also seem to have been the victims of human sacrifice.

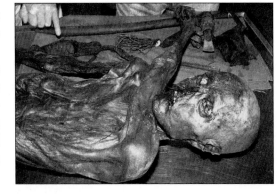

THE SOAP MUMMY

15   One of the oddest mummies ever found was the soap mummy. In the late eighteenth century, a man died in Philadelphia. Not long after his burial, water leaked into his coffin. A chemical process called **hydrolysis** started turning his body fat into soap. His entire body finally became soap. In the 1870s, the mummified body was discovered by accident during a construction project.

THE MYSTERY OF SELF-MUMMIFICATION

16   Perhaps the most unusual form of mummification was practiced in Japan. According to legend, a Buddhist monk who was seeking spiritual enlightenment decided to mummify himself while still alive. Supposedly, he was locked in a room without any food or water. The room was opened 100 days later. The monk was dead, his body perfectly preserved. That may be nothing more than myth. Or perhaps not. Japanese scientists are now studying the well-preserved mummies of other Buddhist monks who died over 200 years ago. Did they also mummify themselves?

Exercises

I. Finding the Correct Pronunciation
Write the letter of the correct pronunciation on the line beside the word.

_____ 1. resin
      a. rĕsʹ ən
      b. rĕzʹ ĭn

_____ 2. avalanche
      a. ăvʹ ə lănch
      b. ā vălʹ ăns

II. Understanding Compound Words
Match each of these compound words (1–10) with its correct definition (a–j).

_____ 1. afterlife		a. without air
_____ 2. waterproof		b. a cold-climate swamp
_____ 3. oxygen-free		c. to make illegal
_____ 4. peat bog		d. a life after death
_____ 5. wind-swept		e. skin, muscle, etc.
_____ 6. freeze-dried		f. gone for a long period of time

_____ 7. linen-wrapped

_____ 8. soft tissue

_____ 9. outlaw

_____ 10. long-vanished

g. dehydrated by cold

h. wrapped in soft cloth

i. exposed to strong air currents

j. something that keeps out moisture

III. Finding the Correct Meaning

Use the dictionary entries given below to choose the correct meaning for each italicized word as it is used in that context. If there is more than one choice give both the part of speech and the number of the definition. Example: <u>n. 3</u>

_____ 1. The Spanish outlawed the _practice_ of embalming.

> **practice** (prăc′ tĭs) _v._ **-ticed, -ticing**. 1. To do or perform habitually. 2. To work at a profession. —_n._ 1. A customary way of doing something. 2. Repeated performance to learn a skill. 3. The business of a professional person.

_____ 2. The mummies were _smoked_ in a way similar to the way meat or fish is preserved.

> **smoke** (smōk) _n._ 1. The vapor made up of small particles from incomplete burning. 2. The act of smoking a form of tobacco. 3. _Inf._ A cigarette or cigar. —_v._ **smoked, smoking** 1. To inhale smoke from cigarette, cigar, or pipe. 2. To give off smoke. 3. To preserve (meat or fish) by exposure to smoke. 4. _Slang_ To kill.

IV. Using New Vocabulary

Choose a word from the Answer Box to complete the following sentences using context clues.

ANSWER BOX

dehydrate	internal	humid	bacteria
resin	victims	glacier	cavity
fungus	tomb	monk	remains

1. In the Andes, the young _____ of human sacrifice were found mummified on the frigid mountain peaks.

2. A _____ is a religious man who often lives and worships in a monastery.

3. The "Ice Man" was found on a melting _____ in Germany.

4. Human _____ will decay rapidly if the body is not embalmed.

5. Whether the mummification is natural or artificial, both _____ and _____ must be destroyed if the soft tissue is to be preserved.

6. The Egyptians coated each mummy in _____ made from plants before wrapping the body in linen.

7. The rainy tropical jungles of New Guinea are very hot and _____.

8. In the scorching-hot Sahara Desert, a body will naturally _____ very quickly.

9. The first step of the Egyptian embalming process was to remove the lungs, stomach, and intestines from the body _____.

10. The Egyptian embalmers removed all the _____ organs except the heart.

V. Finding the Facts
Write the letter of the correct answer on the line provided.

_____ 1. Why did Egyptian embalmers rinse the body in wine?
   a. to wash off the salt
   b. to kill bacteria
   c. to soften the skin
   d. to remove dirt

_____ 2. How old do scientists believe the "Ice Man" is?
   a. 200 years
   b. 500 years
   c. 1,500 years
   d. 5,000 years

_____ 3. In which of these cultures were mummification practices probably the closest to those of the early Egyptians?
   a. Aleuts
   b. Anasazi
   c. Incan
   d. Papua villagers

_____ 4. Which of these cultures is the only one known to have used cold water in their process of mummification?
   a. Aleuts
   b. Anasazi
   c. Inca
   d. Papua villagers

_____ 5. How many Egyptians do historians believe were actually mummified?
   a. 1 million
   b. 3 million
   c. 7 million
   d. 70 million

_____ 6. Very few Incan mummies have been found. Why is that?
   a. Only the kings were mummified.
   b. Only human sacrifices were mummified.
   c. The Spaniards burned most of them.
   d. The mummies were all buried.

_____ 7. In what culture were the mummies placed in caves?
   a. Aleuts
   b. Anasazi
   c. Inca
   d. Papua villagers

_____ 8. Which is *not* true of the Greenland mummies?

a. An entire family was found.
b. CAT scans found food in their stomachs.
c. Even the clothing was preserved.
d. They had been freeze-dried.

_____ 9. What substance did Egyptians not use in their embalming process?

a. resin
b. salt
c. smoke
d. wine

_____ 10. Which form of mummification is not natural?

a. hot, dry air mummification
b. frigid air mummification
c. self-mummification
d. peat bog mummification

VI. Sequencing

The civilizations in the Answer Box all practiced mummification. Place them in sequential order from the most ancient to the most modern.

1. _____

2. _____

3. _____

ANSWER BOX
Chincochoros
Inca
Palomans

VII. Graphic Check

Use the text, your dictionary, and maps if necessary to match the civilizations and people to the continent on which they were found.

_____ 1. Anasazi

_____ 2. Inca

_____ 3. Aleuts

_____ 4. Papua villagers

_____ 5. "Ice Man"

_____ 6. Takla Makan

_____ 7. Peat bog mummies

_____ 8. Palomans

_____ 9. Buddhist monks

_____ 10. Egyptians

a. Africa

b. Asia

c. Europe

d. North America

e. South America

f. Oceania

g. Antarctica

VIII. Finding the Main Idea

Write the number of the sentence in the paragraph that best states the main idea of the paragraph.

_____ 1.   [1]Villagers in hot, humid Papua, New Guinea, found a different way to mummify. [2]Their dead were smoked in a method similar to the way fish or meat is preserved. [3]Once dehydrated by the smoke, the bodies were covered with clay and the mummies propped up on platforms to look down on their villages.

IX. Finding an Implied Main Idea

On the lines below the paragraph, write in your own words a main idea for the paragraph.

The first step Egyptians used in embalming was to make a cut on the left side of the body. The stomach, liver, intestines, and lungs were removed through the cut. The heart was left because it was thought to be the center of thought. The brain was next removed through the nose with a long hook. Afterward, the body was rinsed with wine (alcohol kills bacteria) then packed in salt. Four days later, the salt was removed and the dried body rubbed with oil to soften the skin. It was then stuffed with padding. Finally, the mummy was coated with resin and wrapped in linen.

_____

_____

X. Finding the Central Idea

_____ 1. Which of the following sentences best states the central idea of this reading?
   a. Egyptians practiced mummification for thousands of years.
   b. Many people of the world have practiced mummification.
   c. Mummies, which have been found on every continent except Antarctica, may occur naturally but are usually the result of a complex process of artificial mummification.
   d. The practice of mummification is a complicated process.

XI. Seeing Relationships
Based on what you have read, find the one word or phrase in each set that does not belong and cross it out. On the line, explain the relationship that connects the related words or phrases.

1. heart, liver, stomach, intestines, lungs

   _____

2. Andes mummies, Takla Makan mummies, peat bog mummies, Egyptian mummies

   _____

3. Asia, Europe, South America, Antarctica, Africa

   _____

4. glacier, jungle, high mountain, desert, peat bog

   _____

5. Chincochoros, Spaniards, Inca, Palomans, Anasazi

   _____

XII. Outlining/Mapping
On your own paper, make a map or outline of the following paragraph.

Mummification can happen naturally. Freeze-drying is one way. Just as the cold, dry air in a freezer can dehydrate a piece of chicken, frigid dry air in the cold regions of the world can preserve a body. For example, a person who dies in an avalanche in Alaska might be found perfectly preserved hundreds, even thousands, of years later. Extremely hot, dry air or intense, direct sunlight like that in the Sahara Desert will also mummify a body. Since bacteria and fungus cannot grow without oxygen, it is not surprising that mummies have also been found in peat bogs. A peat bog is like a cold swamp. The peat moss on top of the bog grows so densely that air cannot reach the layers below. Salt, mud, and chemicals can also naturally mummify a body.

READING 6

Black Holes: A Place of No Return

1   **Black holes** are probably the most powerful and unusual phenomena in the universe. No one has ever seen a black hole, and no one ever will because the gravity of a black hole is so strong that not even light can escape from its pull. What is a black hole? Despite its name, a black hole is not a hole. A black hole is, in fact, the remains of a once-gigantic star that has died and collapsed in on itself.

HOW DO BLACK HOLES FORM?

2   To understand black holes, you need to know a few terms, such as *mass* and *density*, from the field of **physics**. The **density** of an object depends on how closely packed the molecules that make up an object are. For example, a balloon and a bowling ball may be the same size. The bowling ball, however, has much greater density because it contains more mass. The **mass** is the actual number of molecules in the object. The bowling ball obviously has greater mass, more molecules more densely packed, than the balloon. That is why it is heavier.

3   Another important term in physics is **gravity**. Gravity is the attraction between objects. Gravity is what makes you fall back to earth after you jump in the air. Gravity is what makes the moon revolve around the earth and the earth around the sun. The amount of gravity something **exerts** on the objects around it depends not on its size but on its mass. The greater the mass is, the stronger the object's gravity.

4   Though it may seem large to us, our sun is a small star compared to many in the universe. Most of the mass of our sun and other stars is made up of hydrogen. This hydrogen burns in a nuclear reaction called **fusion**. Fusion reactions in the sun create the light and heat that our planet depends on. One day, the hydrogen will finally be used up, and our sun, like all stars, will die. Because our sun is small, it does not have enough mass to create a black hole.

5   When a very large star begins to die, it often explodes into a **supernova**, a gigantic superstar. This explosion burns up most of star's remaining fuel. Without the intense heat of nuclear fusion in its core, the

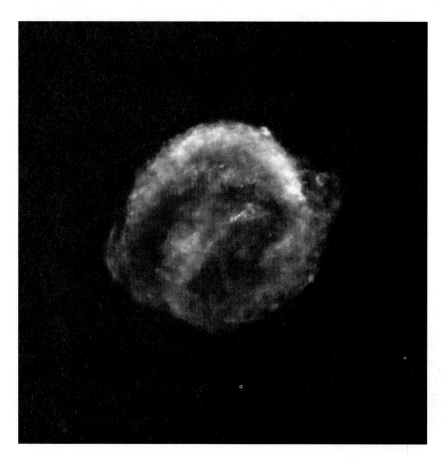

star's own gravity causes the supernova to collapse in on itself. A dying star may eventually stop collapsing and end its final days as a **white dwarf**. The mass of a white dwarf is so dense that a single teaspoon of the white dwarf would weigh $5\frac{1}{2}$ tons in Earth's gravity. If a star is massive enough, it may continue to collapse until it is so dense it becomes a **neutron star**. The mass of a neutron star is so tightly packed a teaspoon would weigh 100 million tons. A super-massive star may continue to collapse until the mass is infinitely small. In other words, it collapses until it is no size at all. If that happens, a black hole is born.

ANATOMY OF A BLACK HOLE

6   It is difficult for the human mind to imagine all the mass of a gigantic star pressed down into a space smaller than the tiniest spot of dust. That infinitely tiny spot at the center of a black hole is called its **singularity**. The mass (the size of the original star) of that singularity, not its size, determines how big the black hole is. That is true because the gravity of a black hole depends on how massive the original star was. The larger the mass of the original star, the bigger the black hole. The size of a black hole is determined by its **event horizon**.

7   To understand the event horizon, you must understand another term from physics—**escape velocity**. To escape the gravity of Earth, a rocket must go faster than a particular speed or it will crash back to earth. The speed an object needs to escape the gravity of another object is called its escape velocity. The closer you come to a singularity, the stronger and stronger the gravitational pull of the black hole becomes. When you reach a distance from the singularity where escape becomes impossible, you have reached the event horizon.

8   A distance where escape is impossible? How can that be? Shouldn't it be possible to increase your speed until the escape velocity is finally reached? The answer is no. Why? Because, according to the physicist Albert Einstein, nothing can travel faster than the **speed of light**. The speed of light is 186,000 miles per second. The gravity anywhere inside the event horizon of a black hole is so strong that you would have to travel faster than the speed of light to escape. That, however, is impossible. Do not think of the event horizon as a line in space, but rather a distance from the singularity, the distance at which your escape velocity would have to be faster than the speed of light.

9   The event horizon is the **point of no return** for anything that crosses it. From a speck of dust to a spacecraft to a star, anything that passes beyond the event horizon is doomed to be crushed down into the **infinite** smallness of the singularity. Black holes may not be holes, but they are indeed black because not even light can escape from inside the event horizon. For that reason, it is impossible to see inside a black hole.

HOW DO SCIENTISTS KNOW BLACK HOLES EXIST?

10   If scientists cannot see black holes, how do they know they exist? Actually physicists as early as the eighteenth century suspected there might be objects in space that were so dense their gravity captured everything,

including light. Ironically, even though Albert Einstein vigorously refused to believe in the possibility of black holes, it was his **theory of relativity** and other mathematical formulas that allowed physicists to develop early theories about black holes. Today, there is compelling evidence that black holes do indeed exist.

11   Black holes may not give off light, but objects such as space dust or even planets that are being pulled into the **gravity well** of a black hole speed up. This increasing speed causes the objects to heat up. When they do, they give off **X-rays**. X-rays cannot penetrate our atmosphere, but astronomers using satellites orbiting above the planet are studying regions in space that are emitting X-rays. They believe that many of these areas may be black holes.

12   Astronomers also look for **rotating stars**. Like planets rotating around the sun, **binary** or **paired stars** rotate around each other. If one of the stars has become a black hole, the second star seems to be rotating around an empty place. Sometimes material from the second star is actually being sucked into the black hole.

13   Another way astronomers locate black holes is by using a technique called **gravity lensing**. The gravity of a black hole is so strong it bends the light of the stars behind it just as a glass lens bends light beams. When an astronomer finds such a distorted area of space, he or she suspects the existence of a black hole.

14   Finding an **acceleration disk** in space is another indication of a black hole. An acceleration disk is the matter revolving around the black hole. An acceleration disk might look something like our own spiral-shaped Milky Way galaxy. In fact, many astronomers now believe that there is probably a black hole in the center of nearly every galaxy.

HOW MANY BLACK HOLES ARE THERE?

15   According to Stephen Hawking, one of today's leading physicists, there may actually be more black holes in the universe than there are visible stars. At least four possible black holes have already been found in our galaxy, not including the one believed to be at its center. In the future, as astronomy and physics improve, more will undoubtedly be discovered.

ARE BLACK HOLES A DANGER?

16   Hollywood movies and space **fantasy** novels may have people believing that black holes are a threat to Earth, but that is not true. The universe is enormous, and the stars (and black holes) are millions of miles apart. The gravity, even of a massive black hole, is too distant to be any threat to us. In the far-distant future, if people do begin long-distance space travel, black holes may present a danger, but to the people of Earth today they are nothing more than one of space's fascinating mysteries.

Exercises

I. Finding the Correct Pronunciation
Write the letter of the correct pronunciation on the line beside the word.

_____ 1. velocity
   a. və lŏs´ ĭ tē
   b. vĕl ŏz´ ə dē

_____ 2. neutron
   a. n‾oo´ trŏn
   b. nēt´ rŏn

_____ 3. exert
   a. ĭg zûrt´
   b. ĕks´ ərt

II. Finding the Correct Meaning
Use the context clues in each sentence to determine the correct meaning of each use of the word space. *Write the correct part of speech and number on the line provided. Example:* <u>n. 3</u>

---

space (spās) *n.* 1. The three-dimensional area in which matter exists. 2. The expanse in which the solar system, galaxy, and stars exist; universe. 3. A blank or empty area. 4. A particular area, such as a place on a train. 5. A period or interval of time.
—*v.* **spaced, spacing** 1. To organize or arrange with spaces in between. 2. *Slang.* To become disoriented from or as if from a drug.

_____ 1. A black hole is not a hole in outer *space*.

_____ 2. A bowling ball has more mass, molecules packed into the same *space*, than a balloon.

_____ 3. Stars are not evenly *spaced* throughout the universe.

_____ 4. There is too much *space* between the pictures. Please move them closer together.

_____ 5. There is still a *space* free on the next rocket to Mars if you would like to go.

III. Using New Vocabulary

Choose a word from the Answer Box to complete the following sentences using context clues.

ANSWER BOX				
acceleration	mass	gravity	physicist	density
astronomer	collapses	visible	distorts	fusion

1. The gravity of a black hole is so strong that it
   _____ the light of stars behind the black hole.

2. An _____ studies not only common things like
   stars and planets but unusual phenomena like black holes and
   quarks.

3. When a massive star _____, it may become a
   black hole.

4. To reach escape velocity, a rocket ship's _____
   must be fast enough to break free of the planet's gravity.

5. The _____ of hydrogen atoms is how a star
   creates energy.

6. The _____ of the singularity determines the
   size of a black hole; in other words, the more molecules in the original star, the bigger the black hole.

7. A _____ studies such phenomena as mass, density, gravity, and velocity.

8. Nothing inside a black hole is _____ to some-
   one beyond the event horizon because not even light can escape the
   gravity of a balloon.

9. A bowling ball has more _____, a larger number of molecules, than a balloon.

10. It is the earth's _____ that keeps the moon or-
    biting around our planet.

IV. Understanding Compound Words
Match each of these compound words with their correct definitions.

_____ 1. escape velocity

_____ 2. binary stars

_____ 3. gravity lensing

_____ 4. white dwarf

_____ 5. neutron star

_____ 6. event horizon

_____ 7. speed of light

_____ 8. theory of relativity

_____ 9. gravity well

_____ 10. acceleration disk

a. Einstein's explanation of the relationship between time and space

b. spiral-shaped collection of matter circling a black hole

c. a collapsed star that is so dense a teaspoon of it weighs $5\frac{1}{2}$ tons

d. the speed needed to get away from the gravity of an object

e. the distance light can travel in a second

f. a collapsed star that is so dense a teaspoon of it weighs 100 million tons

g. the distance from a black hole where escape is no longer possible

h. paired stars that rotate around each other

i. area inside the escape horizon of a black hole

j. the ability of a black hole to bend light

V. Finding Information
Complete the following exercise.

1. List four ways scientists can locate black holes.

a. _____

b. _____

c. _____

d. _____

VI. Sequencing

Put the events in the Answer Box into the correct chronological order.

> The star continues collapsing until it becomes a neutron star.
> The supernova begins to collapse.
> The dying star becomes a black hole.
> A massive star nearing death explodes into a massive superstar.
> The supernova collapses into a white dwarf.

1. _____

2. _____

3. _____

4. _____

5. _____

VII. Finding the Main Idea

Place a check mark on the line next to the sentence that best states the main idea in each set of sentences below.

Set A

_____ 1. Our sun is a small star compared to others.

_____ 2. A dying star may become a supernova.

_____ 3. Stars come in many different sizes.

_____ 4. Some stars are red giants.

_____ 5. A supernova may shrink into a white dwarf.

Set B

_____ 1. At the center of a black hole is an infinitely small singularity.

_____ 2. A black hole is not really a hole.

_____ 3. Just beyond the event horizon is an acceleration disk.

_____ 4. The area of gravity around a black hole where the escape velocity equals the speed of light is called the event horizon.

_____ 5. Though one of the most unusual phenomena in the universe, the makeup of a black hole is actually very simple.

Set C

_____ 1. Because space is enormous, black holes are millions of miles from Earth.

_____ 2. Hollywood movies and space fantasy novels make people believe that black holes are a danger.

_____ 3. However, black holes are not really a danger to people.

_____ 4. Because astronomers can locate black holes even though they cannot be seen, there is little danger that even future space travelers will meet one accidentally.

_____ 5. Even the largest black hole is not able to suck in a planet or even a rocket ship unless that object comes too close to the event horizon.

VIII. Finding the Central Idea

Choose the letter of the sentence that best states the central idea of this reading.

_____ 1. a. Black holes were first suspected in the eighteenth century.

b. Though one of the most unusual phenomena in the universe and impossible to see, black holes are no longer really a mystery to physicists and astronomers.

c. Black holes are not really holes but dead stars.

d. Stephen Hawking believes there is a black hole in the middle of the Milky Way galaxy.

e. A black hole is nothing more than a singularity encircled by an area of space with enormous gravity, a gravity so strong even light cannot escape.

IX. Critical Thinking

State whether the following statements are true (T) or false (F). Read carefully and be prepared to defend your answer.

_____ 1. One day our sun may become a black hole.

_____ 2. Light travels at 186,000 miles per minute.

_____ 3. The gravity of the singularity in a black hole is so strong it can bend light.

_____ 4. Scientists believe there are at least five black holes in our galaxy.

_____ 5. Albert Einstein was the first person to suggest there may be black holes.

_____ 6. Future space travelers may study a black hole from just inside its event horizon.

_____ 7. Objects being pulled into a black hole give off X-rays.

_____ 8. Stephen Hawking believes there may be more black holes in the universe than there are stars we can see.

X. Writing About What You've Read

On your own paper, write a paragraph describing how a black hole is formed.

Chronic Fatigue Syndrome: The Mystery Illness

1   Ten years ago, Paula Cromwell, who is now 45, had a bad case of the flu. She still has not recovered. In fact, her condition is worse. She often sleeps as much as 12 or 14 hours a day, but when she wakes she is still exhausted. Her muscles ache, and her mind is dull. During the last decade, her constant fatigue has caused her to lose her job, her husband, and her house. She now lives with her parents who care for her. Paula is not a **hypochondriac**. Though it took countless visits to several different doctors, Paula was finally diagnosed with chronic fatigue syndrome (CFS).

WHAT IS CHRONIC FATIGUE SYNDROME?

2   Because people who suffer from CFS, as it is also called, have so many different symptoms, even doctors who have been researching this illness for more than 20 years are not certain if CFS is a single disease or several diseases with similar symptoms. Some people call the illness chronic fatigue immune dysfunction syndrome because they believe all the sufferers have some problem with their body's **immune** system. Many doctors, however, do not like this name because they are not certain all people suffering from CFS actually have an immune **dysfunction**.

3   Finding a cure for CFS means raising money for research. Unfortunately, there are other diseases that desperately need funding too. With organizations that research heart disease, cancer, diabetes, and other life-threatening diseases begging for money, it can be difficult convincing **donors** to contribute for a disease with a name like chronic fatigue syndrome. The name seems to suggest that CFS sufferers are nothing more than people who are tired all the time. For that reason, some people want to change the name from CFS to myalgic encephalomyelitis. They believe this name suggests just how serious this illness can be. However, again many researchers are not convinced that everyone suffering from CFS is in fact suffering from myalgic encephalomyelitis, which is an inflammation in the brain.

4   So what then is this mysterious illness? For now, doctors diagnose the disease by using a check list. First, a person must have **severe** fatigue that cannot be explained by work, physical activities, lack of sleep, or illness. Second, this tiredness must have lasted for at least six months. A doctor

will then check for physical causes for the chronic fatigue such as **anemia**, depression, or problems with the adrenal or thyroid glands. If none can be found, the doctor will ask the patient if he or she suffers from any of the following symptoms:

- a sore throat
- tender lymph nodes
- muscle pain
- painful joints that do not have redness or swelling
- loss of short-term memory or mental concentration
- headaches
- insomnia or sleep that leaves the patient still tired
- the feeling of being exhausted for more than a day after activity

5   A patient who answers "yes" to four or more of these symptoms is diagnosed with chronic fatigue syndrome. There are other possible symptoms as well: dizziness, nausea, rashes, irritable bowel, chemical sensitivity, weakness, and constant pain. Often patients of CFS are disabled. Many are housebound. Some are even bedridden.

WHO GETS CFS?

6   In the beginning, researchers believed CFS was rare, affecting mostly white, upper-middle-class women over 30. However, the Centers for Disease Control now believe that as many as 500,000 Americans or more suffer from the disease. A study by DePaul University found that many of the sufferers were, in fact, low-income minorities, though women do seem to get the disease in greater numbers than men. There have been cases of CFS in **adolescents**, but few if any cases have been found in children under 12. People who suffer from allergies also seem to contract CFS in larger numbers than people who do not. Certainly not everyone with allergies, however, gets CFS.

WHAT CAUSES CFS?

7   Again researchers do not have the answers. Over a thousand research articles have been written on the syndrome, but no single cause has been found. Researchers in France have found a virus in the muscles of people suffering from CFS. This virus was not found in the healthy volunteers. Researchers think perhaps a chronic infection caused by the virus may be the cause of CFS. A virus is not the only cause being investigated. Some of the other possible causes being studied are an **imbalance** of the hormones produced by the pituitary, hypothalamus, and adrenal glands, a reduced amount of fatty acids in the brain, low blood pressure, and even stress. Researchers are certain, however, that CFS is not contagious.

WHAT CAN BE DONE TO HELP PEOPLE WITH CFS?

8   Since doctors do not yet know the cause of CFS, they usually treat the patient's symptoms. Pain killers or **anti-inflammatory** drugs might be prescribed for people suffering muscle or joint pain. Sleep aids might be given to patients suffering with insomnia. Patients who sleep too much

may be given **stimulants** to keep them awake during the day. Because CFS can be so devastating to the patient's quality of life, many sufferers of the disease take **antidepressants**. Those with autoimmune problems may take drugs that keep the body from attacking itself. Since many CFS patients also suffer from a sensitivity to medications, doctors can often prescribe smaller doses than with other patients.

9   Drugs, however, are not the only treatments doctors use with CFS patients. Exercise is another. One doctor says the secret for success for his CFS patients is for them to "know how much exercise to do and when to stop." He calls this **paced** exercise. Dr. E. M. Goudsmit offers another technique called "switching activity." He believes his patients should stop an activity before they begin to tire and switch to another. For example, a person with CFS might read for 5 or 10 minutes, then wash a few dishes, rest, then do another activity for a short period of time.

10   Group support is also very important for the people who suffer from CFS as well as for their families and caregivers. Two national organizations—the CFIDS Association of America and the National CFIDS Foundation—offer information for anyone interested in learning more about this disease and what can be done to help those suffering from this life-changing illness.

IS THERE A CURE?

11   Though some people suffering from CFS find that they do recover much of their earlier strength and return to their normal lives in five years or less, few people ever recover completely. Some stay in about the same condition for years, and others continue to get worse. Though research continues, the cause of chronic fatigue has not yet been determined. Once the process of the disease is finally understood, then and only then will researchers be able to begin their search for the cure.

Exercises

I. Finding the Correct Pronounciation

Write the letter of the correction pronunciation on the line beside the word.

_____ 1. anemia
   a. ā nē´ mē ă
   b. ə nē´ mē ə

_____ 2. syndrome
   a. sĭn´ drōm´
   b. sīn´ drəm´

_____ 3. symptom
   a. sĭmp´ təm
   b. sīm´ tōm´

II. Finding the Correct Meaning

Use the dictionary entries given below to choose the correct meaning for each italicized word as it is used in that context. If there is more than one choice, give both the part of speech and the number of the definition. Example: <u>n. 3</u>

_____ 1. "He believes his patients should stop an activity before they begin to tire and *switch* to another."

> **switch** (swĭch) *n.* 1. A slender, flexible rod or stick. 2. A device used to break or open an electrical circuit. 3. A device used to transfer rolling stock from one track to another. —*v.* 1. To whip with a branch or switch. 2. To shift, transfer, or change. 3. To connect or disconnect using a switch.

_____ 2. "A doctor will then check for physical causes for the chronic fatigue such as anemia, *depression*, or problems with the adrenal or thyroid glands."

> **depression** (dĭ prĕsh´ ən) *n.* 1. A sunken area, hollow. 2. *Psychol.* A condition marked by an inability to concentrate, insomnia, and feelings of sadness and hopelessness. 3. A period of drastic decline in the economy. 4. A region of low barometric pressure.

III. Understanding Compound Words

Match each of these compound words (1–10) with its correct definition (a–j).

_____ 1. chemical sensitivity

_____ 2. low-income

_____ 3. antidepressant

_____ 4. anti-inflammatory

_____ 5. blood pressure

_____ 6. housebound

_____ 7. sleep aids

_____ 8. pain killers

a. medication to relieve insomnia

b. medication to relieve extreme sadness

c. medication to relieve swelling and redness

d. medication to relieve aches and pains

e. a response where the body attacks itself

f. the economic status just below wealthy

_____ 9. autoimmune

_____ 10. upper-middle class

g. poor, or economic status of having little money

h. unable to leave home

i. easily affected by drugs or medications

j. measurement of how hard the heart is working to pump blood through the body

IV. Using New Vocabulary

Choose a word from the Answer Box to complete the following sentences using context clues.

ANSWER BOX			
hypochondriac	chronic	syndrome	immune
contagious	minority	adolescent	donation

1. The low-income, _____ populations such as blacks and Hispanics seem to suffer from CFS more than the white middle class, according to research by Purdue University.

2. A _____ condition such as CFS is one that continues to last over a long period of time.

3. Most researchers do not believe CFS is _____; they don't think it can be passed from person to person.

4. CFS is considered a _____ because it seems to be a collection of many different symptoms rather than a single disease.

5. In the beginning of a diagnosis, a doctor may think a CFS sufferer is nothing more than a _____ who has created the symptoms in his or her own mind.

6. Your _____ system may be come weak if you do not eat right and get enough sleep.

7. An _____ is someone who is no longer a child but not yet an adult.

8. Families of CFS suffers will often make a generous _____ to the National CFIDS Foundation to help with CFS research.

V. Finding the Facts
Write the letter of the correct answer on the line provided.

_____ 1. What number of people does the Centers for Disease Control estimate suffers from CFS in the United States?
   a. 500
   b. 5,000
   c. 50,000
   d. 500,000
   e. 5 million

_____ 2. What group seems *least* likely to suffer from CFS?
   a. upper-middle-class women
   b. minorities
   c. low-income men
   d. adolescents
   e. children

_____ 3. Which is *not* a suspected cause of CFS?
   a. having too much fatty acid in the brain
   b. virus in the muscles
   c. stress
   d. a hormone imbalance
   e. low blood pressure

_____ 4. Who suggests a technique called "switching activities" for CFS sufferers?
   a. Dr. Goudsmit
   b. CFS researchers
   c. Centers for Disease Control
   d. National CFIDS Foundation
   e. CFIDS Association of America

_____ 5. To be diagnosed with CFS, a person must suffer from severe exhaustion for at least:
   a. a week
   b. 6 weeks
   c. 6 months
   d. 2 years
   e. 20 years

VI. Finding the Main Idea

Write the letter of the sentence that best states the main idea in each set of sentences below.

_____ 1. a. Those with autoimmune problems may take drugs to keep the body from attacking itself.
   b. Because CFS can be devastating to the patient's quality of life, many sufferers of the disease take antidepressants.
   c. Sleep aids may be given to patients suffering from insomnia.
   d. Since doctors do not yet know the cause of CFS, they usually treat the patient's symptoms.
   e. Pain killers or anti-inflammatory drugs might be prescribed for people suffering muscle or joint pain.

_____ 2. a. People with allergies tend to get CFS more often than people who don't.
   b. In the beginning, researchers believed that CFS was rare and mostly affected white, upper-middle-class women.
   c. In fact, many sufferers of CFS are low-income minorities.
   d. Adolescents have been known to contract CFS, but not often.
   e. Researchers are finding that many different populations suffer from CFS.

VII. Finding the Central Idea

Choose the letter of the sentence that best states the central idea of this reading.

_____ 1. a. Chronic fatigue syndrome is a serious illness.
   b. More than 500,000 people in the United States suffer from chronic fatigue syndrome.
   c. Chronic fatigue syndrome is a complex and serious disease for which neither the cause(s) nor the cure is yet known.
   d. Chronic fatigue syndrome has several different names.

VIII. Seeing Relationships

Based on what you have read, find the one word or phrase in each set that does not belong and cross it out. On the line, explain the relationship that connects the related words or phrases.

1. heart   pituitary   hypothalamus   adrenal   thyroid

        _____

2. muscle pain   cancer   sore throat   insomnia
     short-term memory loss

        _____

3. depression   job loss   allergies   divorce   disabled

        _____

IX. Writing About What You've Read

On your own paper, write a paragraph about why it is so difficult to find funding for CFS research.

X. Making Study Maps and Outlines

On your own paper, make a study map or outline of this reading.

READING 8

Solving the Mystery of Academic Success

1   Why is one person an A student and another a D student? The A student is smarter, right? Not necessarily. Though having a natural ability does make getting top grades a bit easier, in fact, almost any student has the potential to be an A student. How? By knowing the secrets to being a successful student and using them, you too can achieve **academic** success.

SETTING YOUR GOALS

2   The *American Heritage Dictionary* defines success as "the **achievement** of something desired, planned, or attempted." In other words, you are successful when you reach a goal you have set for yourself.

3   If you want to find success, set **realistic** short-term goals that lead you toward a long-term goal. Imagine you are a first-year college student whose long-term goal is to be a **veterinarian**. If you want to succeed, first make a series of short-term goals that are more easily **attainable**. For example, you could set goals like: I'm going to get at least a B in my Biology I class; I want to find a part-time job working with animals; I need to improve my math skills.

4   There are several **advantages** to making a series of short-term goals. First, if you fail at one, you don't have to give up your long-term goal. If you don't pass your biology class the first time around, you don't give up your goal of becoming a vet. You simply admit you will have to work harder and take the biology class over again. Second, having short-term goals means you can find success more quickly. This will help your **self-esteem**. Who wants to wait for years and years to feel successful? Finally, sometimes as you attempt your short-term goals you realize that your long-term goal is either not realistic or not what you want. Changing goals is much easier if the long-term goal is seen as an **option**.

MAKING REALISTIC GOALS

5   So you have decided that you want to be a veterinarian? You know you have many years of difficult courses ahead to reach that goal. What do you do? First, sit down with an academic counselor and map out the courses you will need to take.

6   Many students make the big mistake of wanting to get their course-work over as quickly as possible. They often choose to ignore **recommendations** from assessment tests or counselors and skip recommended **prerequisites** or developmental courses. This is almost certain to guarantee failure. Reading and writing are the foundation of most academic coursework, and basic math is a necessity for anyone pursing a degree in the sciences or technology. Your academic preparation will help determine your success or failure in your chosen career, so it makes no sense to "get over" courses like they are **hurdles** rather than building blocks.

7   Once you have an idea of the courses you are required to take, think carefully about how many courses you can successfully do at one time. This number depends on you and your life. Are you married? Have children? Do you care for your sick mother? Are you working a part-time or even a full-time job? Are there **commitments** to your church or other group that you must meet on a regular basis? Or are you simply the kind of person who needs a little extra time to process material?

8   Academic advisors suggest three hours of worktime outside the classroom for every hour in class. If you take five 3-credit-hour courses, that is 60 hours of work per week and that does not include **commuting** time. That is equal to $1\frac{1}{2}$ work weeks. Do you have that much time to give to your studies? And if you do this, how long can your body and mind take the stress? If you want to be successful, you need to find a class load that is realistic. Students with too many classes often fail one or more of them (or make themselves so sick they must drop out of classes altogether). Remember the old proverb: Slow and steady wins the race.

FRONT AND CENTER

9   Teachers often recognize their A students the very first day of class by where they choose to sit in the classroom. Research shows that most A students sit front and center. This seating position has several advantages. First, being so close forces you to stay **focused**. No sneaking a nap under the very nose of the instructor. Of course, being up front allows you to see and hear more clearly, so you are less likely to miss material. Also, this

position encourages you to become more involved: to ask questions or request **clarifications**. And being front and center also gives the instructor the opportunity to get to know you better. That may seem a bit frightening if you are shy, but in the long run, the closer your relationship with the teacher the more likely you are to ask for help when you need it.

BE PREPARED

10   Come to class every day and come prepared! Have everything you need with you and be organized, ready to go. Many students miss important parts of a lecture because they are trying to find a pen in their backpack or are bothering other students for paper. Especially, be prepared when it comes to your assignments. There is a reason your instructor assigned you to read Chapter 5 before the lecture. A student who has read and familiarized himself with the new vocabulary and concepts can listen and take notes with understanding and then ask questions about confusing material. A student who has not completed the assignment is often lost after the first new vocabulary word. In her struggle to spell the new word, the unprepared student completely misses the next several minutes of lecture. Coming to class prepared not only is a plus for you as a student but also shows respect for your classmates and teacher.

DON'T PROCRASTINATE!

11   It is human nature to want to put things off until tomorrow, but for a student, **procrastination** can lead to failure. An A student knows that it is best to do the assignment as quickly as possible after class. A smart student will take the first free hour after the class, sit down, and complete the homework while the material is still fresh in her mind. A day or two later, the procrastinator may not even remember clearly what the instructor wanted done let alone how to do it. As for tests, top students know that you study bit by bit. Ten or fifteen minutes a day for a week with a longer study session the day before the test is a much better way to learn material than cramming the night before.

FIND A STUDY AREA

12   Another secret to academic success is to have a study spot. If you live alone or have a place at home where you can work without being disturbed, make it your work/study area. Sorry, but your bed is the worst place to do homework or read no matter how tempting it may be. If you have children or a crowded household where you simply do not have privacy, you may want to set aside several hours at school as designated study time. Find a quiet spot in the library or under a shade tree where you can do your assignments without being disturbed. When you do go home, hopefully your work is done and you can give your full attention to your family or friends.

USE YOUR RESOURCES

13   Most colleges and universities have many resources to help their students, from financial aid to mental and physical health services. Take advantage of all the resources available to you. Take particular advantage of any **tutoring** or academic support provided.

14   The **perception** of many people is that only poor students need tutors. In fact, surveys of tutorial services show that many of their **clients** are in fact the top students. One reason they are top students is that these people realize there is always room for improvement, and they willingly seek assistance.

15   The teacher is another resource many students overlook. Most instructors keep set office hours designed specifically for meeting with students. Even if you don't have any questions, drop by a few times during the first few weeks of the course to get acquainted with the instructor. And certainly don't be afraid to go to the instructor with questions; the instructor's job is to help her students learn.

LEARN FROM YOUR MISTAKES

16   Mistakes or failures are only negative if you don't learn from them. When you get a test back, whether it is an A or an F, take a close look at it. If you have made mistakes, take the time to find out the correct answers. If you still don't know why an answer is right or wrong, go to the instructor or to a tutor and find out what you have done wrong. If you don't learn from your mistakes, you are going to keep repeating them.

17   As for the failure, whether of a test or an entire class, that failure should prompt you to ask yourself some basic questions: Did I really prepare for this test? Do I need to take the prerequisite to this course? What more do I need to succeed? Repeated failure of the same test or course may prompt you to ask even harder questions. Do I have the natural abilities to successfully complete this course? Is this really the path I want to follow? Is there another course of action I can take to reach my long-term goal? Just remember your failures as well as your successes are telling you something. Listen and take the necessary action.

SUCCESS

18   Do you have to be an A student to be successful? Only if that is the goal you set for yourself. You are successful, both in school and in life, if you continue to move ahead toward your long-term goals whatever they might be. The only failure is to never strive toward a goal.

Exercises

I. Finding the Correct Pronunciation
Write the letter of the correct pronunciation on the line beside the word.

_____ 1. hurdle
    a. hîr′ dəl
    b. hûr′ dl

_____ 2. procrastinate
    a. prə krăs′ tə nāt′
    b. prŏk′ răs′ tə nət

_____ 3. prerequisite
    a. prē rĕk′ wĭ zĭt′
    b. prē rē′ kwă sīt′

II. Finding the Correct Meaning
Use the dictionary entries given below to choose the correct meaning for each italicized word as it is used in that context. If there is more than one choice, give both the part of speech and the number of the definition. Example: <u>n. 3</u>

_____ 1. Sitting in the front and center of the room forces you to *focus*.

> **focus** (fō′ kəs) *n. pl.* **focuses** or **foci** 1. A center of interest. 2. Concentration or emphasis. 3. A point at which rays of light come together after passing through a lens. 4. The condition or adjustment in which a lens or eye gives its best image. —*v.* **focused, focusing**. 1. To adjust an eye or lens to bring a clearer image. 2. To concentrate, center, or fix on something. [Lat. *hearth*] —**focal**, *adj.* —**focally**, *adv.*

III. Understanding New Vocabulary
Write the letter of the correct definition on the line beside each word.

_____ 1. achievement

_____ 2. advantage

_____ 3. self-esteem

_____ 4. option

_____ 5. recommendation

_____ 6. attainable

_____ 7. clarification

_____ 8. procrastination

_____ 9. commute

_____10. academic

a. to travel between home and school/work

b. related to school or studies

c. pride in oneself

d. putting something off until later

e. having something made clear, easier to understand

f. a thing that is helpful or useful

g. a suggestion or advice

h. a choice

i. reachable

j. a goal reached or other success

IV. Using New Vocabulary

Choose a word from the list in Exercise III to complete the following sentences.

1. Gabriella had an hour _____ every day from home to college.

2. _____ is always dangerous. What happens if you put off studying until the day before the test, then get sick?

3. Skipping a class should not be an _____ unless you are sick or have a personal responsibility you must fulfill.

4. If you learn and practice the secrets of _____ success, you should become more successful in school.

5. Always ask for _____ if there is something that confuses you in a teacher's lecture.

6. Passing your algebra class is a big _____ if you suffer from math anxiety (fear of math).

7. You should not ignore your counselor's _____. She is trained to know what courses will be helpful for you.

8. Don't give up! Your long-term goals are _____. You can reach them by completing one short-term goal at a time.

9. If you start with unrealistic goals, you might suffer failure after failure. In the end, this could destroy your _____.

10. One _____ of making short-term goals is that you can find success more quickly.

V. Finding the Facts
Write the letter of the correct answer on the line provided.

_____ 1. Why should you sit at the front and center of the room?
      a. to stay focused
      b. to see and hear better
      c. to be more involved
      d. to get to know the instructor better
      e. all of the above

_____ 2. Which of the following would not make a good study area?
      a. your kitchen table
      b. a desk in your bedroom or office
      c. a shady spot on a quiet lawn
      d. a table in the library
      e. an empty classroom

_____ 3. Why is it important to have short-term goals?
      a. You can "get over" classes more quickly.
      b. It is impossible to have long-term goals without them.
      c. Short-term goals allow you to have success more quickly.
      d. Your academic counselor recommends them.
      e. You will more likely get A's in your classes.

_____ 4. Which of the following do you need to consider when deciding the appropriate number of classes to take?
      a. your job
      b. your personal commitments
      c. your commuting time
      d. your family responsibilities
      e. all of the above

_____ 5. What is the most important thing you should do when you get a test back?
      a. Look at your grade.
      b. See how many questions you missed.
      c. Talk to the teacher.
      d. Figure out why you made the mistakes you did so you don't make them again.
      e. See a tutor.

VI. Finding the Main Idea
Write the number of the sentence in the paragraphs that best states the main idea of each paragraph.

____ 1.   [1]There are several advantages to making a series of short-term goals. [2]First, if you fail at one, you don't have to give up your long-term goal. [3]If you don't pass your biology class the first time around, you simply take it over again. [4]Second, having short-term goals means you can find success more quickly. [5]This will help your self-esteem. [6]Who wants to wait for years and years to feel successful? [7]Finally, sometimes as you attempt your short-term goals you realize that your long-term goal is either not realistic or not what you want. [8]Changing goals is much easier if the long-term goal is seen as an option.

____ 2.   [1]It is human nature to want to put things off until tomorrow. [2]However, for a student, procrastination can lead to failure. [3]An A student knows that it is best to do the assignment as quickly as possible after class. [4]A smart student will take the first free hour after the class, sit down, and complete the homework while the material is still fresh in her mind. [5]A day or two later, the procrastinator may not even remember clearly what the instructor wanted done let alone how to do it. [6]As for tests, top students know that you study bit by bit. [7]Ten or fifteen minutes a day for a week with a longer study session the day before the test is a much better way to learn material than cramming the night before.

VII. Finding an Implied Main Idea
On the lines below the paragraph, write in your own words a main idea for the paragraph.

Academic advisors suggest three hours of worktime outside the classroom for every hour in class. If you take five 3-credit-hour courses, that is 60 hours of work per week, and that does not include commuting time. That is equal to $1\frac{1}{2}$ work weeks. Do you have that much time to give to your studies? And if you do this, how long can your body and mind take the stress? Students with too many classes often fail one or more of them (or make themselves so sick they must drop out of classes altogether). Remember the old proverb: Slow and steady wins the race.

_____

_____

VIII. Finding the Central Idea

Choose the letter of the sentence that best states the central idea of this reading.

1. ____ a. Always learn from your mistakes.
   b. You must set goals if you want success.
   c. Learn and practice the secrets of academic success.
   d. Making short- and long-term goals is an important part of becoming a better student.

IX. Analogies

Using the information from the reading, choose a word or phrase from the Answer Box to complete the following analogies.

ANSWER BOX			
goal	option	self-esteem	anxiety
future	tutor	negative	procrastination

1. advantage : positive :: disadvantage : _____

2. success : preparation :: failure : _____

3. race : finish line :: achieve : _____

4. rain : drought :: study : _____

5. cooling : temperatures :: failure : _____

6. short-term : long-term :: present : _____

7. teacher : instructor :: choice : _____

8. teacher : aide :: student : _____

X. Writing About What You've Read

Think about your own academic strategies. Then write about your strengths as a student, your weaknesses, and what you can do to improve.

Appendix

Maps

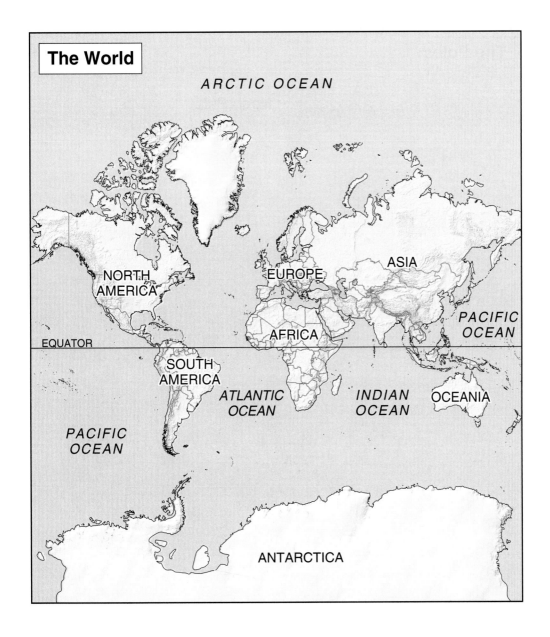

The World

ARCTIC OCEAN

NORTH
AMERICA

EUROPE

ASIA

PACIFIC
OCEAN

AFRICA

EQUATOR

SOUTH
AMERICA

ATLANTIC
OCEAN

INDIAN
OCEAN

OCEANIA

PACIFIC
OCEAN

ANTARCTICA

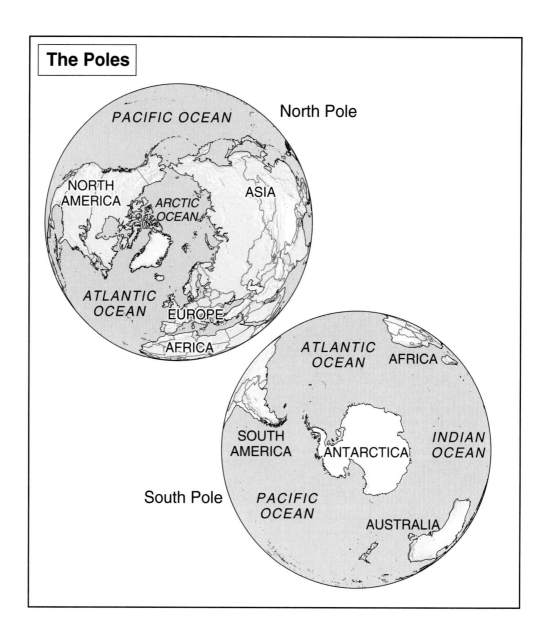

The Poles

PACIFIC OCEAN   North Pole

NORTH
AMERICA   ARCTIC   ASIA
                 OCEAN

ATLANTIC
OCEAN   EUROPE

                 AFRICA

                              ATLANTIC   AFRICA
                              OCEAN

               SOUTH   INDIAN
               AMERICA   ANTARCTICA   OCEAN

South Pole   PACIFIC
               OCEAN

                              AUSTRALIA

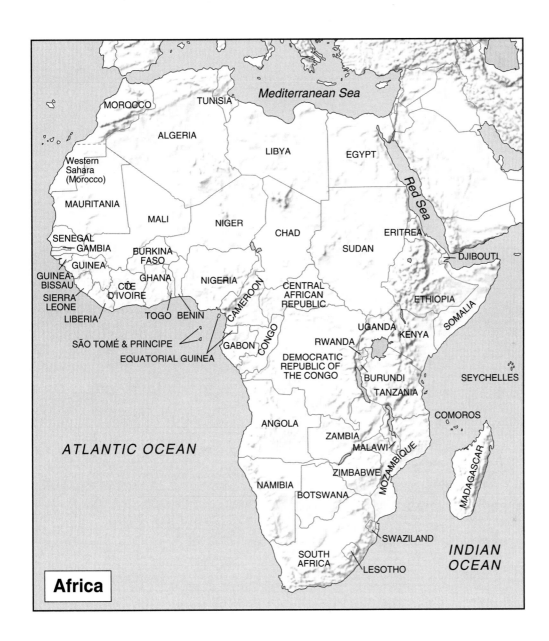

Africa

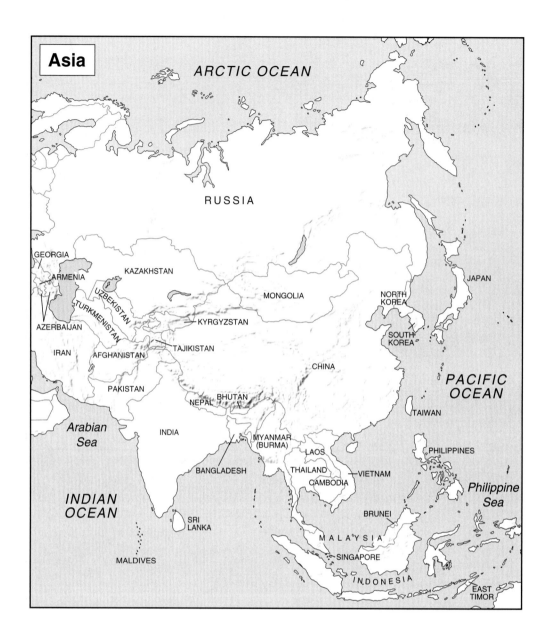

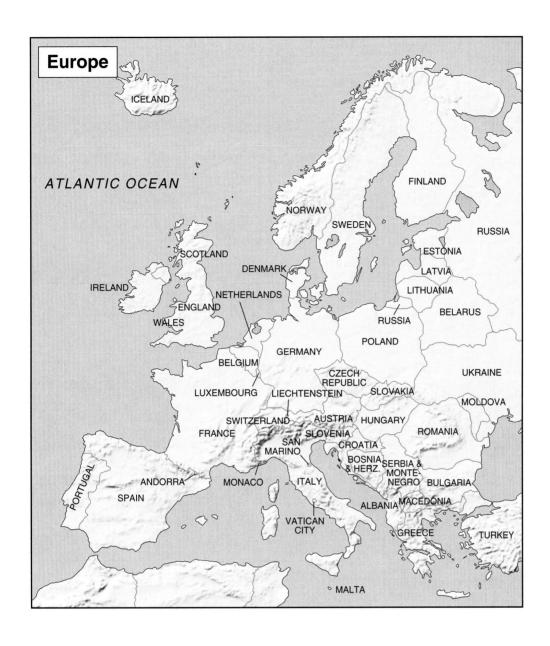

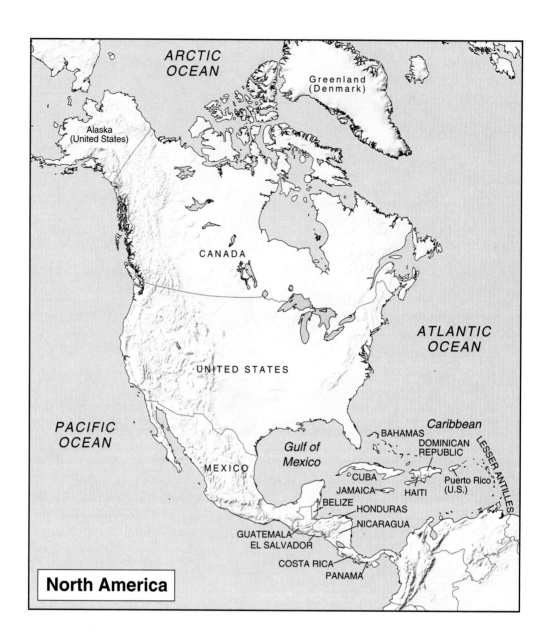

North America

South America

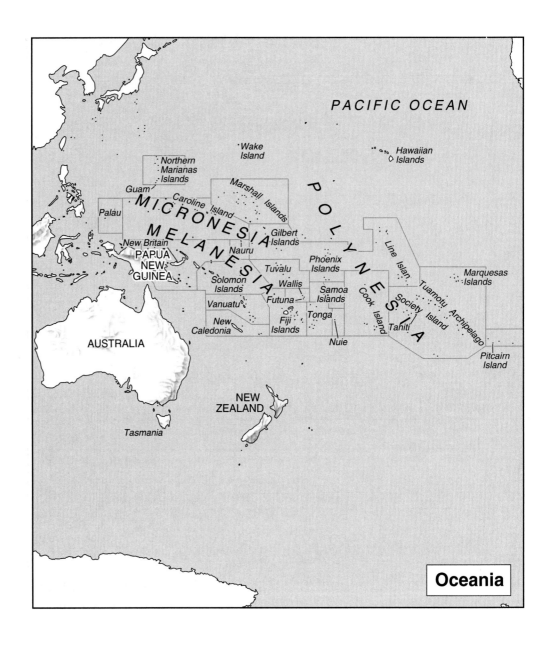

Credits

Page 22, Aladin Abdel Naby/Reuters; page 24, Burke/Triolo Productions/age fotostock, inc.; page 42, Chris R. Sharp/Photo Researchers, Inc.; page 102, Elkhorn Slough Foundation; page 103, Grant Heilman Photography, Inc.; page 134, NASA/JPL; page 135, NASA/JPL; page 164 T, © Dale Stokes/Norbert Wu Productions; page 164 B, Ralph White/CORBIS; page 188, D. Roddy (U.S. Geological Survey), Lunar and Planetary Institute; page 242, Burke/Triolo Productions/age fotostock, inc.; page 291, Bettmann/CORBIS; page 313, Doug Scott/age fotostock, inc.; page 32, ©Eastcott/Momatiuk/The Image Works; page 334, Rykoff Collection/CORBIS; page 34, Reuters/CORBIS; page 351, Chandra X-Ray Observatory/NASA

Index